S0-BOK-970

The Sense of Well-Being in America

The Sense of Well-Being in America

Recent Patterns and Trends

Angus Campbell

McGraw-Hill Book Company
New York St. Louis San Francisco Auckland
Bogotá Singapore Johannesburg London
Madrid Mexico Montreal New Delhi
Panama São Paulo Hamburg
Sydney Tokyo Paris
Toronto

1 2 3 4 5 6 7 8 9 RRD RRD 8 1 6 5 4 3 2 1

Thomas H. Quinn and Michael Hennelly were the editors of this book. Mark Safran was the designer. Thomas G. Kowalczyk supervised the production. It was set in Electra by David Seham, Inc. and was printed and bound by R. R. Donnelley and Sons.

Library of Congress Cataloging in Publication Data

Campbell, Angus

The sense of well-being in America.

Reports the major findings of a series of national surveys conducted by the Institute for Social Research between 1957 and 1978.

Bibliography: p.

Includes index.

1. United States—Social conditions—1960- —Public opinion. 2. United States—Economic conditions—1961- —Public opinion. 3. Social indicators—United States. 4. Economic indicators—United States. 5. Public opinion—United States. I. Michigan. University. Institute for Social Research. II. Title.

HN59.C29 973.92 80-14379

ISBN 0-07-009683-X

To Jean, Bruce,
Joan, and Carol

Contents

PART 2
Conditions of Well-Being 53

PART 3
The Quality of Life 221

Appendices

Preface

In this book I have reported the major findings of a series of national surveys conducted by the Institute for Social Research between the years 1957 and 1978. I have attempted to describe, without the aid of charts, statistics or professional jargon, the state of psychological well-being of the American people during this period and the changes which have occurred over these two eventful decades.

Support for these surveys has come from several different sources, both public and private. The 1957 study was conducted at the request of the Joint Commission on Mental Illness and Health and was reported in the 1960 book, *Americans View Their Mental Health*, by Gerald Gurin, Joseph Veroff and Sheila Feld. In 1967, Philip E. Converse and I were asked by Dr. Eleanor B. Sheldon and Dr. Wilbert E. Moore, then of the Russell Sage Foundation, to organize a contributed volume of review articles showing the state of research on the psychological aspects of social change. Russell Sage published this book in 1972 under the title *The Human Meaning of Social Change*. During the preparation of this volume, Dr. Sheldon and Dr. Orville G. Brim, Jr. encouraged Converse and me to undertake a survey of the psychological quality of life of the national population. This project went into the field in 1971 and the results of the study were reported in *The Quality of American Life*, published by the Russell Sage Foundation in 1976. Willard L. Rodgers was associated with Converse and me in this study. During this same period our colleagues, Frank M. Andrews and Stephen B. Withey, were carrying out a major study of methodologies in the measurement of subjective well-being, supported by a grant from the National Science Foundation. Their book, *Social Indicators of Well-being*, was published by Plenum Press in 1976. In 1975 Elizabeth Douvan and Joseph Veroff received a grant from the National Institute of Mental Health to replicate the original 1957 study. A book reporting this study is in preparation. In 1977 Converse and I received support from the National Science Foundation to make possible a national study, repeating and extending our 1971 study. This survey was carried out in 1978. In acknowledging the support of these various donors, I must of course absolve them from responsibility for any and all statements made in this book.

These studies were all based on personal interviews taken in the homes of the respondents. The respondents were chosen by procedures of probability sampling which have the effect of listing every person over the age of 18 in the contiguous 48 states and choosing among them in such a way that each has an equal chance of being chosen. The interviews, averaging something over an hour in length, were conducted by the interviewing staff of the Institute for Social Research. Refusals, illness, language problems, and failures to find the designated respondents at home after repeated calls resulted in a loss of between 15 and 25 percent of the designated sample of the five surveys. The actual number of respondents interviewed in these surveys was 2,460 in 1957, 2,164 in 1971, 2,369 in 1972 (1,297 in the spring and 1,072 in the fall), 2,264 in 1971, and 3,692 in 1978.

In writing this book I have drawn on the research of a number of my colleagues at the Institute for Social Research and I am pleased to name them here: Frank M. Andrews, Philip E. Converse, Elizabeth Douvan, Sheila Feld, Gerald Gurin, Robert L. Kahn, Robert W. Marans, Arthur H. Miller, Warren E. Miller, Robert P. Quinn, Willard L. Rodgers, Stanley E. Seashore, Burkhard Strumpel, Joseph Veroff, and Stephen B. Withey. I am especially indebted to Philip E. Converse with whom I have been associated in various scholarly activities for over 20 years. I also owe a particular debt to Dr. Norman Garmezy of the University of Minnesota, with whom I first discussed the concept of this book and whose reading of the original manuscript contributed greatly to its quality. Frank M. Andrews, Jean Campbell, and Richard Kamman also read the manuscript and offered helpful suggestions.

All surveys at the Institute depend on the support of its service sections, particularly the Sampling Section headed by Irene Hess and Leslie Kish, the Field Section headed by John C. Scott, the Coding Section headed by Joan M. Scheffler, and the Computing Service Facility headed by Duane Thomas. The numerous very competent interviewers, coders, samplers, statisticians, and computer technologists directed by these people were all essential to the conduct of these studies. Assistance in the preparation of data for this book was effectively provided by Giovanna Morchio. Betty Jennings took responsibility for the preparation of the manuscript and contributed to the proofreading and editing, as she has with previous books with which I have been associated. She was assisted by Garland Montalvo. To all these associates and friends I express my thanks.

I am aware of the fact that some readers of this book will be frustrated that relatively few of the many statements of fact presented are supported by a display of numbers. There are several tables in the Appendix and a few in the text but in general an attempt was made to avoid the direct presentation of data. All of the basic data on which the book is based are archived at the Institute for Social Research and are available for secondary analysis to interested scholars.

September 1980 **Angus Campbell**

The Sense of Well-Being in America

1
Introduction

The mind is its own place and in itself
Can make a Heaven of Hell, a Hell of Heaven.

In this passage from *Paradise Lost*, John Milton expressed the belief that the quality of human experiences lies in the spirit, that the mind "in itself" can overcome the circumstances in which people find themselves and can make life a heaven or a hell.

The world has become more secular since Milton's time, and we have come to believe that we can judge people's lives by the objective circumstances in which they live. The mind is not its own place but is located within a physical situation that determines what it perceives and what the quality of that perception is. It is not the mind that makes our world a paradise or a purgatory, that makes us happy or miserable, but the conditions in which we live.

This book does not attempt to defend a purely subjective position, but it will contend that we cannot understand the psychological quality of a person's life simply from a knowledge of the circumstances in which that person lives. There are many good reasons for knowing the context of people's lives—their environmental condition, their economic status, their work life—but none of this information gives us more than a partial explanation of why some people find their lives enjoyable and satisfying and some do not. The mind does indeed influence our perception of the world, not without limits, to be sure, but to a sufficient degree that the correspondence between our objective conditions and our subjective experience is very imperfect. If we try to explain the population's sense of well-being on the basis of objective circumstances, we will leave unaccounted for most of what we are trying to explain.

Material Well-Being

For the past hundred years we have had a prevailing faith in the power of economic affluence to elevate the good life in America. We are internationally known as a money-oriented society, although whether our national values are more materialistic than those of any other nation is difficult to demonstrate. In any case it is clear that we have become an increasingly affluent people over the past century, and it would be hard to argue that the life of the average American has not been enhanced therewith. We are better fed and housed, we live longer, we are better educated, we work many fewer hours per week, and we are inclined to believe that we are the most favored nation in the world.

We have become so entranced with our economic indicators as guidelines to the good life that we have come to identify economic affluence with the good life. As recently as 1969 a government publication put the issue about as bluntly as it can be put, "Economic indicators have become so much a part of our thinking that we tend to equate a rising national income with national well-being."

National well-being is a concept with many meanings. We might reasonably define it in terms of public health. As the great advances have been made in sanitation, nutrition, and immunization, our days of sickness have decreased, our life expectancy is greater, and our well-being is enhanced. Ecologists now seek to identify well-being with the quality of the environment, and they urge reduction in the pollution of air and water and the protection of natural beauty as a contribution to the quality of our lives. Sociologists relate well-being to measures of crime, suicide, public violence, family disintegration, and other aspects of social pathology. But primarily we have learned to associate national well-being with economic welfare.

Welfare is commonly defined by economists in terms of the goods and services an individual can command. Current income is taken as a convenient estimate of individual welfare and gross national income has become a widely accepted indicator of the nation's welfare. Governments become concerned about economic welfare because they believe it is the major determiner of psychological well-being. They assume that if they can raise the average family income and reduce the number of families in poverty, they will lift the general level of happiness of the nation. This is an article of faith not only of our government but of governments around the world.

It is difficult to doubt that economic welfare contributes something critical to the psychological quality of life. Certainly as income has increased over the nation's history, the proportion of the citizenry living pleasant and satisfying lives must also have increased. And, as we will see later, studies comparing measures of satisfaction with life in countries at various levels of economic development typically find the highest sense of well-being in the countries with the highest per capita income.

But tracing changes in the quality of American life over the past 200 years or comparing levels of well-being in the developed and underdeveloped countries of the world is quite a different matter from explaining why some contemporary Americans find their lives joyful and satisfying and others find them miserable. A factor which may be significant in explaining international differences may have little value for accounting for individual differences within any particular nation. There may have been a time in this country's history when economic status was a dependable predictor of individual sense of well-being, when most people lived under oppressive circumstances which guaranteed a life of deprivation, and when those few at the top enjoyed lives of unquestioning pleasure. Our society is surely not that simple today; if economic needs were once the preeminent determiner of happiness and satisfaction, they now share that stage with many other needs of a nonmaterial character.

The Quality of Life

There have always been social critics who deplored the "economic philistinism" of American life, our blatant materialism, our obsession with things rather than human values. These critics were for many years largely disregarded in governmental circles where the only practical solution to the nation's problems seemed to be to put more money into the hands of more people. Sometime after the Second World War, however, there began to enter into political rhetoric a theme that the good life in America implied something more than material affluence; it implied the fulfillment of needs which cannot be expressed in monetary terms. An early spokesman for Lyndon Johnson's Great Society expressed this theme in the following language:

> The task of the Great Society is to ensure our people the environment, the capacities, and the social structures which will give them a meaningful chance to pursue their individual happiness. Thus the Great Society is concerned not with how much, but with how good—not with the quantity of goods, but the quality of our lives.

A few years later in his annual State of the Union message (1970) Richard Nixon included this statement:

> In the next 10 years we will increase our wealth by 50 percent. The profound question is, does this mean that we will be 50 percent richer in any real sense, 50 percent better off, 50 percent happier?

Neither of these philosophical observations suggested that life in this country might be improved by a reduction in the consumption of material goods, but the inference was clear that Americans should expect something more from life than the gratification of material needs. The phrase "quality of life" had entered the public vocabulary and, while seldom precisely defined, it became a dependable staple of political discourse.

Despite this rhetoric, there has been a great deal of reluctance on the part of national planners and decision makers to give up income and other measures of welfare as the essential indicators of public well-being. Economic accounts have a degree of precision and elegance which makes them adaptable to the kinds of analysis of costs and benefits which governmental officials are wont to do. Not that the Council of Economic Advisers and the other people responsible for the production of our economic indicators are unaware of the fact that a rising national income is not precisely the same as a rising sense of well-being. As one of them has put it, "The goods and services produced by the economic system, with rare exceptions, constitute instrumental rather than ultimate outputs of the system." The ultimate output is the individual utilities, the satisfactions and pleasure, that flow from the supply of goods and services.

But the economic profession has been raised for generations in the conviction that these satisfactions and pleasures cannot be measured directly. Alfred Marshall laid down the word for his fellow economists in 1890 with the declaration, "It cannot be too much insisted that to measure directly—either desire or satisfaction—is impossible, if not inconceivable," and for the most part his descendants have not questioned his advice. Economists have set about finding indicators that can be precisely counted (usually in dollars) to serve as proxies or surrogates for what they consider unmeasurable. Thus the amount of money spent on tickets to artistic performances of one sort or another might serve as an indicator of the public's level of aesthetic pleasure, the number of vacation days taken might be taken as an indicator of the total amount of enjoyment of leisure, changes in the average wage level might serve to indicate changes in satisfaction with work, the amount of money spent on do-it-yourself tools could give an indication of the pleasure people derive from hobbies. There is no doubt that economists have been very inventive in suggesting ways of using monetary indicators to estimate what they call individual utilities, or what we will call sense of well-being. All of them depend ultimately on the assumption that economic welfare and psychological well-being have an intimate and necessary association.

Sometime during the 30 years following the Second World War, however, something went wrong with this simple tie between welfare and well-being. During this period, Americans experienced one of the most dazzling rises in economic affluence in the nation's history. Average family income went up by about two-thirds in constant dollars between 1945 and 1973. The proportion of people living below the poverty line dropped from the prewar high of near one in three to closer to one in eight. It was a remarkable achievement. But in increasing the number of families whose income was sufficient to purchase an adequate diet and the associated necessities of life, we did not increase the sense of confidence with which Americans walked the streets of their cities, we did not increase the feeling of attachment to one's community or the feeling of satisfaction working people found in their jobs, we did not strengthen the bonds that held families together, we did not prevent the alienation of a generation of young people or the development of a small army of people dependent on drugs, and, least of all, did we increase the citizenry's trust in its elected officials. None of these improvements in the quality of

American life occurred; and it can be argued that as economic welfare increased in this country during the postwar period, psychological well-being declined.

How are we to explain this paradox? It is our belief that this country is entering an era in which public aspirations and values can no longer be as fully satisfied by simple increases in economic affluence as they may have been at an earlier time in our history. This does not imply that the general public is no longer moved by economic values; this is surely not true. But there appear to be a growing number of people in this country for whom values other than those of an economic character have become important enough that they are prepared to trade off economic return in order to achieve them. When a cross section of Americans was asked in 1973, "What does the quality of life mean to you—that is, what would you say the overall quality of your life depends on?" their most frequent answers were in order: (1) economic security, (2) family life, (3) personal strengths (honesty, fortitude, and intelligence), (4) friendships, and (5) the attractiveness of their physical environment. For the most part these people were talking about values that cannot be counted in dollars.

Psychological Man

Forty years ago Edward Chace Tolman, a well-known American psychologist, observed that American society had been dominated historically by the concept of "economic man," by the belief that human welfare and happiness depended primarily on the satisfaction of man's economic needs, his needs for material things. Tolman predicted that this phase of man's development would pass, that economic man would be replaced by psychological man, who would be motivated not only by material needs but also by the need for social prestige, group identification, sense of achievement, and other psychological satisfactions.

Although Professor Tolman could not have foreseen in 1940 the five years of the Second World War or the great wave of economic prosperity in this country in the years following thereafter, it is the basic premise of this book that he did correctly anticipate the gradual development within American society of a concern for values which are not specifically economic. Americans have always given great importance to what are called "spiritual" values, usually associated with their religious beliefs, but Tolman was proposing the development of psychological values, primarily associated with people's perceptions of their social relationships and of themselves. It is the preeminence of these values that distinguishes "psychological man."

During the 1950s Abraham Maslow proposed in his well-known books that human needs arrange themselves in a hierarchy, that people must first fulfill their "basic needs" for food and shelter; as these needs are met, they are then motivated by the "higher needs" for social support, belongingness, love, self-esteem, the respect of others, and finally self-fulfillment.

Erik Allardt has recently suggested a simplified version of this hierarchy, which we will utilize in subsequent pages. He classifies the basic human needs under having, relating ("loving" in his original language), and being. The need for *having* is satisfied through "the material and impersonal resources an individual has and can master." The need for *relating* is concerned with "love, companionship, and solidarity." The need for *being* denotes "self-actualization and the obverse of alienation." The satisfaction of each of these needs is assumed to contribute independently to the individual's sense of well-being.

We are now entering the decade of the 1980s and it is still too early to say that the age of psychological man has arrived in this country. There are far too many million American families living in a state of economic desperation to justify any such characterization, and there is too much evidence that economic motives still have high priority for most Americans. But there are interesting signs in the air: the growing concern about the despoliation of the natural environment, the protests against the boredom and meaninglessness of much industrial and white-collar work, the reluctance to join the "rat race" of competition for promotion in business enterprise, and the current increase in the flow of population into the rural areas of the country. It would be hazardous to predict what the ultimate importance of any of these manifestations will be, but they all seem to indicate a growing concern with values other than those that can be evaluated directly in monetary terms.

We believe that some form of emergent change toward a greater concern with what Allardt calls the needs for "relating" and "being" has been taking place in this country since the Second World War. This change has been supported by two critical developments in American life, the great increase in economic affluence and the substantial rise in the educational levels of successive generations. The affluence has diminished the fear of economic disaster which hung over earlier generations, especially those which had experienced the Great Depression of the 1930s, Doing without the necessities of life is no longer a realistic prospect for most Americans; their sense of insecurity in the face of unpredictable economic events has been reduced. The great increase in the number of college graduates has brought into the labor market a growing proportion of people entering professional, technical, and managerial occupations, relatively well-protected against the threat of unemployment and more liberated than most to concern themselves with the "higher needs." Their college education has not only provided them a passport into these favored occupations, it has also tended to broaden their horizons, cultivate their humanistic interests, and increase their appetite for challenge and new experience.

We believe these college graduates are the forerunners of psychological man in American society. As we shall see, their levels of subjective well-being seem much less dependent on their levels of economic affluence than those of people with more limited education. Their orientation toward their work is quite different from that of other people. They concern themselves with problems of the environment and other noneconomic issues far more than the rest of the population. One may ask whether their pattern of values, less dominated by the need for having and more concerned with the needs for relating and being, will in time become the pattern of a larger proportion of the population. College-educated people are very visible and very influential, but there is no guarantee that their values will diffuse into the population at large. Our expectations would be that their values will become more common as their conditions of life become more widespread, that psychological needs will become more prominent in American life as economic needs are more widely gratified. We are not likely to see a time when concern with economic income will disappear, but if we can find a way to extend the kind of economic security that our more advantaged citizens apparently feel, we may hope to enlarge the lives of an increasing number of people beyond the constraints of an obsessive concern with meeting the material needs of everyday life.

Affluence has not lifted American society to utopian levels of social harmony and personal fulfillment, but it has helped raise national aspirations to the attainment of those goals. The concept of quality of life has taken on new dimensions in this country, and the national concern has turned increasingly from its focus on the economic needs of the "ill-housed, ill-clad, and ill-nourished" to the needs of all the people for equity, participation, respect, challenge, and personal growth. For many Americans the "revolution of rising expectations" may be simply a desire for a larger house and a second car, but for some it is a growing demand for the fulfillment of needs which are not basically material but are primarily psychological needs for a larger and more satisfying life experience.

part 1

Concepts, Definitions, and Methods

When Thomas Jefferson included the pursuit of happiness as one of mankind's endowed rights in his draft of the Declaration of Independence, he was not proposing a concept which was unfamiliar to his contemporaries. "Happiness," as Garry Wills points out, was a "constant preoccupation of the eighteenth century," and he demonstrates that the writings of the time abound with discussions of the nature of happiness and the conditions of its achievement.

In 1725, the Scottish minister and philosopher Francis Hutcheson argued in his treatise on beauty and virtue, "That action is best which accomplishes the greatest happiness for the greatest numbers." The implications of this formula for the role of government were widely perceived, and happiness, which had been largely the preserve of theologians, became the central concern of political economists. Happiness was seen both in its manifestations in the individual's experience and in society, as the sum of the individuals. And it was assumed that it was a measurable quantity and that governments could be judged in terms of their success in creating public happiness.

In 1776, Jeremy Bentham proclaimed what he called his fundamental axiom, "It is the greatest happiness of the greatest number that is the measure of right and wrong." This utilitarian doctrine became accepted writ among the philosophical radicals of the nineteenth century and its influence still persists. By the end of the century, however, references to pleasure, good, or happiness had been largely displaced by the ambiguous term "utility," and Bentham's assumption that happiness was a measurable variable had been virtually abandoned. The economists busied themselves with goods and services which they were sure they knew how to count and gave up any attempt at a direct assessment of the impact the presence or absence of these commodities might have on the quality of individual experience.

But the concept of the public happiness is as important today as it has ever been, and even though the word seems to have gone out of style the desire to learn something about the way people experience their lives has, if anything, increased. Psychologists and sociologists throughout the world have experimented with measures of what is variously called "positive affect," "quality of life," "sense of well-being"—all concerned in essence with what the early philosophers called happiness. There is no gainsaying the fact that the measurement of these subjective feelings presents many hazards and requires assumptions that are subject to challenge. There is no psychological litmus paper that will tell us without question who is happy and who is miserable. Perceptions and feelings are certainly subjective but they are real to the person who experiences them. People are able to describe the quality of their own lives, not as precisely or with as great a degree of interpersonal comparability as one might like, but with a kind of direct validity that more objective measures do not have. Subjective experiences can only be measured subjectively, and we will have to accept the degree of imprecision this requirement implies.

The three chapters which make up Part One of this book are concerned primarily with concepts, definitions, and methodologies. Chapter 2 discusses the concept of well-being, the various ways it has been defined, and the methods which have been used to assess it. It presents the basic themes around which the content of the book is organized. Chapter 3 describes the major studies of subjective well-being which have been carried out in this country in the last 20 years and considers evidence of stability and change in the American population during that time. Chapter 4 is concerned with satisfactions in the major domains of life and the way in which they contribute to the individual's general sense of well-being.

2

The Concept of Well-Being

The World Health Organization (WHO) has defined health as "not only the absence of infirmity and disease but also a state of physical, mental, and social well-being." Concern with health has historically dealt with illness, injury, and death. WHO asks for a positive definition of health—physical, mental, and social well-being. It is concerned not only with those individuals in the population who suffer from illness, accident, or loss of function but with the entire population.

Our interest in this book is with the mental well-being of the American people. We will review certain limited information about the physical well-being of the population and we will take note at various points of certain indicators of social well-being, but our primary concern is with the experience of well-being.

Mental well-being may be defined in different ways. If society defines it, through its rewards and sanctions, it tends to emphasize the individual's stability, predictability, and conformity to the social code. Societies are generally not amused by transgressors and are quick to apply the label "sick" to those individuals who do not display a reasonable amount of conforming behavior. Some societies carry this attitude to its logical extreme and confine their dissidents in mental institutions.

If a psychiatrist or psychologist defines mental well-being (more likely to be called "mental health" by them), he or she would tend to evaluate an individual in terms of some theory of a "healthy" personality structure. A person who might appear quite "normal" in society's eyes might be seen by a psychiatrist as having an unhealthy life adjustment, based on an immature ego development and dependent personal relationships.

When individuals themselves evaluate their well-being, they are not likely to judge themselves on the basis of either society's or the psychiatrist's criteria. They depend on the quality of their own experience, their feeling of being happy and contented, their sense of well-being. In this definition well-being is entirely subjective, known directly to the individual person and known to others only through that person's behavior or verbal report.

It is this third definition that we follow in writing this book. The research from which the book is drawn is based on personal interviews taken with individuals who are asked to describe their experiences, feelings, moods, satisfactions, and frustrations. It is their sense of well-being with which we are concerned. We will discuss the problems of defining and measuring this subjective feeling, its relationship to the circumstances in which people live, and the characteristics of its changes through time. Our data all originate from individual respondents, but they will be aggregated so that we are typically speaking about the American population as a whole or comparing various of its component segments.

In choosing this particular focus, we do not undervalue the significance of social and physical well-being. These aspects of national well-being are the subject of frequent analysis, however, and we will assume that they do not need to be reviewed here. The reader is surely aware that economic indicators are far more commonly used as measures of national well-being than is any form of subjective measure. Indeed, as we have observed, we have tended very strongly in this country to identify economic welfare with the good life and to equate a rising national income with general well-being. It will be our argument in these pages that economic welfare may be a necessary condition for public well-being but it is not a sufficient one.

Many Americans are also aware of the statistics which appear periodically reporting the incidence of marriages, divorces, birth, crimes, college graduates, employed women, and the like. The range of these "social indicators" has been greatly extended in recent years, partly as a consequence of a growing dissatisfaction with purely economic measures. Some of these statistics can be taken as unequivocal indicators of national well-being or ill-being, the crime rate for example; others are more difficult to interpret. It is not immediately clear whether a rising divorce rate, for example, should be regarded as positive or negative or whether a continually rising number of college graduates necessarily contributes to national health. A zero-population-growth birthrate would have been regarded as a catastrophe during the days of Theodore Roosevelt, but it is now a popular and even a patriotic cause.

No one would contest the assumption that the status of the nation's physical health is a measure of national well-being. Whenever people are asked what they consider to be the essential requirements of a good life, good health is invariably near the top of the list. The nation has a growing repertoire of health statistics that tell us how likely we are to survive the first year of life, what kinds of sickness and accidents we may expect, how much health care we will require, and how long we may expect to live. We can see that over the years our national health has gradually improved and we can also see, perhaps surprisingly, that in such vital indicators as infant mortality and life expectancy we do not compare favorably with a number of other countries considerably less affluent than we are. We cannot demonstrate that subjective well-being has been enhanced as the nation's health has improved because our measures of perceived well-being do not go back far enough in time. But we can hardly doubt that the dramatic improvements in public health over the years have increased the amount of happiness and contentment Americans find in their lives.

All these indicators of the nation's social, economic, and physical health tell us a great deal about the way people live their lives in this country, but it has become increasingly evident in recent years that they do not tell us all we want to know. It is reasonable to assume that a rising national income will have a generally favorable effect on people's lives, that improving medical facilities will reduce the amount of misery associated with illness, and that rising educational achievements will create a more informed and more capable population. These facts tell us about the circumstances of people's lives, but they tell us only inferentially how people feel about their lives—to what extent they find them pleasant and rewarding, stimulating and joyful, supportive and secure.

If we knew that people's sense of well-being was highly predictable from a knowledge of these objective circumstances of life, we would not need to search for ways of measuring subjective well-being directly. But we know from commonplace observation that this relationship cannot be very high. There are too many affluent people receiving psychiatric attention, too many physically handicapped people with positive outlooks on life, too many people whose apparent sense of well-being seems not to fit the objective situation in which they live.

How Can We Assess Sense of Well-Being?

Mankind seems to have always been concerned with trying to understand the qualities of the "good life." Through the ages philosophers have written on the subject, usually in rather broad terms, since the concept seems quite resistant to precise definition—so resistant, in fact, that we have depended heavily on measures of economic, social, and physical well-being as surrogate indicators of subjective well-being.

Can the feeling of life be measured? Is it possible to say that a person is more happy or more miserable on one day of the week than on another? Or that one person has a more positive sense of well-being than another? Our everyday experience tells us that these kinds of differences do exist among the people we know although we would find it difficult to say how much more or less happy one person is than another. Subjective variables such as attitudes, values, or states of well-being surely cannot be measured in the same sense that we measure monetary income, square feet, or minutes on the clock. We can seldom go beyond simple ordering in which one person may be said to be higher or lower on a scale than another person, without having a precise estimate of how much higher or lower.

It is self-evident that the only source of information from which we can learn something directly about the feeling of life is the individual person; the man or woman who is living the life is the only one who can tell us how it feels. The feeling of well-being or ill-being is a private experience, and we can only learn about it if the person is willing to tell us about it. Fortunately most people are.

In order to probe into a subject as personal and as subjective as sense of well-being, one might think first of using the techniques of the depth interview of the psychotherapist or social anthropologist. Certainly no procedure is better adapted to bringing out the details of personal experience than the many-houred interviews these scholars typically use. And no technique can produce the intimate insight into individual lives which these detailed case histories provide. After months and often years of continued communication, they are likely to know as much about their subject's state of well-being or ill-being as it is possible for another person to know.

Unfortunately psychiatry is a very expensive method of gathering information and is practiced very largely on the small fraction of the population who can afford it. And social anthropology seems much better adapted to the study of small societies than of large ones. The problem in both cases is one of representation; both procedures describe highly selected segments of the population very well, but they are not able to guarantee that all parts of the population will be represented in their proper proportions. What these procedures gain in depth they lose in scope.

Since our interest in this book is in the sense of well-being of the American population, we cannot be satisfied with evidence from isolated case studies. The method of choice for portraying all the variety of a large heterogeneous population is clearly that of the sample survey. Ever since statisticians and social scientists learned how to draw a sample from a large universe in such a way that every member of the universe has an equal chance of being chosen, it has been possible to describe the national population accurately by obtaining information from a few thousand carefully selected individuals.

The sample survey is able to overcome the problem of accurate representation, but it has two major shortcomings with which we must be concerned. The first is the severe limitation on time in the conduct of survey interviews. Instead of the many hours of contact which the psychotherapists or anthropologists might expect to have with their subjects, the survey interviewer must complete her questioning within an hour or two. She must also follow a rigidly formalized questionnaire in order to create comparability between one interview and the next. These restrictions raise questions about the depth to which the interview penetrates the respondent's feelings, whether there is a "latent structure" to a person's feelings which may differ from the "manifest structure" which is available to a short interview. If latent feelings can only be unearthed by extended clinical interviewing, they will obviously not be revealed in a survey. We must be content with those feelings which the respondent is conscious of and is willing to describe. No doubt something is lost in this procedure, but a great deal is learned.

The second weakness of the survey method is its lack of time depth. It takes a recording at a specific point in time, and a single interview cannot record the fluctuations in a respondent's feelings that may occur from day to day or week to week. This does not create a problem in representing the average sense of well-being of the population at large since these fluctuations tend to average out, but it reduces our ability to account for the level of well-being of individual respondents. Although the respondents are asked to describe their lives "these days" or "in general," it is very likely that in some cases their responses are influenced by recent events or swings in mood of a short-term character. We assume that some individuals are very stable in their levels of affect and satisfaction with life but others are more variable, and it is these latter people who contribute to the unreliability of quality-of-life measures. Even so we know from earlier studies that there is a good deal of consistency in the way national samples answer these questions, even after an interval of several months. People's feelings of well-being change over time in response to changing circumstances, but this is not capricious as we will find when we examine measures of these feelings which have been recorded over the last 20 years.

Much as one might want to capture the best features of these various methodologies, if we insist on describing the national population, there is no alternative to reliance on the sample survey. One may use lengthy exploratory interviews to get a sense of how people talk about the quality of their lives and a feeling for how to develop questions, but ultimately one is forced into the practical constraints of the survey methodology. Since we are concerned in this book with the adult population of the United States, we will be relying throughout on data gathered from sample surveys. Most of these studies were conducted by the Institute for Social Research, and we will be drawing heavily from five Institute studies conducted in 1957, 1971, 1972, 1976, and 1978.

What Determines Sense of Well-Being?

We do not need to conduct any systematic research to know that people differ substantially in their general sense of well-being. Some seem to find their lives wholly gratifying and positive, while for others life is an unrewarding and depressing experience. How can we explain these differences?

Economic explanations of behavior typically begin with the assumption that there is a universal human impulse to maximize one's supply of goods and services. We take as our basic assumption that people are primarily motivated to maximize their sense of well-being. They seek to make their lives as happy and as satisfying as possible. We assume that the accumulation of goods and services commonly serves as an instrument through which people enhance their feelings of well-being, but we do not assume that there is a strong and necessary relationship between the affluence of their objective circumstances and the quality of their subjective well-being. People respond to the world around them not as it objectively is but as they perceive it, and it is our belief that they strive to perceive it as positively as possible. There are limits of course to their ability to reconstruct objective reality, and some kinds of circumstances will facilitate their wish to see their world positively and others will inhibit it. In general we would expect economic affluence to be a facilitating circumstance, but there are clearly many noneconomic conditions which make it difficult for people to see their lives positively—ill health, marital troubles, low status, discrimination, and social isolation, for example.

We assume that everyone's private world contains a mixture of facilitating and inhibiting conditions which make easy or difficult his or her effort to achieve a positive feeling of well-being. This balance differs from one person to another and may differ at different points in the same person's life span. We assume there are also differences between individuals in their ability to see this combination of conditions positively. We all tend to see what it pleases us to see, but some of us have a greater capacity to accomplish this than others. In the popular idiom, some people can "see the best in everything" while others are "never satisfied."

The ultimate level of perceived well-being which an individual will achieve will depend in part on the balance of facilitating and inhibiting conditions within which that person lives and in part on the success of that person's impulse to see his or her world positively. Because "the mind is its own place," we cannot expect to explain the level of well-being of this or that segment of the population solely on the basis of the objective circumstances within which it lives. But we do expect that there are some circumstances of life which will on the average make it easier to see life as a heaven and some which will make it more difficult.

In the following chapters we will be concerned with those objective conditions of life which are commonly thought to have the greatest influence on the individual's sense of well-being. We will find that segments of the population that live in different circumstances may show quite different patterns of well-being, although sometimes less different than one might have expected. We will have less to say than we would like about the contribution made to levels of well-being by personality differences, not because we regard their contribution as unimportant but because we have relatively little information about them.

The Domains of Life

Although most people have little trouble evaluating the quality of their lives as a whole, they are clearly more satisfied and pleased with some aspects of their lives than with others. A recently divorced man may be very unhappy about his marriage but very well-pleased with his work, his health, and his apartment, and he would be able to describe his feelings about each of those areas of his life. The number of discrete bits of their experience people can describe in this way is probably very large, but we will assume that we will capture most of this by considering the major divisions of life which we will call "domains." Thus, in the following chapters we will consider at some length the way people evaluate their marriage, their family and friends, their standard of living, their work, their community, their neighborhood, the nation, their housing, and themselves, and we will have somewhat less to say about their health and their education.

We must assume that an individual's general sense of well-being is determined in large degree by that person's satisfaction with his or her experience in these important domains of life. For most people, this appears to be a simple additive process: the more domains the person feels positive about, the stronger the sense of well-being. But there may be some people whose lives are dominated by a single central experience—an excruciating illness, a bad marriage, an exciting job. Very likely a domain which makes a relatively minor contribution to the global sense of well-being at one point in a person's life may make a major one at another time. Young people, for example, typically do not attach great importance to health, but for older people it often becomes the central domain of life. The domain of work seems to have more influence on a person's general sense of well-being during the middle years of life than it does during the earlier or later years. We will be concerned with the various domains of life both for the interest each of them has in its own right and for the pattern they form as components of general well-being.

At some points in the following pages we will change our focus from well-being to ill-being. One of the first things we will discover about the American people is that most of them succeed in perceiving their lives as satisfying, pleasant, and free of stress. But located here and there in this general atmosphere of well-being are groups of people who have a strong sense of ill-being. Prominent among these are those individuals who would like to work and do not have a job. In percentage terms, they are not a very large part of the population, but they receive a great deal of political attention which does not, unfortunately, appear to provide them a very positive life. On a more personal basis, divorced men and women also demonstrate a great sense of ill-being. Some segments of society find some aspects of their experience positive but others negative; widows, for example, are as satisfied with their lives in general as married women and are as free of stress, but they are much less likely to describe their lives as enjoyable, friendly, or happy. These pockets of ill-being, and others we will describe, attract our attention as exceptions to a generally favorable picture of quality of life in America. In some cases they seem to result from the failure of our society to provide the conditions necessary for a good life and in others they apparently grow out of the personal problems of individuals for which society itself does not seem capable of providing a solution.

Affect, Satisfaction, and Strain

The first time a national cross section of the American people was asked to assess their level of subjective well-being was in a national survey carried out by Gurin, Veroff, and Feld in 1957. They asked their 2,500 respondents to describe their feelings of happiness, their worries, and their experiences in marriage and on the job. In 1965 Norman Bradburn, at the University of Chicago, moved on from simply asking about happiness to asking people to recall "positive and negative feeling states" they had experienced in the preceding few weeks, how many times they had felt pleased, proud, excited, successful, on top of the world or restless, bored, depressed, lonely, or upset. Various other devices have been used to probe these *affective experiences* or what might be called the "pleasure-misery dimension" of well-being. They all seek to represent the positive and negative feelings which are associated with everyday experiences, and we will draw on them at appropriate points in the pages that follow.

Satisfaction, like pleasure, is also an attribute of daily experience which gives life its color. Sense of satisfaction often carries with it a strong element of pleasure, even exhilaration, and there is no doubt that happiness and satisfaction have something in common. But there is also a difference. Satisfaction does not have the spontaneous lift-of-the-spirits quality which distinguishes happiness. Satisfaction implies an act of judgment, a comparison of what people have to what they think they deserve, expect, or may reasonably aspire to. If this discrepancy is small, the result is satisfaction; if it is large, there is dissatisfaction. Satisfaction may be associated with strong feelings of pleasure, as at the moment of great achievement, but it may also be a satisfaction of resignation, when one comes to understand that what once seemed possible is no longer so and the best must be made of it. Dissatisfaction may have a dash of misery if it is associated with a failure experience, but on the contrary, it may be characterized by frustration, which is quite different from misery. Misery, on the other hand, is commonly associated with sadness, a feeling not typical of dissatisfaction.

The third contributor to one's general sense of well-being is the feeling of *strain* which people experience in their confrontation with the daily problems of their lives. Strain is a very complicated experience, the unraveling of which consumes an untold number of hours on psychiatrists' couches. The more severe kinds of anxiety which develop from stressful circumstances often have a physiological component; they are associated with a fast heart beat, sweating hands, headaches, and other similar symptoms. Although we will refer to studies of these symptoms in the following pages, we will focus on a more benign form of strain which is perceived as feeling tied down, feeling life is hard, being worried about money or other threats and, at the extreme, worrying about a nervous breakdown. This is the kind of strain that most people feel at one time or another, usually not severe enough to send them looking for professional help but detracting from their sense of well-being. This aspect of experience is basically affective, reflecting primarily negative affect. People who are free of strain also tend to describe their lives as satisfying and pleasant, but the relationship is not very strong and as we will see later, people in some walks of life show us quite uneven patterns of these three measures.

These are the three major dimensions of life experience—affect, satisfaction, and strain—which we will be considering in this book. Each of them taps at a somewhat different angle into that quality of human experience which we are calling the "sense of well-being." We will not add them together into a single index because we believe we can maintain a truer picture of how people describe their lives if we keep them separate. Our use of these measures is based on the assumption that all the countless experiences people go through from day to day add to these general global feelings of well-being, that these feelings remain relatively constant over extended periods, and that people can describe them with candor and accuracy.

Basic Themes

The reader will find that the body of this book is organized around a series of assumptions concerning the nature of the experience of well-being. We present them at this point to provide a setting for what is to follow.

1. People react to the world as they perceive it, not as it objectively is. Perception of objective fact is always influenced by the values, expectations, and personality traits the individual brings to the situation.

2. Sense of well-being is an attribute of human experience that derives from people's perceptions of their contemporary situation. It is always dependent on the subjective characteristics of the person and the objective characteristics of the situation.

3. Sense of well-being is an individual experience. Social well-being is the sum of individual experiences.

4. There is a general human impulse to maximize one's sense of well-being, to perceive one's objective circumstances as positively as possible.

5. Sense of well-being largely comprises two central components,

satisfaction-dissatisfaction and positive and negative affect. Sense of strain is an aspect of negative affect. Satisfaction and affect are related, but they are not identical and in some circumstances they move in opposite directions.

6. Satisfaction-dissatisfaction is a function of the gap the individual perceives between his or her present situation or status and the situation or status he or she aspires to, expects, or feels entitled to. Change in satisfaction level may result from a change in perceived situation or a change in aspiration level or both.

7. Affect reflects the spontaneous feelings of pleasure and misery associated with events in the individual's immediate experience. These events are both positively and negatively toned, and their sum determines the individual's affect balance.

8. Satisfaction and affect are both associated with specific domains of life. They are also experienced at the level of life as a whole.

9. Changes in sense of well-being follow either from changes in the individual's objective circumstances or in changes in the psychological perspective from which the individual perceives these circumstances.

Conclusion

This is a book about the way people feel about their lives. It is not a book of case studies; it is not the kind of book a psychiatrist or clinical psychologist would write. It is a book about the American public in all its fascinating diversity: young people, retired people, housewives, college graduates, childless couples, divorced men and women, farmers, black people, suburbanites, Southerners, Catholics, widows, and working women. At some points we will be describing the total population, but more commonly we will be teasing out these segments of the total population, comparing them with each other and identifying wherever we can what it is about their circumstances which makes them feel as they do about their lives. To the extent possible, we will take note of changes which may be occurring in the qualities of these people's experience.

In 1929, President Hoover asked the leading social scientists of the day to draw together a description of trends in American life. In the introduction to the resulting volume, called *Social Trends,* the authors remarked,

"Happiness and unhappiness have been little studied by science, yet happiness is one of our most cherished goals." Twenty years later Clyde Kluckhohn and Henry Murray, in their well-known book on personality, observed,

> One of the strangest, least interpretable symptoms of our time is the neglect by psychologists of the problem of happiness, the inner state which Plato, Aristotle, and almost all succeeding thinkers of the first rank assumed to be the "highest of all good achievable by action." Although the crucial role of dissatisfaction and of satisfaction is implicit in much that is said about motivation, activity, and reinforcement, psychologists are generally disposed to shun these terms as well as all their synonyms.

Because we have not felt confident about how to define or measure happiness we have contented ourselves with measuring those things we felt sure we could count, income and material goods. We have made economic welfare a surrogate for well-being because well-being is "too subjective." This book is specifically concerned with sense of well-being, a wholly subjective experience which can only be assessed by asking people to describe their lives. The findings we present are based on measures which are still experimental and imprecise, but they confront the problem with which we are concerned, the psychological well-being of the American people.

3

Measuring the Sense of Well-Being

Life is undoubtedly experienced in bits and segments, by the hour and by the day, but it also has a whole quality which the individual feels as something more than any of the parts. People may be more or less satisfied or pleased with their marriage, their job, their housing, or their health, but they are also more or less satisfied and pleased with their life as a whole. We will consider those major domains of life in the later chapters, but we begin by thinking about this global sense of well-being, the general feeling people have about the quality of their lives.

There is unfortunately no infallible test we can administer to people around the country to give us a precise reading of their general sense of well-being. We must rely on the various imperfect scales which have been used over the last 20 years, and we will consider in order those intended to assess affect, satisfaction, and perceived strain. We will also take account so far as possible of changes in the way the American people have described their lives over these two decades.

Happiness

The simplest and most straightforward question we could ask to ascertain a person's general feeling about life is, "Taking all things together, how would you say things are these days—would you say you are very happy, pretty happy, or not too happy?" It is not a wholly satisfying question;

happiness is a word with many meanings and we cannot tell from this categorical question what people have in mind when they answer it. But it has one great advantage; it has been asked repeatedly in this precise form over the last 20 years, and it is one of the very few indicators we have of how feelings of well-being have changed in this country over those two decades.

When we first asked this question of the American people in 1957, we found that about one person in three described himself or herself as "very happy," about half as "pretty happy," and about one in ten as "not too happy." This raw finding foreshadowed many similar distributions which social scientists have reported since—most people give positive answers when asked to evaluate their lives. However the question is asked, there is always a clustering of cases toward the upper end of the scale and a trailing off to a small number of unhappy people at the negative extreme. And this is not a characteristic of Americans alone; studies in countries much less affluent than our own, Britain for example, show a similar pattern. People seem to try hard to see their lives in a positive light.

Of course not all segments of the population are as willing to say they are "very happy" as others are. Not only are there dramatic contrasts between individual men and women who find their lives a delight or a misery, there are also substantial differences between classes of people who live in different circumstances. Part Two of this book will be primarily concerned with comparing the way Americans in differing conditions of life describe their lives. Are the affluent happier and more satisfied than the poor, the college graduate more than the high school dropout, the married person more than the widowed or divorced person, the young person starting life more than the older person, the white more than the black? One of the major purposes of this book is to test a number of commonly held hypotheses concerning those circumstances of life which are associated with feelings of well-being or ill-being and examine the extent to which these associations have changed over the last 20 years.

Between 1957 and the early 1970s there was a decline in the proportion of the American population prepared to describe itself as very happy. As we see in the accompanying comparison, this proportion fell from its high point of 35 percent in 1957 to a low of 24 percent in 1972. It then rose again in the latter part of the decade to 30 percent. These shifts are

	Very happy	Pretty happy	Not too happy
1957	35%	54%	11%
1971	29%	61%	10%
1972	24%	66%	10%
1976	30%	60%	10%
1978	30%	62%	8%

larger than might be attributed to sheer chance, and they are particularly interesting because they moved in direct opposition to the national economic trends of the ime.

If we accepted the common assumption that the state of the national economy is the major contributor to fluctuations in the national sense of well-being, we would find these changes in reported happiness rather difficult to explain. The decline between 1957 and 1972 took place during a period when the country was experiencing one of its greatest surges of prosperity in history. It is obvious that some other event of a noneconomic nature must have impressed itself on the national consciousness during this period. The 1960s was a decade of great social turmoil—political assassinations, racial conflict, revolt on the campuses, rising rates of crime and violence, and, perhaps most traumatic of all, the tragedy of Vietnam. We do not know specifically the impact of these events on the average American's feelings, but we cannot doubt that their general influence was negative and we do not find it surprising that the number of Americans who could describe themselves as "very happy" declined during these years.

American participation in the Vietnam conflict ended in 1973, street demonstrations diminished, and the campuses began to return to their prewar calm; racial issues still held high priority, but the atmosphere of confrontation had cooled substantially. Crime rates remained very high although they began to drop in the latter part of the decade. These changes were of a positive character and might have been expected to raise public spirits somewhat, but they were offset by the unprecedented political crisis growing out of the Watergate exposé and by the severe depression of 1974–1975 and the ensuing problems of unemployment, inflation, and a stagnant economy. the slight rise in reported well-being between 1972 and 1976 paralleled the 1974–1975 recession, and if economic considerations were accepted as the preeminent determiners of public well-being, we should have expected happiness levels to decline during the 1972–1978 period. But in fact they improved modestly, obviously for reasons that were not economic.

The Indices of Affect

Happiness, as we have observed, is a many-faceted experience and the simple "Are you happy?" question which has been asked over the last two decades gives us very little of the flavor life has for people. A broader and more reliable measure of the feel of life may be obtained by asking about the kinds of affectively toned experience people have had in the recent past. Have they felt particularly excited or interested in something, proud at having been complimented, pleased at having accomplished something, on top of the world, or that things were going their way? These are positive experiences which we would expect to be related to people's expressions of general happiness with life. There are also negative experiences—feeling too restless to sit still, feeling lonely, bored, depressed, or upset because of having been criticized—that contribute to a feeling of negative affect and that we would expect to relate inversely to general happiness. These are the indices of positive and negative affect which were developed by Norman Bradburn in 1965 and were asked of national samples by the Institute for Social Research in 1972 and 1978.

When Bradburn first asked these questions in 1965, he found that people were generally more likely to remember positive experiences than negative ones (see Appendix Table 1). The specific percentages obtained in his survey depended of course on the particular wording of the questions, but the generally positive pattern which he found is consistent with the findings of other research. There appears to be a persistent human impulse to see the world positively, to feel positively about it, to remember it positively, and to use positive language in describing it.

When the same series of questions was asked in 1972, the proportions of people recalling positive and negative experiences were very similar to what they had been in 1965. This is rather perplexing in view of the decline in levels of reported happiness which occurred during this same period. In view of the relationship which we know to exist between reported happiness and the two indices of affect, a decline in recalled positive experiences and an increase in recalled negative experiences might have been expected. But it did not happen.

Between 1972 and 1978, however, there was a significant rise in the Index of Positive Affect, paralleling the increase in the number of people who described themselves as "very happy." These two measures appear to reflect a brightening of national mood during this period. But the Index of Negative Affect remained unchanged in 1978 from its 1972 level or indeed from its level in 1965. Bradburn demonstrated in his early research that these two indices are not mirror images of each other, that a person who reports many positive experiences may also report many negative ones. They clearly did not move together during the 1972–1978 period, and they appear to be measuring different aspects of the individual's affective experience. We will treat them as separate measures in the following pages and give particular attention to those instances in which they move independently of each other.

Are You Satisfied with Your Life?

One of the basic facts that research on feelings of well-being has taught us is that being satisfied is not quite the same as being happy. People may be happy with their lives but still not satisfied because they aspire to something beyond what they have. They may also be satisfied with life because they have accommodated themselves to its inevitabilities, but they do not find it a happy life. Satisfaction tends to be a more stable quality of experience; happiness is more susceptible to fluctuations of mood which may vary from day to day. Satisfaction and affect are the two major dimensions of sense of well-being which we will consider in this book. They are certainly related, but they are also different, and the differences will give us a fuller understanding of the experience of well-being.

People's feelings of satisfaction may be associated with a virtually unlimited variety of experiences; people may be satisfied with the climate, their health, their job, their marriage, their government, their neighborhood, and countless other aspects of life. They may also be satisfied or dissatisfied with their life as a whole. We assume that their satisfactions with the specific domains of life contribute to their general satisfaction with life, and we will see in the next chapter that some of these domains seem to make a much greater contribution than others.

Just as with the questions concerning happiness and general affect, when people are asked, "How satisfied are you with your life as a whole these days?" they are far more likely to give a positive answer than a negative one. When a cross section of Americans was asked this question in 1971, 22 percent of them described themselves as "completely satisfied." No more than 1 percent were "completely dissatisfied," although an additional 6 percent were dissatisfied in some lesser degree. The total number of people dissatisfied with their lives was not very different from the number who said they were "not too happy," and of course they tended to be the same people. In 1978 the proportions of satisfied and dissatisfied people were almost precisely the same as they had been eight years earlier: 22 percent were now completely satisfied and a total of 7 percent dissatisfied in some degree.

This persistence in the levels of life satisfaction during a period when the proportion of "very happy" people was increasing raises questions on whether this was a peculiarity of the 1970s or whether satisfaction as a general experience is inherently more stable than the more direct measures of affect. Although there are no directly comparable data from earlier years, there is a series of studies beginning in 1959 and running through 1974 that suggest that the latter hypothesis is probably correct. During the 1950s Hadley Cantril developed what he called "the self-anchoring striving scale." He asked his subjects to think of the best possible life they could imagine and the worst possible life. They were then asked to indicate on a scale where they thought their present life would stand between these extremes. These people were not asked specifically how satisfied they were with their lives, but the discrepancy they saw between their actual life and the best life they could imagine can be thought of as a measure of their satisfaction. As we will see, Americans rate their lives quite high on this scale compared with people in other countries, but the interesting fact is that over the 15 years this measure has been used in this country, there has been no consistent trend in the assessment people make of their lives. The rating in 1974 was the same as it had been in 1959.

Other studies have also shown an impressive consistency in indicators of public satisfaction over time. In 1955 a cross section of housewives living in Detroit was asked, "How do you feel about your standard of living—the kind of house, clothes, car, and so forth?" The same question was asked again of a comparable sample in 1971, and the proportions of women describing themselves as satisfied were almost identical. There is little doubt that the average standard of living of these people had in fact improved during this 16-year period; the average income of Detroit families increased over 40 percent in constant dollars during that time. But satisfaction with standard of living did not change.

Similarly the General Social Survey found almost no variability from year to year between 1972 and 1977 in expressed satisfaction with "your present financial situation." While these annual national surveys carried out by the National Opinion Research Center recorded a consistent decline in the proportion of people who felt their financial situation was "getting better," their average satisfaction levels remained constant throughout this five-year period. It is not surprising that the severe depression of 1974–1975 was associated with a drop in perceived economic status; the impressive fact is that it was not accompanied by a decline in level of satisfaction.

These indicators of satisfaction are obviously behaving differently than the measure of happiness. While avowed happiness declined from the late 1950s to the early 1970s, levels of satisfaction with life stood still. Satisfaction is a more cognitive process than feeling the pleasant and unpleasant experiences of life, less immediate, more dependent on a judgmental comparison of one's present circumstances with what is thought to be an appropriate standard. People's circumstances change but their standards of judgment tend to accommodate to these changes and their levels of satisfaction tend to remain constant. As we will see, some life events are so traumatic that most people cannot accept them as satisfying—unemployment, divorce, ill health—but the less dramatic changes of circumstances that a person encounters can be adjusted to, and on the average people appear to be successful in modifying their aspirations and expectations upward or downward to accommodate to these changes.

In the 1978 Institute for Social Research survey a question was presented which asked people to consider their satisfaction with life in a somewhat different light. The question came at the end of the interview and it read, "Considering everything, would you say that up to now you have had all the happiness a person can reasonably expect in life or have you had less than your share or more than your share?" This is again a question which forces the individual to make a judgment, a comparison of his or her life experiences with what he or she might have "reasonably expected." The time reference is not to "these days" but to the persons's life "up to now." Six out of ten of a national sample of the population said they had had all the happiness they were entitled to and an additional one in six felt they had had more than their share. But over one in five of these people (22 percent) felt that, all things considered, their measure of happiness in life had fallen short of what they thought of as their proper share. These people who see their happiness as going beyond or falling short of what they consider to be a reasonable expectation present an interesting contrast, and we will have occasion to examine their other characteristics at various points in the following pages.

The fact that general levels of public satisfaction remain as constant as they do does not mean of course that every individual remains constant in his or her satisfaction with life. People differ substantially in the degree of satisfaction they appear to derive from their lives, partly we assume because some people are simply easier to satisfy than others and partly because the circumstances of their lives fulfill or fail to fulfill their aspirations. Personality differences, whether inherited or acquired, undoubtedly account for some part of the differences we see between people in their satisfaction with life, but it also matters whether they have gained or lost a spouse, a promotion, a job, their health, or some other of the "goods" of life. And it matters whether they are young or old, black or white, urban or rural. While the average American appears to be quite satisfied with life, there are a good many Americans who are not, and the circumstances which are associated with being satisfied or dissatisfied will become evident as we move into Part Two.

Do You Feel under Stress?

Strain is a feeling of being burdened, hemmed in, worried, pressured. In the extreme it sends people for psychiatric help; for most people it is an aspect of life experience, not quite like general affect or satisfaction and contributing in a different way to the subjective quality of their lives.

As we have noted, research on strain often depends on physiological symptoms as the crucial indicators—headaches, loss of appetite, dizziness, and the like. This is a different measure from the one we are concerned with, which is entirely psychological: do people see their lives as hard rather than easy, tied down rather than free, do they worry about money or other threats to themselves or their families, do they worry about a nervous breakdown? No doubt this is a thin substitute for the kind of interview a psychiatrist would consider necessary for an assessment of a patient's feelings of strain, but in studying the general public, simplified measures are imperative and, as we shall see, this one reveals some interesting facts about people that the other measures do not.

In 1971 nearly half of the people in this country admitted that there was something about their lives that "made them feel frightened or worried." Most commonly this something was a concern with health, either their own or their family's. Some people were worried about their jobs or their general financial situation. A few were concerned about international tensions, Communism, or declining moral standards. For the most part the things that made people feel "frightened or worried" were personal and family matters rather than concerns with the larger world. Somewhat fewer than one person in five said they worried all the time or most of the time about money. One person in four described their lives as "hard" rather than "easy" and one in seven said they felt "tied down" rather than "free." One person in seven said they sometimes worried that they might have a nervous breakdown. People who reported one kind of worry or stress were likely to report others; these five questions all tap an aspect of experience we are calling "*perceived strain*."

As we might expect, people who perceive their lives as strained are not as likely to describe themselves as very happy or very satisfied with life as those people who do not report worries and pressures of the kind these questions are concerned with. When these five questions are combined into an Index of Perceived Strain, it is apparent that the dimension of experience measured is inversely associated with the other two measures. Strain is a negative experience and is predominantly affective rather than cognitive. In these respects it resembles the kinds of feelings expressed in the Bradburn Index of Negative Affect. The two measures are not identical, but to a significant degree they are measuring the same thing.

The measure of perceived strain was not used in surveys prior to 1971, and we cannot compare its movement during the 1960s with that of the measure of happiness. But we can compare 1971 and 1978, and we discover that over this period reported feelings of strain changed very little.

Although the measures of happiness and positive affect moved upward during these years, this measure stood still, just as the Index of Negative Affect did. It may seem curious that people were more likely to report positive experiences in 1978 than they had been in 1971 but were no more nor less likely to report negative experiences. It seems natural to assume that as people find more positive experiences in their lives, they will also find fewer negative ones. But the incidences of these two kinds of events have been repeatedly shown to be more independent of each other than one might be inclined to expect. Whether the positive events are inherently more variable in number and the negative ones more fixed we do not know, but the evidence we have suggests that this may be the case.

Conclusions

If someone asked us whether Americans are honest people, a religious people, or an intelligent people, we would have to ask in return, compared with whom? If we are asked, Are Americans a happy people? We will have the same problem. We can see that most Americans describe their lives as at least "pretty happy," mostly satisfying, and free of strain. But that might have been true a hundred years ago, and it may be true in other countries today.

Unfortunately we do not have the wealth of international comparisons of psychological well-being that we have for economic welfare. There is a flood of economic indicators that describe the objective circumstances of the people of many nations and have done so for decades. Moreover these indicators are typically counted in units which are relatively easily compared from one country to another so that it is possible to say that a larger proportion of the families of one country than of another own an automobile or that the average living space in one country is so many square feet more than that of another. The measurement of subjective well-being is a much more recent development, much less standardized and much more subject to the ambiguities of language differences. But beginnings have been made and Americans seem to view their lives quite favorably in comparison to the people of other countries.

In the early 1960s Cantril carried out sample surveys in 13 widely scattered countries, using his self-anchoring scale to assess the perceived quality of life. Americans saw their current lives as closer to the best life they could imagine than any of the other nationalities. An international Gallup survey in 1965 found a larger proportion of Americans describing themselves as very happy than any of several other nationalities except the British, whose percent very happy was slightly higher. More recently (1976) the Gallup Organization reported a comparative study of 60 countries which showed North Americans to stand more favorably on various indicators of subjective well-being than people in any of the other areas of the world. None of these studies was as definitive as one might like, but they all showed that reported feelings of well-being in this country were at least as high as they were elsewhere and considerably higher than in many other countries.

It has been argued that this high level of perceived well-being is the natural consequence of this country's material affluence, that as nations move up the ladder of economic welfare they also raise their level of social welfare (the term economists use to describe what we are calling *sense of well-being*). Cantril concluded from his study that the richer countries are indeed the happier countries, but the differences between the most advantaged countries and the least developed in his study were rather irregular and the relationship between affluence and happiness was not very strong. Gallup reported more positively from his 1976 survey that "economic privation seems to affect the spirit as well as the body. Poverty adversely colors attitudes and perceptions. Although one probably could find isolated places in the world where the inhabitants are very poor but happy, this study failed to discover any area that met this test. The nations with the highest per capita income almost invariably top every test of psychological well-being and satisfaction in major aspects of life."

The findings of these studies support the contention that national sense of well-being depends in part on the level of that nation's economic development. Although there are inconsistencies in the data, especially in the Cantril study, when nations as economically different as the United States and India are compared, there is little doubt that associated differences in subjective well-being will be found. It is also true of course that within every country where studies have been done, affluent individuals on the average describe their lives more positively than do poor people. It is probably true that an individual's sense of well-being depends more on how his economic status compares with that of other people within his own country than on how his country's economic status compares with that of other countries. But the conditions of life in the affluent countries seem clearly more propitious for the development of positive evaluations of individual well-being than the circumstances in which people of the poorer countries live. There are limits to the individual's ability to accept deprivations without damage to his or her feelings of happiness and satisfaction.

Whether or not Americans compare favorably with other nationalities in their evaluation of the subjective quality of their lives is probably not as significant a question as whether feelings of well-being in America have improved or declined over the last 20 years. This question requires a mixed answer. In number of people who described their lives as "very happy," this country declined quite sharply between 1957 and 1972 but then turned upward again in the later 1970s. The proportion who said they were "satisfied" with life maintained an even level throughout this period. Happiness, which would appear to be a more spontaneous experience than satisfaction, seemed to respond directly to the flow of change in the circumstances of national life. Satisfaction, which seems more judgmental, appeared to accommodate itself to these changes.

The fact that these two indicators record different patterns of change over the 20 years of our observations makes it apparent that they are measuring somewhat different components of the individual's general sense of well-being. These components are surely related, happy people tend also to be satisfied people, but they are sufficiently independent that they do not always move together. We will find repeated examples in the following chapters of life situations in which they move in opposite directions. We also find circumstances in which the measure of perceived strain diverges from the other two measures and gives us an insight we would not otherwise have had.

4
Domains of Life

People live their lives in many settings. To the conventional housewife, life may seem bounded by the concerns of marriage and children. Her husband spends half of his day at a place of work and his experience there may dominate his life. They both are concerned with the economic status of their household, their standard of living, and their savings. During periods of good health, they may not give much thought to their physical condition, but at times of illness considerations of health may become oppressive. Their house and neighborhood concern them, enough on occasion to lead them to change their residence. Their experiences in these and other domains of life contribute in some additive way to their general sense of well-being.

We might, if we tried, list several hundred different aspects of people's lives that contribute to their general feeling of satisfaction and pleasure in life. A balky bit of plumbing or a sick household pet may produce total misery. It is not practical to try to trace the impact of isolated experiences of this kind; the effort would be overwhelming. It is possible, however, to identify the major regions or domains of life in which these experiences occur and to consider the level of satisfaction people associate with each of them.

The Pattern of Domains

There is certainly no common pattern of concerns to which all Americans conform. Some people's lives revolve around the collection of postage stamps, others around sports or music. But there are a certain number of areas of life which concern almost everyone, and when we consider the population at large, we find that satisfaction or dissatisfaction with these specific domains is largely reponsible for satisfaction with life in general. We will consider 12 such domains in the following chapters.

Marriage Not everyone marries in this country, but sooner or later over 90 percent of the population do. Some of them do not stay married, an increasing number, but most of those who divorce get married again. Marriage is obviously the core of much emotional experience; the quality of one's marriage has far-reaching implications for the quality of one's life.

Most Americans, both men and women, describe themselves as very well satisfied with their marriage, over half of them saying in both 1971 and 1978 that they are completely satisfied (see Appendix Table 2). In view of this country's high divorce rate, these declarations of high satisfaction may seem somewhat paradoxical; one might have expected a much stronger expression of dissatisfaction. Perhaps the ordinary person is reluctant to admit that his or her marriage is something less than satisfying, perhaps people compare their marriage to the alternatives of no marriage, perhaps most marriages are satisfying and those that aren't have long since ended in divorce. We will return to these questions in Chapter 6.

Family Life Not everyone is married but virtually everyone has or has had a family. Family includes parents, siblings, and children; death or divorce may end a marriage but they do not typically end family life. Widowed people are as satisfied with their family life as people still married, even though their own marriages have dissolved. For married people marriage and family life are intertwined of course, and satisfaction with one is likely to be accompanied by satisfaction with the other. But not always—a well-married couple may be estranged from their children, and a husband and wife may feel their marriage has wilted but they still feel close to their parents or siblings.

Most people express high satisfaction with their family life. They are not so often "completely satisfied" as they are with their marriages, but people in general are more satisfied with their family life than with any domain other than marriage. There was an increase between 1971 and 1978 in the proportion of the population which was divorced or never married, and there was an associated decrease in the proportion that described itself as completely satisfied with family life. We will explore this relationship more fully in Chapter 7.

Friendships While marriage and the family undoubtedly provide the most intimate interpersonal associations, most people find additional social support in their friends. Having good friends "you can count on in case of trouble" may not be important to people who do not have troubles, but they may be crucial to those who do. Not everyone is interested in having a great many friends; indeed those people who report having fewer friends than average are less interested than average in making additional friends. But, in general, those people with the most friends are most likely to describe themselves as very satisfied with their friendships.

Friendships vary in degree of intimacy, from the confidante with whom one would feel comfortable discussing the most personal kinds of problems to the people who live across the street whom one knows by name but never visits. Most Americans feel they have at least one friend to whom they can tell anything, but one person in six in the population seems to be totally without such a confidential friend. As one might expect, these isolated people tend to be unmarried, younger than average, and residents of large metropolitan centers. For the most part, however, people in this country seem to be well supplied with friends and the general level of satisfaction with friendships was relatively high throughout the population in both 1971 and 1978.

Standard of Living The accumulation of material goods is often taken to be an American obsession, the essential demonstration of the philistinism of American life. Whether material belongings are more important to Americans than they are to other people may well be questioned; they are probably important to most people everywhere. When Americans are asked to tell an interviewer what the quality of life means to them, their most frequent type of response makes some reference to income security. When they are asked to describe the ways their quality of life falls short of what they would like it to be, their most frequent response is that they do not have enough money. These people evidently consider a degree of economic security to be a necessary condition for a happy and contented life; we will see later the extent to which economic status is in itself a sufficient condition for such a life.

In the 1971 and 1978 surveys economic status was determined by questions about standard of living, "the things people have—housing, cars, furniture, recreation, and the like," and about savings and investments. People are considerably more likely to say they are satisfied with their standard of living than they are with their savings, and in both cases the number who claim to be "completely satisfied" is comparatively low. The average income of the population (in constant dollars) changed very little in the period between the two surveys, but there had been substantial rises both in the cost of living and unemployment and there was a decline in the number of people who felt satisfied with their economic circumstances.

Work Despite occasional predictions that advances in the technology of production will soon make work anachronistic, the fact is that the proportion of adult Americans who are employed has continued to rise and now stands at an all-time high. And in spite of continuing controversy regarding the four-day workweek and other proposals intended to reduce the number of hours at work, the average workweek in this country has stubbornly maintained itself at 40 hours for the past several decades.

The psychological meaning of work has inspired thousands of research inquiries and countless commentaries. One of Karl Marx's earliest pronouncements was that people's essential being is intimately bound up in their work and that the mechanization and specialization of labor which developed under industrial capitalism had forced people into a dehumanized existence. Because the product of their labor had no real meaning to them, workers became estranged, not only from their work but from themselves. This theory of alienated labor has demonstrated remarkable vitality; it is still a popular theme of criticism of Western society. "For most Americans," writes Charles Reich, "work is mindless, exhausting, boring, servile and hateful, something to be endured while 'life' is confined to 'time-off.'"

In light of this continuing drumbeat of criticism, one has to be impressed with how well-disposed toward their jobs American working people, both men and women, seem to be. When asked if they would want to continue to work if they were to come into enough money "to live as comfortably as you'd like for the rest of your life," the large majority assert that they would. And, when they are asked how satisfied they are with the work they are doing, four out of five say they are at least moderately satisfied. Perhaps there is some element of "false consciousness" involved in these assessments, but there is no doubt their jobs have value for these people that has little to do with the economic return which the work provides.

Neighborhood What does it mean to a person to live in a particular neighborhood, a particular town or city, a particular nation? What kinds of psychological value do these surrounding communities provide the individual citizen? To what extent is our general satisfaction with life influenced by the fact that we live in this community rather than another? Is it true, as some believe, that community identification is declining in this country and that we are becoming increasingly alienated and uninterested in community life? To what degree can we assess the level of satisfaction people get from their communities from a knowledge of such objective indicators as extent of park space, intensity of traffic noise, level of air pollution, density of population, extremes of weather, and the like?

As we see in Appendix Table 2, most people seem quite satisfied with their local neighborhoods, more so than they are with their city or the nation at large. And this satisfaction was no less strong in 1978 than it had been in 1971. Nonetheless, as we will see, not all neighborhoods are equally attractive.

City or Town or Residence From the earliest days of the Republic there has been a steady flow of migration from the farms and open country into the towns and cities. Only during the latter part of the 1970s did this movement of population reverse. People move for different reasons, but there is little doubt that economic motives have a high priority. For generations the cities have promised opportunity and success and millions of Americans from the rural areas have responded. But economic opportunity is not the only criterion by which people judge the community in which they live, and in these nonmaterial values the large cities compare very badly with the smaller places. People are less willing to say they are fully satisfied with their city than they are with their neighborhood, and a substantial number (one in four) do not admit to being even moderately satisfied.

Newspaper polls in recent years have reported that many people living in urban centers say they would prefer to live in a small town. When we compare the levels of satisfaction with their community expressed by people living in urban and rural areas, we see why the polls come out as they do. The larger the community people live in, the less satisfying they find it. The metropolitan centers, which have been losing population steadily over the last decade, were seen as the least satisfying by the people who live there, the suburbs were considerably more satisfying, but to the residents of small towns and rural areas their locales were clearly the most satisfying of all.

The Nation The ultimate social identification for most people is their status as citizens. The nation intrudes in their lives in a good many ways and such experiences are not always pleasant. In 1971 one American out of three thought that "all things considered" things in this country were getting worse, twice the proportion who thought they were getting better. But fewer than 10 percent were prepared to say that they were dissatisfied with "life in the United States today." People found many things to criticize, but most of them were unwilling to say that they were dissatisfied with their country. In 1978 the national situation had changed dramatically with the end of the Vietnam war and the civil turmoil associated with it. Watergate had come and gone as well as the recession of 1974–75. But deep concerns about inflation, unemployment, and related economic stresses and strains remained, and the number of people who described themselves as satisfied with life in this country was no higher than it had been in 1971.

Housing Housing has both a physical and a psychological meaning. A dwelling is a structure of a certain number of square feet and other physical qualities, but it is also the locus of family life, a man's castle, a symbol of status, a retreat from the world, and for many the object of much sentiment and nostalgia. In most cases a house is a home. Governments all over the world take great interest in building new housing on the apparent assumption that people's sense of well-being depends in some essential way on how well they are housed. In comparison to other countries, Americans are generally well housed; the number of homes without the basic amenities has declined to very small numbers. But the general level of satisfaction with housing is not high compared with that with other domains of life, and over one family in four says it would like to move from its present dwelling. Of course many of these potential movers are simply looking for space more appropriate to their needs which have changed because of a change in family size, retirement, or other circumstances of life. Many people who live in what by objective standards would have to be called very modest housing seem entirely satisfied with it, and the proportion who expressed dissatisfaction with their housing did not exceed one in ten in the population in either 1971 or 1978. As we will see, satisfaction with housing has much less influence on one's general satisfaction with life than one might expect.

Education For generations Americans have seen education as the road to success and the good life, especially those Americans who were not well-supplied with either of those conditions. The nation has given very high priority to public education and the average American spends more years in school than do the citizens of any other country. The longer people in this country have spent in school the more likely they are to say they are satisfied with their educational achievement (with some interesting exceptions which we will consider later), but there are a great many Americans who do not feel satisfied with the amount of education they have received.

There were notable changes in the educational achievements of the American population during the 1970s. There was a substantial decline in the number of people who progressed no further than grade school, accounted for very largely by the gradual disappearance of an older, poorly educated generation. There was an increase in the number of people who had completed a college degree and a substantial change in the proportion of the population who had attended college but had not finished a four-year degree, reflecting the great increase in junior college and community college enrollment around the country. With this general upgrading of educational levels there was, paradoxically enough, a small decline between 1971 and 1978 in the degree of satisfaction Americans felt with their education. This surprising trend was contributed in large part by the increasing numbers of people who started college but did not complete a degree. As we will see, these people express more dissatisfaction than either high school graduates or college graduates, not only in the extent of their education but in other domains of life as well.

Health There is probably no experience in people's lives more exclusively personal than their perception of their own health. No one else is involved; the experience comes from within. When the message is bad, it can make life a misery. Like some other aspects of human experience, health seldom commands a very high priority in the individual's awareness until it begins to give trouble. For most of their lives, people give very little thought to their health and when they are asked if they are satisfied with their health, they respond affirmatively. They are satisfied with the fact that they are not sick or infirm. When physical problems begin to appear, as they do with advancing years, satisfaction declines. Poor health seems uniquely difficult to accommodate to with resignation and good spirit. In both 1971 and 1978, however, a relatively small proportion of the people in this country expressed dissatisfaction with their health, approximately one person in ten in each year. One wonders what this proportion would have been in the nineteenth century, before the great advances in sanitation and immunization revolutionized standards of public health in this country.

The Self Asking people to report how satisfied they are with themselves may seem to put a severe strain on their powers of introspection and their ability to assess their own merits and demerits. There are a great many ways individuals might evaluate themselves as persons. They may be satisfied with themselves because they have accomplished something they had aspired to or because they feel they have handled difficulties well. They may feel dissatisfied that they are not as generous, religious, thoughtful, or loving a person as they would like to be. In fact most people do not find this question difficult to answer and they do not always give themselves high marks. In 1978 the proportion who expressed themselves as "completely satisfied" with themselves was relatively small, some one in five, one of the lowest levels of complete satisfaction expressed in any of these 12 major domains of life. But the proportion who described themselves as dissatisfied in any degree was even smaller, only six percent. People obviously avoid the extremes in responding to this question. One may guess that some people find it immodest to claim to be completely satisfied with themselves; they prefer to admit to some reservations. But for the most part they are not ready to say they are generally dissatisfied with themselves and, as we will see, those few who do find a good many other shortcomings in their lives.

These are the 12 domains of experience with which we will be primarily concerned in the chapters which follow. These domains are not independent of each other; they tend to form clusters. Satisfaction with family life is associated with satisfaction with marriage and with friendships; standard of living and savings go together; satisfaction with housing, community, and neighborhood are related; and satisfaction with the nation is on the boundary of this cluster. Satisfaction with education is closer to the economic cluster than to any other, and satisfaction with work also has a moderate association with this group of domains. Satisfaction with health seems to stand by itself; it is only weakly related to general satisfaction with life and to the other domain satisfactions. Satisfaction with self has moderate relationships with a number of the other domains, and it is more closely related to satisfaction with life in general than is satisfaction in any of the other domains.

We clearly do not exhaust the total range of life experience in concentrating on these 12 domains. There are many other concerns which are important for some segments of the population—church activities, hobbies, volunteer work, for example—but they do not add a great deal to our understanding of the sense of well-being of the population as a whole. Knowing how satisfied people are in these 12 basic domains tells us a great deal about their level of satisfaction with life in general.

Which Domains of Life Seem Most Satisfying?

We do not expect everyone to be satisfied with the same things in life, and it is clear that the different domains of life do not seem equally satisfying to everyone. When we put these domains in order according to the average level of satisfaction people express with each of them (Appendix Table 2), the differences between the domains become apparent and they suggest something of why it is that some domains of life seem more satisfying than others.

As we see, Americans are most likely to express high satisfaction with their marriage and their family life and low satisfaction with their economic status and their education. It can be argued that marital and family relationships have a uniquely intimate character that makes them inherently rewarding while the more impersonal domains of standard of living and education are less central to the emotional life of the person and are less capable of giving satisfaction. It may be, however, that levels of satisfaction in these various domains of life are influenced by a very different consideration, the presence or absence of external objective standards to which the individual's present status can be compared. People may be most able to feel satisfaction with those domains of their lives for which it is most difficult to find such an objective standard and least able in those domains for which such a standard clearly exists. A person's image of a satisfying marriage is very largely a matter of his or her definition of such a marriage; there is no generally accepted standard he or she can take as a point of reference. Economic status and educational level, however, are very countable and readily compared to societal averages. The sense of discrepancy in these areas of life may be immediate.

It is apparent, of course, that the most internal, personal domains of a person's life are also the ones for which it is most difficult to find an objective standard of comparison—marriage, family life, friendship, the self. The most external domains are the most readily compared to objective reality, standard of living, educational level, and housing. Neighborhood and work, both of which imply some degree of personal interaction, lie toward the upper side of this scale. The city and the nation at large lie toward the lower, more external side.

Which Domains Contribute Most to Satisfaction with Life in General?

As we have noted, an individual's life may be dominated from day to day by a variety of different concerns, and different individuals may have an overwhelming concern with some aspect of life which dominates their feelings over long periods of time. For the population at large, however, we must assume that some domains of life experience are generally more central than others and, on the average, have greater influence on people's general satisfaction with life.

We undertake to assess the contribution each of the various domains makes to one's general level of satisfaction by relating the level of satisfaction in each of the domains to the level of satisfaction with life in general. We assume that if, in the population at large, people who are highly satisfied with their marriage, for example, tend also to be highly satisfied with life in general and the opposite for those who are not satisfied with their marriage, then people's feelings about their marriage must be an important contributor to their satisfaction with life in general. When we perform this analysis for each of the 12 domains of life we are considering, we find that satisfaction with self has the strongest relationship with general life satisfaction; satisfaction with standard of living is second and satisfaction with family life is a close third (see Appendix Table 3). Satisfaction with marriage is also high on the list, as are satisfaction with friends and work.

Satisfaction in these domains—*self, standard of living, family life, marriage, friends*, and *work*—has the greatest influence in accounting for the level of satisfaction people feel with their life in general. The other domains are of diminished importance. Less significant are the domains relating to the environment—the community, the neighborhood, housing, and the nation at large. The degree of satisfaction people in general feel with their health and their education is also only weakly related to how satisfied they feel with life in general. There are undoubtedly particular individuals for whom these domains have transcendent importance. People with severe health problems, for example, are typically dissatisfied with their health and with life in general. But there are fortunately relatively few such people; most people have no difficulties with their health, and their general feelings of well-being are influenced by their experiences in other domains of life which have high priority at the moment. Most people say, when asked, that good health is a very important requirement for a good life, but they appear to take for granted the good health they have and their satisfaction with it has relatively little impact on their expressed feelings of well-being.

The order of importance of the domains listed in Appendix Table 3 changed very little in the national surveys taken in 1971 and 1978. Satisfaction with self was not asked in 1971, but other studies at the same period indicated that it would rank high and it is not surprising that it takes the high position it does in the 1978 survey. Specific individuals depart dramatically from this general pattern as the circumstances of their lives differ from the average, but the pattern for the population at large was very stable through the decade of the 1970s.

Conclusions

We know that satisfaction with life in general and satisfactions in the various domains of life are related, but we do not know for sure which is primary and fundamental. We know that the former can be quite well predicted from a knowledge of the latter; experience in the different domains appears to contribute additively to general life satisfaction or dissatisfaction. But it may well be that some people have a general orientation toward life, more or less accepting or demanding, that is reflected in their readiness to express satisfaction both with the specific domains of life and with life in general. In all probability both of these mechanisms are important. A misfortune in one area of life, marital estrangement, for example, may well have a depressing effect generally, but a basically optimistic person may be able to contain the effects of such a disaster and maintain the positive quality of other life domains. To an individual who habitually finds the worst in everything, every domain may seem less than acceptable. Such a person, as the saying goes, "is hard to satisfy."

We are impressed again with the generally positive quality in the assessments people make of the various domains of their lives. We have seen how reluctant Americans are to describe themselves as "not too happy" or not satisfied with life, and we see that when they talk about the specific areas of their lives they are much more likely to be positive than negative. This cannot be attributed to a characteristic American tendency to see the best in everything; similar distributions, although not quite so positive, are reported when Europeans are asked similar questions.

Of course not everyone is satisfied with everything, and when we begin to disaggregate the total population and look at people living in different circumstances, we will see that in some of these groups—unemployed, divorced, disabled, for example—life does not have a very positive quality. These are people who have had the experience of moving from a more satisfying condition of life to a much less satisfying one, a move which is so traumatic that they cannot accommodate to it. For most people life does not bring such dramatic reversals; the life course in this country has been typically characterized by a gradual improvement of circumstances, and even though aspiration levels tend to rise as achievement levels rise, they appear to remain in a relationship to each other which is experienced as satisfying by most people.

The fact that the different domains of life contribute unequally to the determination of general life satisfaction confirms commonsense expectation, and the priority of marriage, family life, self, and standard of living occasions no surprises. It is noteworthy, however, how inadequately a simple theory of economic determinism would explain differences in life satisfaction. As we will see in Chapter 5, satisfaction with the economic circumstances of life increases the more affluent these circumstances are, even though there are a good many people in the wrong cells—satisfied poor people and dissatisfied people who are well-off. Economic satisfaction clearly contributes to life satisfaction, but it is not the only contributor nor even the preeminent one. We find, in sum, that satisfaction with life is powerfully affected by domains in which satisfaction has no relationship with income levels, and if we attempt to account for life satisfaction on the basis of economic satisfaction alone, we discover that we have left most of the differences between individuals unexplained.

part 2

Conditions of Well-Being

Social scientists are seldom in a position to say that some specific aspect of a person's experience or behavior is caused by some attribute of the circumstances in which that person lives. The survey method from which much of our information comes does not permit us to go beyond saying with some confidence that people living in certain kinds of circumstances are more likely to feel or behave this way or that than people living in different circumstances. The implication of causation is often present, but what has been demonstrated does not in fact go beyond a relationship of more or less strength.

In the following chapters we will examine a series of relationships between people's feelings of well-being and the circumstances in which they live. External circumstances vary in countless ways of course, and we will have to restrict ourselves to those major attributes of people's lives which social theory or earlier research has suggested would have an important association with the subjective quality of life. We will be asking the following questions.

Chapter 5. Status: Do people of high status—economic, educational, or occupational—enjoy more pleasant and more satisfying lives than people of low status?

Chapter 6. Marriage: Are married people happier and more satisfied with life than people who are not married? Under what circumstances is marriage most and least likely to be satisfying?

Chapter 7. Social Networks: To what extent are people supported by a network of neighbors, relatives, and friends, and in what way are these relationships associated with feelings of well-being?

Chapter 8. Employment: Are the lives of men who work more pleasant and more satisfying than those who do not—unemployed and retired men? Are some kinds of work more satisfying than others?

Chapter 9. Women at Work: Are the lives of married women who are employed outside the home perceived as more pleasant and fulfilling than the lives of homemakers who are not so employed?

Chapter 10. Neighborhoods and Housing: Do the physical circumstances in which people live relate in meaningful ways to their feelings of well-being? Are clement weather, low density of population, well-kept neighborhoods, and spacious housing associated with positive feelings of well-being?

Chapter 11. The Nation: Is satisfaction with life in the United States strongly associated with sense of well-being? Is disaffection increasing?

Chapter 12. Aging and the Life Span: Do feelings of well-being change in predictable ways as people move through the life span, declining from a generally positive pattern in the younger years to a more negative pattern in later life?

Chapter 13. Health: Do physical health and attractiveness contribute to satisfaction with oneself as a person, to one's sense of controlling one's fate, and to a sense of well-being?

These are the major conditions of life that are commonly thought to influence psychological well-being in the general population. In the nine chapters in this part of the book, we will discover that some popular hypotheses about the conditions of a happy life are supported by the evidence and some are not. We will also see that some aspects of American life changed between 1971 and 1978, but many others did not.

5

Having High Status

People have high status when they stand high in the attributes to which their society accords privilege and respect. What is more reasonable than the expectation that those people who stand nearest the top and have the most would have the most pleasant and satisfying lives? Of course we know that it is primarily the well-positioned who fill the psychiatrists' offices, and it is not uncommon to find people of very modest circumstances who seem to be much more content than one might expect them to be. But if we set aside individual cases and think of averages, we would confidently expect that feelings of well-being would decline as we move down the status ladder.

We expect people with high status to report a high sense of well-being for two reasons. First, we believe people are more likely to have pleasant things happen to them if they are at the top of the ladder than if they are at the bottom. They are more likely to be treated with respect, deferred to, and complimented; they are more likely to have success experiences rather than failure experiences; they are more likely to have access to pleasant situations, entertainment, sports, travel, and vacation activities; they are more likely to enjoy good health; and they are more likely to own consumer goods that give pleasure, a special house, an attractive location, new rather than worn-out automobiles and appliances. The opportunities for affectively positive experience are simply more frequent for these people. Second, it seems clear that since these people stand above most of their fellows, they can hardly fail to see their advantage and we would expect them to feel some degree of satisfaction with it. People at the bottom, like the small boy with his nose against the candy store window, are looking at things they do not have.

Status implies position in respect to other people, and it can be measured in different ways. Inherited family position is thought by some to be the ultimate in social status, especially so in societies with aristocratic pretensions. Economic affluence is a more commonplace standard but a very popular one. Educational achievement is also taken as a mark of status, more respected in some societies than others. Occupation is widely recognized as giving status, most people having very clear ideas on what are the high- and low-prestige occupations.

Although there have been a number of studies of social class in this country which have given prominence to the importance of inherited family status, those studies have not represented the entire population and they have not been repeated through time. We turn then to the other indicators of status, and the most important of these is affluence.

Affluence

"The happy man," Aristotle wrote some two thousand years ago, "is one whose activity accords with perfect virtue and who is adequately furnished with external goods." Modern Americans would probably have some difficulty defining "perfect virtue," but they understand the importance of "external goods." Affluence seems to be recognized universally as the door to many good things, and while it may not guarantee a high sense of well-being, it is commonly thought to make it more likely.

Affluence is usually measured by current income. This is not a wholly satisfactory measure since it does not take account of the individual's accumulated assets and in some cases, retired people for instance, income and assets may not be very closely related. But assets are difficult to get records for, and in their absence income is in most cases an acceptable substitute. Income is easily counted and, with proper modifications for inflation, income levels can be compared through time and with appropriate conversions can be compared from one country to another.

There is no doubt that over the last 20 years, high-income people in the United States have been more likely to describe themselves as "very happy" than those with low incomes. Looking at five national surveys conducted between 1957 and 1978, we find an unmistakable pattern (see Appendix Table 4). In each of these years the proportion of "very happy" people is higher as we move from low- to high-income levels. A very stable relationship but by no means an exclusive one. Even among the most affluent, there are a large majority who describe themselves as less than very happy and a sizable minority of the least affluent claim that they are very happy. Happiness is far from the exclusive domain of the well-to-do.

We saw in Chapter 3 that the proportion of the American population who call themselves "very happy" fell between 1957 and 1972. Now we see that this decline was most marked among the most affluent, while people in the lowest income quartile maintained their low position without change. The most affluent were the most likely to call themselves "very happy" throughout this period, but the substantial difference in levels of perceived happiness that separated high-and low-income people in 1957 diminished significantly during the prosperous period of the 1960s and early 1970s and was much smaller in 1972 than it had been 15 years earlier. There was no Institute for Social Research survey of psychological well-being during the 1974–75 recession, but in 1976 this trend was reversed; income level regained most of its association with perceived happiness. If we assume that this reversal reflected the psychological impact of the recession, we must conclude that the effect was very short-lived since by 1978 the happiness levels of the different income groups had again drawn closer together. High income seemed to have less power to produce feelings of happiness at the end of the 1970s than it had had in 1957.

In 1978 high-income people still stood at the top of the happiness ladder, and they also scored well when they were asked to recall pleasant and unpleasant experiences in the recent past. The ability to remember being excited or interested in something, proud, pleased, on top of the world, or feeling that things were going your way is clearly highest among people with the largest incomes, and it declines gradually through the lower income levels. Conversely the memory of negative experiences is highest among the people with the lowest incomes, although this difference is not entirely consistent, and income has a weaker relationship to negative experiences than it does to positive.

These scales of positive and negative affect were first used in a national survey in 1965, again in 1972, and most recently in 1978. In all three years the pattern was the same: high income went with high positive affect and somewhat less strongly with low negative affect. Positive affect was higher for the total population in 1978 than it had been in 1965 and 1972. High-income people became more positive during this period, but so also did low-income people; the distance between them did not narrow.

It is not surprising to find that people with high incomes have a greater positive feeling about their lives, and we might expect to find that they are also more satisfied with their lives. But when people of different income are asked, "How satisfied are you with your life as a whole these days?" we find that reported satisfaction with "life as a whole" does not differ as greatly through the income scale as the reports of positive affect do. High income is consistently associated with greater satisfaction with life, but the relationship is very modest.

Knowing people's incomes does not tell us a great deal about their general satisfaction with life, but it does tell us something about their satisfaction with those domains of life which are most closely associated with the need for having—income, standard of living, and savings. With these material considerations, people with high incomes tend to be well-satisfied, clearly more satisfied on the average than people with low incomes. Level of income is also positively related to satisfaction with health and much less strongly to satisfaction with level of education, work, neighborhood, and housing. Income level seems to have nothing to do, however, with levels of satisfaction of an interpersonal character—marriage, family life, and friendships—and it is totally unrelated to people's satisfaction with themselves. A high income undoubtedly increases the likelihood of being satisfied with the material things of life, but it has very little to do with people's evaluation of some of the most important aspects of their life experience, those associated with their needs for relating and being.

Feelings of strain are a negative experience, and like the events making up the Bradburn Scale of Negative Affect, they tend to be more common among people of low income. Low-income people are more likely to find their lives to be "hard" and worrisome in one way or another. They are more often concerned about having a "nervous breakdown." Affluent people are clearly in an advantaged position to receive positive experiences, and while they cannot altogether avoid negative ones, they succeed more often than poor people do.

A further demonstration of the relationship of income to feelings of well-being appears when people are asked if they feel they have had "all the happiness a person can reasonably expect in life." When people undertake to evaluate their whole life "up to now," the differences between income groups are similar to those shown when they express their degree of happiness in their lives "these days." Over a third of the people in the lowest 10 percent of the income distribution say they feel they have had less than their share of happiness in life; at the top of the income ladder, the proportion is close to one in ten. These people were not being asked if they thought they had received all the income a person might reasonably expect, but it is quite evident that they find it easier to believe they have had their share of happiness in life if they have had more than an average share of income. It is important to note, however, that a majority (60 percent) of the population feels they have experienced about the share of happiness they could reasonably expect in life, that some dauntless souls find more than their share of happiness with very low incomes, and that some very-high-income people do not believe their lives have been as happy as they should have been.

It is clear from all this evidence that income has something to do with people's sense of well-being. This relationship has been found repeatedly in every country in which studies of well-being have been conducted. It is always better to be rich than poor. This is a fact which is universally understood; what is not so well-recognized is how modest this relationship is and how many other influences come into play in determining an individual's feelings of well-being.

Satisfaction with Income

Of course income is not the same as satisfaction with income and with the standard of living that goes with income. Satisfaction with these material aspects of life is far more strongly related to the affect and satisfaction measures of well-being than is income itself. People who express high satisfaction with their standard of living tend also to be well-satisfied in the other domains of life, even in those domains involving interpersonal relations and the self, with which income itself has no relation whatsoever. We see here what we will see again at later points in this book; if we undertake to describe people's general feelings of well-being, it is much less helpful to know the objective facts of people's circumstances than to know how people perceive these circumstances. Income and standard of living are important objective circumstances of life, but they do not in themselves make possible a very firm prediction of how a person feels about his or her life. A knowledge of people's levels of satisfaction with these material conditions of life provides a much stronger indication of their general sense of well-being.

Education

The status associated with education derives in part from the status associated with income, since education and income tend to go together. The relationship is not as close as it once was, to be sure; many craftsmen in blue collars earn more than professionals and semiprofessionals in white collars. And if we consider family incomes, the presence of two workers in a family may raise the family income considerably above the expected income for their level of education. A significant relationship remains however; on the average, higher education means higher incomes.

Educational level is even less dependable as a predictor of perceived happiness than income is (see Appendix Table 5). Those people with the most limited education (no more than grade school) were generally the least likely to call themselves very happy throughout the 1957–1978 period. College graduates, who were an increasing proportion of the population over these 20 years, were the most likely to describe their lives as very happy. But the range of difference in reported happiness between the well and poorly educated diminished substantially between 1957 and 1978, resulting in the same kind of contraction we saw between contrasting levels of income. People at the bottom of the educational ladder changed very little during this period, but those at the top moved downward and the gap between them narrowed.

Like people of high income, people with college degrees are more likely than other people to report positive affective experiences in their recent past. They are clearly more likely to say they remember being excited, pleased, proud, and the like than people with limited education.

Curiously enough, however, they are not less likely to say they remember being bored, upset, depressed, lonely, or restless. These negative experiences seem to be about as frequent at one educational level as another. So also are the experiences of strain, a different form of negative feelings. Years of education do not appear to protect a person from seeing life as hard, feeling tied down, being frightened or worried, although they do reduce one's concern about meeting the household bills.

We see again that positive affect and negative affect are not two sides of the same coin. Both income and education appear to make it more likely that people will encounter pleasant, stimulating, rewarding experiences in their daily lives. This is in no way surprising, considering what we know about the life-styles of people who are well-placed in these respects. We might have expected that they would be more successful in avoiding the disagreeable, worrisome experiences of life than they apparently are. Alas, even the very rich do not fully succeed in achieving this, and a college diploma seems to be a very inadequate defense.

We have seen above that satisfaction with life as a whole and with the material domains of life tends to increase modestly from low- to high-income people. When we compare people of different educational levels, we find a different pattern. College graduates are somewhat more satisfied with their lives than other people, but otherwise amount of education does not appear to have much influence so far as general satisfaction with life is concerned. It has a very substantial influence, however, on how satisfied people are with their own education. People who complete college are over twice as likely to say they are very satisfied with the amount of education they have than those who do not complete high school. There is one striking departure from this general pattern of more satisfaction associated with more education. Those people who attended college but did not complete a degree are less satisfied with their level of education than are high school graduates and of course much less so than college graduates.

People seem to be well-aware of how their educational achievement compares with the standards toward which most Americans aspire, high school or college graduation. They also appear to attach great value to years of schooling, and the fewer years they have the greater their sense of deprivation and the lower their feelings of satisfaction. The case of those people who went to college but did not complete a degree is particularly interesting. Many of them must have gone with hopes of completing a four-year degree. Their college experience might be expected to strengthen their aspiration to the occupational, economic, and social goals they see associated with a college degree. When for whatever reason they drop out of college, they are left with a particularly acute sense of falling short of their goal and the attendant feelings of dissatisfaction. This scenario does not fit everyone who stops short of a four-year degree to be sure, but the general pattern seems clear. If one starts college, it is better to finish.

Years of education, like level of income, is also positively related to satisfaction in one other important domain of life, physical health. The more education people have, the more likely they are to say they are satisfied with their health. On the face of it this might appear to mean that well-educated people are more likely than average to have superior health care and to avoid environmental or dietary conditions which might diminish their health. It is also true, however, that educational levels in this country are correlated with age; most of those people who did not reach high school are beyond middle-age and most of those who have reached college are below middle-age. And of course health and satisfaction with health are also correlated with age. Thus part of the relationship we see between education and satisfaction with health is produced by the influence of the third factor, age. When this influence is removed statistically, the relationship between education and satisfaction with health is diminished but it does not disappear.

In these domains of health and education, educational level has a clear positive association with satisfaction, but in other areas of life the picture is quite different. Indeed people with the most limited education express a surprisingly high degree of satisfaction with many domains of their lives. The general pattern of satisfaction with housing, work, community, and self is high among the least educated, tends downward through the education ladder to a low point among people with some college, and then turns up again among college graduates. This pattern, clearly present in both 1971 and 1978, tells us something about the influence of education. Exposure to formal education expands people's horizons, makes them aware of alternatives, and, unless they have clear objective evidence of their own advantages (as in the areas of health and education), makes them less willing to describe the various domains of their lives as fully satisfying. Their aspiration levels rise as their experience broadens, and their satisfaction levels decline.

The college graduates tend to reverse this pattern; they are clearly more satisfied in these other domains than people who do not finish college. As we will see at various points in later pages, college graduates have other unique characteristics that will attract our attention. Their aspiration levels are presumably higher than those of people at the lower educational levels, but their circumstances are also very favorable in many respects.

College graduates, like people with high incomes, are considerably more likely than average to say they "have had all the happiness they could reasonably expect in life" or more. Those people who dropped out before they reached high school are much more likely to say they have had less than their share than more (30 percent to 8 percent); the college graduates show the opposite balance (14 percent to 28 percent). Of course in both groups over half say they feel they have had no more or less happiness than they regard as reasonable. In other words, most people appear to be satisfied with the level of happiness they have experienced in their lives, but the more years they have spent in school the more likely they are to say they are more than satisfied.

Satisfaction with Education

Being satisfied with one's education is a much poorer indicator of one's general feelings of well-being than being satisfied with one's income or standard of living. As we know, education and income are rather substantially related but satisfaction with the economic aspects of life is one of the strongest predictors of positive affect and life satisfaction, and satisfaction with education is one of the weakest. Most adults have completed their education, of course, and they have had to accommodate to whatever level they have attained. Since few of them see any likelihood that they will be able to improve their educational status, whatever dissatisfaction they feel may tend to be contained and to have little influence on their general outlook on life. This seems peculiarly not true, however, of people who start college but do not finish. They not only have higher levels of dissatisfaction with their education than one might have expected but also with their income, their work, and, in lesser degree, with other aspects of their lives. Their failure to complete a college degree appears to be associated with diffuse and persistent discontent.

Income and Education

Knowing a person's income is clearly a better basis for predicting a person's sense of well-being than knowing his or her educational level. But income and education are both moderately related to feelings of well-being, and we might expect that people with the highest income and the most advanced education would report the highest levels of satisfaction and pleasure in life. This turns out not to be the case; the picture is not as simple as it might appear.

Over the 20 years of these studies, people with high incomes have consistently reported high levels of affect and satisfaction with life regardless of what their educational attainments were; college graduates with high incomes were no more positive in these respects than people with equally high income who had less formal education. At this level of income, education had no clear relationship to level of perceived well-being. However, among people who had less than an average income, educational level did make a difference but not the expected one. On the average, college graduates with low incomes expressed more positive feelings of well-being than any of the less-educated groups who had low incomes. A low income appeared to have a more depressing effect on the well-being of people without a college degree than it did on those who had such a degree.

The contrast between people who have some college but not a degree and those who have a degree is striking. One might have expected people in both of these groups to show low levels of well-being if they fell in the low-income brackets, on the assumption that their advanced education would have given them high-income expectations which would be frustrated by their low-income experience. This is in fact an accurate description of the some-college group; if they have low incomes their affect and satisfaction is generally negative compared with the other groups. The low-income college graduates, who might have been predicted to be the most negative of all, are in fact the most positive. This is a surprising finding, and it compels one to ask whether income means something different to college graduates than it does to other people.

We have suggested in an earlier chapter that the educational experience and occupational advantages of college graduates have freed them in part from the demands of purely material needs and broadened their concern with values relating to social relationships and self-evaluation. We will return to this theme at later points in this book.

Occupation

Occupation is a well-recognized mark of status in this country and most others, and people have very clear and well-established concepts of what the high- and low-prestige occupations are. Doctors, judges, and scientists head the list, and the low-skilled service occupations are at the bottom. The prestige order does not follow income levels precisely; ministers, for example, are higher in prestige than they are in income, but there is of course a degree of relationship with both income and education.

National surveys are typically not large enough to permit the comparison of such specific occupations as teacher, nurse, or truck driver, but they do make possible comparisons of categories of occupations. When we make the customary groupings, we find that they differ in interesting ways on the various indicators of well-being and the ordering is for the most part about what one might have expected. Throughout the 20-year period of the Institute for Social Research surveys, people in the white-collar occupations have been somewhat more likely to describe themselves as very happy than people whose occupations are blue-collar. People in the prestige categories of professionals, managers, and proprietors do not differ greatly among themselves in this respect nor from the much more modest, and modestly paid, clerical and sales occupations. Unskilled operatives, service workers, and farmers hold the bottom rungs on this scale, and they also differ rather little from each other.

The same division of white-collar and blue-collar appears when people are asked about recent positive experiences, with the former somewhat more likely to recall being excited, pleased, proud, and the like. But the negative experiences are quite a different story. Farmers are clearly the least likely to report feeling restless, lonely, bored, depressed, or upset, and they are followed by the self-employed proprietors. The other occupations do not differ in any systematic way. As individual enterprisers, farmers and proprietors have a different occupational experience than other people do, one which is characterized by unusual rewards, as we will see in Chapter 8.

Satisfaction with life, like perceived happiness and positive affect, tends to follow the prestige ordering of occupations, with the notable exception of farmers. Although farmers rank very low in their expressions of happiness, they are among the highest in describing themselves as satisfied with their lives. They also exceed people in other occupations in their satisfaction with other domains of life. They have particularly high satisfaction with their work, along with self-employed proprietors who also rank high in this domain. The life of the farmer is clearly different from that of other workers, and while it is not especially well-paid on the average and is not characterized by the kind of experience that is described as "happy," nevertheless it appears to be particularly satisfying to that diminishing number of Americans who choose it as their lifework.

As one might expect, it is the prestige occupations that tend to believe they have had more happiness in their life than they might have reasonably expected and the blue-collar workers who feel they have had less. People in clerical and sales jobs are on the fence. Although white-collar, their jobs are not highly paid or very prestigious, and they are as likely to feel they have had more than their share of happiness as to feel they have had less. Farmers, however, who are neither white-collar, highly paid, or prestigious, are on balance positive in their sense of receiving their share of happiness in life, another indication that their way of life seems peculiarly satisfying to them.

These comparisons of people in the different occupations reveal small differences of an interesting character, but they make it clear that the high or low status associated with occupational level does not account for very much of the differences we find in people's sense of well-being. And if we removed the influence of income from the comparison of the different occupations, even these small differences would be diminished, although farmers would still be unique.

The importance of occupation does not become fully apparent, however, until we look at those people who do not have an occupation—those who are unemployed. We then discover that the absence of an occupation has very substantial implications for feelings of well-being. These people are far less likely than any of the employed groups to speak of themselves as very happy or satisfied with their lives. This pattern has been very stable throughout the years these measurements have been made, and it is not simply a consequence of the fact that unemployed people typically have restricted incomes. Even when the income differences are removed by statistical controls, the low levels of well-being remain. We will return to this subject in Chapter 8, but we can see immediately that if one is in the labor force, it is surely better to be employed than unemployed.

There is one further large segment of the population who work, although they are not usually said to be employed. They are homemakers. Their level of professed happiness has resembled that of the population at large in the years between 1971 and 1978, following the same fluctuations that the total population has. They are also very similar to the rest of the population in their general level of satisfaction with life. We will have a great deal more to say about the lives of homemakers in Chapter 9.

Conclusions

American society is not made up of a privileged minority who find life very pleasant and a much greater majority who find it miserable, as some social theorists would apparently like us to believe. Most people describe their lives in relatively positive terms, although some are more positive than others. In some part these differences result from their positions on the status ladder; those who stand near the top tend to be happier and more satisfied with life than those who stand on the lower rungs.

There is certainly nothing surprising in the fact that this ordering has been found repeatedly in surveys in this country and elsewhere. High-status people lead privileged lives; one would expect them to enjoy them. The puzzling question is why they do not differ more than they do from people of more modest status. One would expect that people of high incomes would be more likely to call themselves "very happy" than people of lower income levels, and they clearly did throughout the 20-year period of these studies. But a sizable proportion of the very lowest income level also called themselves "very happy," half or more the proportion of the most affluent.

Income, of course, is an imperfect measure of social status, but of all the "objective" facts we can know about people, it probably tells us more about the circumstances of their lives than any other. It tells us something about people's sense of well-being as well, but it leaves a great deal unexplained. Income level relates significantly to people's satisfactions with the economic aspects of their lives, but it scarcely predicts at all their satisfaction with the interpersonal domains of their lives—friendships, marriage, family life—or their satisfaction with themselves. A person's general sense of well-being depends heavily on these underlying life domains. High income is associated with satisfaction in some of these domains and not in others and its relation to general sense of well-being is dependable and universal but only moderate and far from preemptive.

It has been repeatedly shown that when people are asked how the quality of their lives might be improved, they tend to answer in terms of more income. But, as we see, income is not a panacea for the shortcomings of life and in some of life's most central domains, it is totally ineffective. People appear to overestimate the beneficial effects that additional income will have on their lives. There is no reason to believe that increased income will on the average decrease feelings of well-being, but its ability to enhance these feelings appears to be restricted largely to those material domains of life which relate to the need for having, which in turn has only a limited relationship to a person's general sense of well-being.

In some respects a person's educational level is a more valid indicator of social status than income, but education is a limited indicator of sense of well-being. The kinds of experience that are perceived as pleasant and enjoyable are clearly more numerous the more years of schooling a person has, and over the years those people with the least education have been least likely to describe their lives as very happy. Satisfaction, however, is a different experience than happiness, depending more on a judgmental evaluation of one's situation and less on spontaneous experiences of pleasure or misery. In those domains of life in which education is clearly associated with advantage, health, and education itself, satisfaction is substantially highest among the college graduates and lowest among those with only limited schooling. For satisfaction in most other domains of life, higher education is of little or no advantage.

Income level appears to have a direct transitive relationship to the various indicators of well-being—the higher the income the more positive the affect and satisfaction levels. Education is more ambiguous. People who are well-educated are substantially more likely to express high positive affect than people lower on the educational scale. In this respect income and education are similar. But education does not have the same relationship to satisfaction with life or the domains of life that income has. In some domains of life, people with limited education appear to have rather modest aspirations, and they do not feel their circumstances fall short of these aspirations; their level of satisfaction is as high as that of college graduates. In these domains aspirations appear to rise with increasing education, but achievement lags behind and satisfaction levels fall, reaching their lowest point among the people with some college education. Among college graduates satisfaction levels tend to be high; at this level the discrepancy between aspirations and achievements appears to have closed, presumably because of the greater advantages college graduates enjoy.

The situation of this small proportion of the population who have graduated from college is especially intriguing. On the average they tend to rank relatively high on the various measures of well-being. But in comparison with people at the other educational levels, their sense of well-being seems to be least dependent on their income level. Gratification of the needs that income itself will not satisfy apparently plays a larger role in these people's lives than it does in those of the rest of the population. The possession of a college degree clearly means something more than just a few additional years of schooling. It increases the priority of the "higher needs," for relating and being.

The three status variables—income, education, and occupation—are undoubtedly powerful descriptors of the objective circumstances in which people live. Knowing these facts about people, we can predict a great deal about their physical situation and their life-style. But we would not do well at all in predicting their sense of well-being. Of all the influences that determine people's happiness and satisfaction, these three indicators—income, education, and occupation—make up no more than 10 percent.

At an earlier time in our history, this figure may have been considerably higher. It is an impressive fact that since our first assessment of professed happiness in 1957, the relationship of this measure to these indicators of social status has declined substantially. The happiness levels of high-status and low-status people have gradually come closer together, not because the low-status people have become on the average more happy about their lives but because the people in high-income and educational status have become less happy.

This decline in the ability of income-related status to guarantee a high level of positive affect invites speculation. One argument proposes that the period following the tranquil 1950s was a time of increasing turmoil—political assassinations, racial confrontation, rising crime rates, deceit and malpractice in government, and perhaps most significant of all, the Vietnam war—and that this turmoil intruded itself with particular force into the awareness of high-income and high-education people, who are the most responsive to such stimuli, and that the impact on the feelings of well-being of these people was negative. Thus during a period of rising economic prosperity, the economic contributions to well-being were offset by forces of a noneconomic character. Presumably if these noneconomic influences were to disappear, economic forces would reassert themselves and the pattern of the 1950s would return.

It has been alternatively argued that as a society passes a certain level of affluence, people begin to seek satisfactions of a nonmaterial kind and those whose material wants are most adequately fulfilled are the first to turn to these nonmaterial sources of satisfaction. This theory would place less emphasis on the specific events of the last 20 years and assume that high-income people become more like low-income people in their patterns of well-being because their economic advantage has become less important in their total picture of wants and satisfactions. Assuming a continuation or expansion of general affluence, the differences in levels of well-being would depend less and less on the gratification of economic needs.

It is probably too early to choose between these two theories. There is evidence from studies in Canada and in affluent West European countries that has shown the same weakening of material values as determiners of the well-being that has occurred in this country. Affluence in itself appears to be changing satisfaction patterns in these countries. On the other hand, it is hard to doubt that in the American case the series of disturbing events during the 1960s and 1970s had some impact on the sense of well-being of people who were sensitive enough to be moved by them or who were directly affected by them. It may be that the decline in perceived happiness would have occurred among these people even if this country had been spared its trials of the last 20 years, and it is probable that the loss was greater because they did occur.

Governments around the world place great store in raising the economic and educational levels of their populations because they consider these to be essential attributes of a high quality of life. To some degree, this strategy must be regarded as successful since we have seen from repeated surveys that expressions of well-being are highest in the most affluent societies. But within the American population during the recent past, individual differences in affect and satisfaction are much more dependent on factors other than income and education than they are on these two factors alone. Being wealthy and a college graduate is an advantage no doubt, but we must also ask whether the person is black or white, younger or older, healthy or disabled, single or married, widowed or divorced, living in a city or a small town. Does he or she feel satisfied with himself or herself, feel in control of life rather than controlled by outside forces? We turn now to these and other questions, and we will find that there is much more to well-being than simply being well-off.

6
Being Married

Abraham Maslow argued in his theory of the hierarchy of human needs that the need for love and belonging follows immediately after the basic need for food and shelter. As a society succeeds in providing an adequate diet and protection from the extremes of climate and other natural dangers, interpersonal relationships which provide affection and support assume high priority. In Allardt's language this is the need for relating. Of the various mechanisms societies provide to meet this need, marriage and the family appear to be the most universal and the most fulfilling. It is hard to imagine an individual who is immersed in an unhappy marriage living a pleasant and satisfying life. It is difficult to believe that people whose marriages are dissolved by death or divorce do not suffer damage to their feelings of well-being. One may doubt that the minority of women and men who never marry find the quality of their lives as fulfilling as those who do.

The simple statistics of who gets married and how often suffice to show that despite a certain amount of liberated criticism, marriage is a very hardy institution indeed. Of those people in this country who are in their 40's or older, 95 percent have married at least once. About 15 percent have married a second time and a few determined souls (2 to 3 percent) have taken the plunge three times or more. Three of every four women whose first marriage ended in divorce eventually marry a second time and five out of six divorced men remarry. Widowed people, being older, are somewhat less likely to remarry although approximately half do marry a second time, with men again being more likely than women to return to the married state. Americans are a marrying people, with much smaller numbers who never marry than are found in most other Western societies.

We are also of course a divorcing people. Our divorce rate has traditionally been high and in recent years, since 1963, it has doubled. The divorce rate has been increasing with each succeeding generation; of men and women born in the first years of this century who subsequently married, only 5 percent had divorced by the time they were 35. For people born in the early thirties, this figure is about 12 percent. It is now estimated that over one-third of married people now between 25 and 35 years of age will ultimately end their first marriage in divorce. The comparable figure for ever-married persons now in their 70's is 13 percent.

The decade of the 1970s was a period of changes in attitudes toward the institution of marriage, changes which are reflected in a comparison of the marital status of Americans in 1971 and 1978. During that period the proportion of the adult population who were married had declined. The number divorced or separated had increased as had the number who had never married. In 1978 a small number of people described themselves as living in a companionate relationship with a person to whom they were not married; they are combined with the more conventionally married people in the following pages.

Satisfaction with Marriage

For over 50 years psychologists and sociologists have been trying to identify the characteristics of a successful marriage. It has not been an easy task because there is no objective standard by which a marriage can be judged. A marriage that dissolves has obviously not been successful, but the fact that a marriage persists does not guarantee that it has been a good marriage. It is quite clear that people are capable of living together in continuing discord if for financial, religious, parental, or other reasons they do not choose to divorce. In the absence of objective criteria, researchers have turned to the experience of marriage with the reasonable logic that a marriage is successful if the two people concerned believe it to be. Some studies have asked, "Taking things all together, how would you describe your marriage? Would you say that your marriage is very happy, pretty happy, or not too happy?" This question tends to emphasize the affective side of experience, and the person is likely to respond in terms of the positive or negative experiences he or she associates with his or her marriage. Other research has asked, "All things considered, how satisfied are you with your marriage?" In responding to this question, the person tends to ask, "Compared with what?"—to the glamorized marriages of fiction and the movies, to one's parents' marriage, to the marriages of one's associates, or to no marriage at all? A person might be satisfied with a marriage but not very happy in it. As we have seen, happiness and satisfaction are related but not identical components of one's sense of well-being.

Despite the fact that an increasing number of people find their marriages so unsatisfactory they feel compelled to dissolve them, when people are asked to evaluate their marriage, their responses are typically very favorable. About seven out of ten married people say they are "very happy" with their marriage and nearly six out of ten say they are "completely satisfied." Perhaps marital difficulties are so traumatic that people must deny them in order to maintain their feelings of security and self-regard. On the other hand, in a society where divorce is easy, it is not likely that many couples will remain for long in an unsatisfactory marriage. The ones who remain married are those who are left after those who found their marriage intolerable have departed. There will still be some who have not yet reached the point of breakup, but at any particular time they will be a small proportion of the total. The number of married people who describe their marriages as "unhappy" or "unsatisfactory," although small, is ample to provide for the new departures. Marriage, of all human experiences, appears to have unrivaled potential for joy and torment, fulfillment and frustration. For most people the positives outweigh the negatives, and their feeling of the quality of their marriage contributes crucially to their perception of the quality of their lives.

Although the majority of married people speak very positively of their marital relationship, there are a great many who are not without reservations and some who are frankly negative. When we look at the various segments of the population to see where the positive or negative attitudes are most prevalent, we find that they exist everywhere; marriage brings out about the same range of reactions at all levels of society.

Women and Men

Traditionally in our society marriage and family have been thought to be the indispensable core of a woman's life, but somewhat less important in the life of a man. In recent years many long-standing beliefs about the marital relationship have been challenged, among them the assumption that marriage is a more fulfilling experience to women than it is to men. The argument has been advanced that marriage is in fact destructive to the emotional health of the typical housewife, that housework is "pathogenic." At the extreme the implication is given that the traditional role of wife and mother is so traumatic that women would be well-advised not to enter into it.

Concepts of women's role are undoubtedly changing in this country, but repeated studies over the last 20 years fail to produce any evidence that happiness in marriage is any less common among women than it is among men. When women and men are asked to rate their marriage on a scale of happiness, a large majority of both choose a "very happy" or "above average" category, and their total distributions are very similar. Those studies which have asked about both happiness in marriage and happiness in life in general find that the two are more closely associated among women than they are among men.

When people are asked how satisfied they are with their marriage, rather than how happy, most women and men describe themselves as "completely" or "almost completely" satisfied. Men, however, are slightly more likely to rate their marriages in these very high categories than women are. There is no evidence that men are generally more satisfied with various other aspects of their lives than women are; it would appear either that the realities of marriage are intrinsically less satisfying to women than they are to men or that women's expectations from marriage are higher than those of men and thus more subject to disappointment. This difference between men and women is not very great, but it may be growing. The proportion of married women who expressed some reservation about their marriage increased slightly between 1971 and 1978, and there was no such movement among men. As the current concern for equal sharing in marriage increasingly confronts the traditional patriarchal patterns of family life in this country, the potential for conflicting expectations is likely to grow.

Income

As we have seen, expressions of positive affect and satisfaction with life in general rise steadily as we compare people of increasingly affluent income levels. This relationship fades dramatically when we ask people to evaluate their marriage. When people with low incomes are asked how *happy* they are with their marriage they are a little less willing to describe their marriage as very happy than are those with higher incomes, but the difference is not substantial. Low-income women are the least likely to say they have a happy marriage. When people are asked how *satisfied* they are with their marriage, the pattern is rather curious. In both 1971 and 1978 the proportions of people who said they were "completely satisfied" with their marriage were considerably higher in the lower-income groups than in the higher. But the average level of satisfaction with marriage did not differ from one income group to another. We will see in the later chapters that people of modest income and education seem to be more willing to choose the extreme category of satisfaction in these scales; more sophisticated people appear to be more discriminating and less ready to describe themselves as "completely satisfied."

Education

The early studies of marriage found a substantially higher report of marital happiness among people with more formal education than among those with less, and this relationship was about as strong among women as men. Subsequent surveys have found the same pattern. We know that people with more education are more likely to describe themselves as happy with their lives and it is not surprising that they are also more happy with their marriages. As we have seen, marital happiness is one of the most important contributors to happiness with life as a whole.

Satisfaction with marriage, on the other hand, relates to education in much the same way as it does to income level. The proportion who declare themselves to be "completely satisfied" with their marriage declines progressively from those with no more than grade school (near 70 percent) to college graduates (less than 50 percent). But the number who are neutral or negative about their marriage is higher among the former than the latter, although small in both groups. Married women with only a grade-school education show an especially high incidence of dissatisfaction; one in five of them find their marriages less than satisfying.

How can we explain the fact that professed *happiness* with one's marriage increases as education increases and complete *satisfaction* decreases? We can start with the finding that advantaged people (high income, high education) are generally more likely to describe themselves as leading happy lives. We assume that happiness reflects the feelings one has in response to the events of the day, and we have seen in the recall of pleasant experiences that advantaged people do indeed more often than disadvantaged people encounter "good" events rather than "bad" events. Surely not an unreasonable expectation, and no one is surprised that advantaged people are as happy as they say they are. Satisfaction, however, is a more thoughtful experience implying a comparison of what one has to some criterion—expected, aspired to, or thought appropriate. Education appears to make judgment of one's marriage a more complicated process, bringing in images of perfection that a less-sophisticated person does not have in mind. College people, for example, are considerably more likely than other people to see inadequacies in their own performance in the marital role and to perceive difficulties in their relationship with their spouse. Gurin and his associates believe that the "effect of education is to increase the salience of the more internal, intrinsic aspects of marriage, making marrige, in a sense, more central to one's life." College people are less able, because of their more sophisticated aspirations and their sense of personal shortcomings, to see themselves as "completely" satisfied with their marriage. But they are less likely to enter into a marriage which turns out to be unsatisfactory, partly we may assume because they marry somewhat later in life than people of limited education and partly because they may be somewhat more discriminating in the person they choose to marry.

Age

Americans tend to marry young. In 1978 the average age of first marriage for women was 21.8 years; for men it was 24.2 years. The long-term trend in this country has been toward earlier marriages, but in recent years the age of first marriage has been rising slightly.

Early studies of marital happiness (1957) showed younger married people most likely to describe their marriages as "very happy," with older people somewhat less willing to do so. But in the midseventies, surveys found no differences among younger and older married people. As we will see in later pages, the ebullient feelings of youth seem to have been generally dampened during this 20-year period.

Satisfaction with marriage follows quite a different pattern. Younger married people (18–24), most of them married a rather short time, are more likely than the married population at large to express satisfaction with their marriage. But then the curve takes a dip and through their 30's and 40's, married people are not so confident that their marriages are all they expect them to be. Once they are safely into their 50's, however, their evaluations of what they have and ought to have appear to come into closer agreement, and their satisfaction levels are much higher. This pattern conforms to the age distribution of divorces. First marriages which end in divorce last on the average a little over six years; second marriages go on a little longer before they dissolve. If the couple manage to stay together through age 50, they are very likely to make it the rest of the way.

We have seen earlier that general life satisfaction tends to turn upward after age 50, and we will see later that this pattern tends to reappear in most domains of life. In the case of marriage we might argue that the relatively high satisfaction of the very young reflects the general exhilaration of early marriage and the absence of the family responsibilities which are yet to come. With the arrival of children and mortgages, difficulties may develop and the marriage may seem less satisfying. In the 50's and later many of these pressures have relaxed, the children have grown up, the marriage is more tranquil, the couple have learned to live with each other, and the marriage seems more as the individual expects and wants it to be. In support of this argument, we know that when people are asked to describe "problems" they have in their marriage, the frequency of these problems follows the same pattern we saw with expressed satisfaction, with an increase in the years following the 18–24 period and a subsequent decrease in the older decades. Feelings of inadequacy in one's marital role also decrease with age, perhaps because the decline in problems encountered makes it easier to perform this role in a satisfying manner.

It may be, however, that satisfaction with marriage is higher in the older age groups not because the circumstances of marriage improve but because over time people tend to lower their aspirations and resign themselves to realities they cannot change. We think it likely as a general principle that, where a situation is fixed for a person over a long term, there is a tendency toward accommodation to it, which is reflected in gradual increases in level of satisfaction. Thus people who for 10 or 20 years have chafed over the shortcomings of an imperfect marriage are likely in the end to face the fact that they do not live in a perfect world, to decide the marriage is probably as good as most, and to accept it as satisfactory.

We cannot say with certainty how much the age differences in marital satisfaction can be attributed to either of these explanations. Probably both have some influence. We do not doubt that the mechanism of accommodation plays a significant role in marriage as it appears to in other domains of experience. But there are changes in the circumstances of a person moving through the stages of married life which must in themselves make life seem more or less satisfying. We will consider these in detail in Chapter 12, where we compare levels of well-being at successive stages of the life cycle.

As a note of caution we must remind the reader that these observations are based on the comparison of different age cohorts and not on the longitudinal study of married couples. It is possible to argue that the greater satisfaction with marriage of people in their later years results either from a generational difference (older people were born in a generation that learned to be satisfied with one's marriage) or from a progressive loss of unsatisfied married people (people who are not satisfied with their marriage seek a divorce, leaving only the satisfied couples in the married portion of their age cohort). Neither of these explanations is very convincing. One wonders in the first case why the older generation who learned to be satisfied with their marriges did not learn to be happy with them as well. And we have seen that the absence of divorced people from the ranks of the married is typically rather brief. The older cohorts are not characterized by an unusually high proportion of divorced people. We incline to the belief that the age differences in satisfaction with marriage are for the most part the consequence of growing older, with the attendant changes in circumstances and expectations which occur as one moves through the life cycle.

Religion

Religion and marriage are closely associated in this country, as they are in most societies. The marriage ceremony is strongly flavored with religious imagery and is usually performed by an officer of the church. The children are baptized in the church. The different religions take strong positions regarding the sanctity of the family, and some do not recognize divorce. There are many wholly secular marriages in America, and many families that have no contact with a church. But the majority pattern is still very clear: religion and marriage are interconnected.

We can sort out Americans either by the church they identify with or by the importance they assign to their religious attachment. If we look first at the followers of the two major churches, we discover that Protestants and Catholics in this country differ very little in the degree of satisfaction they report from their marriages. Despite the fact that the doctrine of the Catholic church regarding divorce may keep a certain number of parishioners in marriages they might wish to leave, Catholics are no less likely to describe their marriages as satisfying than Protestants. That small part of the population who call themselves agnostic or atheist or have no preference among the various religions are on the average most critical of their marriages: they are also the most likely to have been divorced from an earlier marriage. This may indicate that a religious attachment tends to enhance the quality of a marriage. But it may also suggest that people with no religious association have a generally critical outlook on life which is expressed not only in their attitudes toward religion but also in their evaluation of their marriage and of other aspects of their lives. The fact that they are less likely than religious people to describe themselves as happy and satisfied with life in general inclines one to this view.

A good many people have only a nominal relation to the church with which they identify, and we come closer to the meaning of religious attachment when we classify them according to how "religious-minded" they are. About one married person in seven in this country says "very" when asked, "In general, how religious-minded would you say you are?" This figure differs only slightly between Protestants and Catholics. Those people who say they have no religious preference are of course least concerned with religion; half of them say they are not at all religious-minded.

As we might have predicted, religious-minded people are clearly more likely to say they are satisfied with their marriage than people for whom religion is less important, and this is true of both the major religious groups. On the face of it, this finding would appear to support what is probably a widespread belief that religious convictions tend to strengthen and enhance marriage, that "people who pray together stay together." But as we have suggested above, it may be that people whose religious attachments are weaker than those of the general population may also differ in other ways which make them poor prospects for a successful marriage. They may, for example, have antiestablishmentarian attitudes that incline them to find fault with both religion and marriage. We cannot demonstrate that this is true, and we are not inclined to reject the suggestion that religious conviction does increase the probability of a satisfactory marriage.

Family Background

The early studies of marriage leaned heavily on the childhood circumstances of a person's life as predictors of ultimate matrimonial experience. They did not perform very effectively then and they do not tell us very much now. It has been assumed, for example, that people who grow up in a broken home would be less likely themselves to be able to establish a satisfactory marriage. The evidence does incline in this direction, but the difference between people who have grown up with both parents and those who have not is very modest and an inadequate explanation of what predisposes to a satisfying marriage. The same can be said for the effect of a rural background. It might be supposed that a person growing up in the more traditional culture of a small town might be more likely to be satisfied with his or her marriage than the child of a big city, and this is true but only marginally so. People who attended religious services regularly as children are slightly more satisfied with their marriages than those who did not. None of these presumably important attributes of a person's childhood experience is very helpful in extending our understanding of why some people find their marriages satisfying and others do not.

* * * *

We have seen in these pages that the majority of people in all the major social categories are content with their marriages, and some are miserable. There is no part of the population which appears to have found a special secret to a satisfying marriage. Differences in income and education, which are important in other domains of life, do not have much influence here. The quality of marriage does change in significant ways as people move from their early years to later maturity, and we will pursue this fact in Chapter 12.

Perceptions of Marital Relationships

There is no single attribute of an individual's circumstances or status which comes through strongly as a predictor of marital satisfaction. Our search among these "objective" variables has proved disappointing. But when we examine the way people experience that aspect of their marriage which would appear to be most central to its success, their relationship with their spouse, we find that this subjective measure brings us closer to an understanding of what makes a marriage satisfying.

Various studies have asked an assortment of questions about the relationship between man and wife. Two of the most extensive asked the following four questions:

"How often do you disagree with your (wife-husband) about how much money to spend on various things?"

"How well do you think your (wife-husband) understands you—your feelings, your likes and dislikes, and any problems you may have?"

"How well do you understand your (wife-husband)?"

"How much companionship do you and your (wife-husband) have—how often do you do things together?"

These questions tap different aspects of the marital experience and they give illuminating insights into how people see their marriages.

Women and Men

About one married woman in five says she never disagrees with her husband about spending money, and over half say they rarely or never do (see Appendix Table 6). The proportions of husbands who give these answers are very nearly the same. Four women out of ten say they think their husband understands them very well; husbands are somewhat more likely to believe their wives understand them very well. Wives and husbands do not differ significantly when it comes to understanding their spouse; close to half of the wives think they understand their husbands very well, and about the same number of husbands are that sure they understand their wives. And finally, somewhat over a third of the wives say they share companionship with their husbands all the time; the husbands have very much the same picture of their companionship with their wives. As one might guess, the answers to these questions tend to be interrelated: people who see their relationship with their spouse positively in one respect are likely to see it positively in others as well.

Two aspects of the responses to these questions are striking. To three of these questions, women and men give very similar answers. They appear to define arguments and companionship in the same way and to perceive the realities of their married life in the same way. By contrast, however, both women and men are somewhat more likely to believe that the wife has a better understanding of the husband than he has of her. It is not a large difference, but it suggests a greater sensitivity on the part of the wife, a reflection perhaps of a greater reality of feelings among women. Also impressive is the great similarity in the way these questions were answered in 1971 and 1978. We might have expected that with all the questions about sex roles in marriage that have come to prominence during the 1970s, there would have been changes in the way people see their marital relationships. Whatever changes occurred, they did not influence the way wives and husbands answered these questions.

As we see, married people are more willing to be critical in describing how they get along with their spouse than they are in expressing dissatisfaction with their marriage. Of course, those women and men who are most positive about their relationship with their spouse are generally very satisfied with their marriage; those who are less positive are also less satisfied. But even those people who admit to disagreements and misunderstandings do not often say they are dissatisfied with their marriage; they are not completely satisfied to be sure, but neither are they generally discontented. People clearly do not find it easy to admit that their marriage is a failure.

Once the marriage has come unhinged and the couple are separated or divorced, however, the difficulties the wife and husband had in their relationship become apparent. Very few of these people remember their marital relationships favorably. The women seem to be a little more likely to describe their failed marriage in negative terms than the men, although they are not more willing to admit they did not understand their spouse very well. Women and men are both more ready to attribute lack of understanding to their spouse, however, than to admit it in themselves. Women and men who are separated but not yet divorced give a clearly more negative description of their relationship with their spouse than do those who are now divorced. Presumably this is a function of the recency of the unpleasantness involved; if these separated people eventually complete a divorce, we would expect their memories of the marriage to moderate in the direction of the currently divorced.

Women and men who are widowed present an interesting contrast to those who are separated or divorced, describing their terminated marriages in even more favorable terms than do those women and men who are still married. A marriage which ends with a death is not typically characterized by the kind of discord usually associated with divorce, and it may be that widowed people tend to romanticize their marriages and to remember their relations with their spouse as more pleasant than they actually were. We must remember, however, that widows are on the average considerably older than people who are still married and in most cases their marriages had persisted for a good many years. It is not unlikely, therefore, that marriages which end in death are in fact more successful than the average of those marriages still extant and that the reports of marital relations given by widowed women and men simply reflect this fact.

We also see in Appendix Table 6 that a small fraction, about 10 percent, of the currently married women and men show the same pattern of criticism of their relations with their spouse as shown by those whose marriages have dissolved. They would appear to be likely candidates for the divorce court themselves.

Marital harmony, as expressed in agreement, understanding and companionship, and satisfaction with marriage, gives us an indicator of the quality of an individual's marital experience, which is related but not identical. Logically one might think of a perception of harmony with one's spouse as causally antecedent to a feeling of satisfaction with one's marriage. True as this may be, the questions on marital harmony tell us something additional about the quality of the marriage experience, and we look now to see how people in different circumstances of life answer them.

Income

As we have seen earlier, high income does not produce an unusually high number of completely satisfactory marriages; neither does it produce a high proportion of very harmonious marriages. Surprising as it may seem, low-income people are more likely to say they never disagree with their spouse about money than people in the higher income brackets. They also are more likely to claim they do things together with their spouse "all the time" than high-income people do. Differences in perceived level of understanding of the spouse are not so clear, but the lower-income people are no less positive in answering these questions.

The expectations that women and men of different income levels have of their marriage and their definitions of their respective roles undoubtedly differ. Low-income people may perceive fewer arguments about money because in these families it is more commonly assumed (than in more affluent families) that the man of the house makes the decisions regarding money without consultation with his wife. High-income people may see themselves somewhat less commonly spending "all their time" together because wife and husband at this level are more likely to have separate interests and activities. The impressive fact about the perceptions these people have of their marital relationships is that they are so similar. Considering the objective differences in the lives these families live, great contrasts in their perceptions might not have been surprising. But knowing a person's income tells us very little about the way that person sees his or her marriage. A high income may be an effective cure for many of the aches and pains of life, but it does not seem to contribute very much to harmonious relationships between the partners of a marriage.

Education

People with advanced education are generally better off financially than people with limited schooling, and the relationship of perceived marital relations to educational level is about the same as it is to income level. Married people with the most restricted education are most likely to claim that they never argue with their spouse about money and that they "do things together" all the time. The more education a person has, the less willing he or she is to make these categorical statements. They are also less willing, however, to use the most negative descriptions of their marital relationships. This is a similar picture to that we saw when we were comparing the number of people "completely satisfied" with their marriage; in that case this proportion also declined with increasing education. Advanced education seems to create higher expectations, and college people seem to feel more constrained in the terms they use to describe their lives. We will encounter this phenomenon again in later chapters.

Age

In general, the older people are, the more likely they are to say their marriages are entirely harmonious. Very young married couples (under 25) are far more likely to disagree about money than older couples, even more than retired people whose financial problems are often severe. They are also less likely to believe that they understand each other very well. They do, however, report a relatively high amount of companionship, doing things together all the time or very often. Many of these young couples are still childless at this stage of their lives and, as one might expect, when we look at slightly older married people, we see that their reported companionship takes a dip and does not recover until they are into their 40's.

All this appears to be as it should be. If a couple are sufficiently compatible to stay married, one would surely expect that their relationships would become more comfortable as time passed. The drop in amount of companionship following the first years of marriage undoubtedly reflects the presence of children in the home and the demands they put on their parents' time. As this stressful period passes, the marriage becomes more harmonious and satisfying.

Religion

We did not find any difference between the two major religious groups in their expressed satisfaction with their marriages, and we do not find differences of any consequence in their reported relationships with their spouses. Protestants and Catholics seem to disagree about money with their wives and husbands about equally as frequent, and neither group differs from those people who profess to have no religion. Nor do they differ in their perceived understanding of their spouses, although Catholics seem a little more companionable. People with no religious preference report somewhat less mutual understanding and clearly less companionship.

We have pointed out earlier that belonging nominally to one of the major religious sects does not tell us much about the individual's concern with religion. When we do consider the extent to which people consider themselves to be religious-minded, we discover that among both Protestants and Catholics, marital harmony is somewhat higher among those with the highest sense of religiosity than among those with the lowest. These differences are not very substantial, but they were present in both the 1971 and 1978 surveys. They are also consistent with the differences we saw in levels of satisfaction with one's marriage. Men and women whose religion is important to them are a little more likely to have an understanding, companionable relationship with their spouse, a little more likely to be very satisfied with their marriage, and a little more likely to stay married.

Family Background

Satisfaction with marriage is relatively little influenced by the conditions in which a person grew up, and the quality of marital relationships also seems to depend only slightly on these early experiences. It may seem surprising that a person who has grown up in an intact family should not report more harmonious marital relations than a person whose parents were separated, but in fact such people differ very little. It is apparent that how a person gets along with wife or husband cannot be explained by whether or not he or she grew up in a religious home, a rural community, an educated family, or an intact family. These childhood experiences do not appear to influence people's later marital adjustment nearly as much as they are often assumed to.

* * * *

Asking married people to describe their relationship with their spouse is not quite the same as asking them how satisfying their marriage is. They seem more willing to admit the various imperfections in their marriages than they are to express general dissatisfaction. In those cases where the marriage has dissolved, these imperfections appear to have been overwhelming. There are a good many marriages that fall considerably short of total compatibility, but the participants still find them satisfying. Most people seem to bring a sense of realism into their evaluation of their marriage; they realize that human relationships are not often without flaw, and they balance the shortcomings of their marriage against its benefits, in most cases to the advantage of the latter. Of course the fewer the shortcomings, the greater is their satisfaction with their marriage.

Having Children

Most people who marry ultimately have children. Bearing a child is an act surrounded by all manner of religious, legal, economic, sociological, and psychological implications. For the church the child consummates the marriage; one of the major purposes of the marriage is to produce children. For the family the child becomes a protection against old age and a carrier of the family name, especially in the case of a son. For the state the child helps maintain the national population so that it does not appear to weaken in the face of international competition. For the individual parent the child may be the cherished answer to a lifetime dream or it may be an unwelcome encumbrance.

Attitudes toward the bearing of children have been one of the most sharply changing beliefs in recent American history. It has been only two generations ago that contraception was a practice known only to a minority of the population, prosecuted by the law in most states, and condemned by many religious leaders. Married couples accepted the number of children "God sent them," partly because they felt it was their moral duty to bear children and partly because they had no effective way of avoiding it.

Since World War II contraceptive practices have spread throughout the population; they are not used universally to be sure, either for religious or other convictions or because of lack of foresight, but the number of couples who report currently using some method of controlling birth is approaching 80 percent. The diffusion of these acts of family limitation reflects not only the spread of information about contraception but also profound changes in popular attitudes toward childbearing. As recently as 1955 the average married woman in this country regarded three to four children as the "ideal" family size. Twenty years later the image of the ideal family had fallen to no more than two children. A quiet revolution had taken place, and the falling birthrate which reached an all-time low was one of the consequences. There was no great increase in the number of couples with no children nor in the number of people who regarded "none" as the ideal number of children. Children were still desired by a large majority of married people, but they wanted and were having fewer children than was true of any preceding generation.

In view of the fact that in spite of widespread public knowledge about contraceptive practices over 90 percent of the married couples in this country who are physically capable of childbearing do have at least one child, we can hardly fail to conclude that children are highly valued in our society. We would not be surprised to find that the quality of a marriage would be enhanced by the presence of children and a childless marriage would suffer in comparison. The facts of the matter are rather more complicated than that, however, and they suggest that the contributions of children to the quality of their parents' lives can also be painful.

If we simply look at those married couples who have no children in the home and those who have one or more, we find that those marriages without children seem at least as successful as those with, both in satisfaction with the marriage and in expressed compatibility. But a marriage may be without children for different reasons: the couple may be young and not yet have had a child; the couple may be older and not have had children, either because they chose not to or were unable to; or the couple may be in the "empty nest" stage, having had children who have grown up and moved away. We will consider each of these stages in the life cycle in Chapter 12, and we will see that the indicators of marital success are quite positive in all of them, although these people differ quite markedly in other respects.

When we consider only those couples who have at least one child at home with them, we discover that marital satisfaction and compatibility do not increase as the number of children increases. The parents of several children are no more positive in these respects than the parents of one child. The presence of numerous children does appear, however, to increase the psychological burden of parenting, particularly for the mother. In those families with four or more children in the home, the mothers are less likely than mothers with fewer children to say that being a parent has always been enjoyable and they are more likely to admit that they often or occasionally wish they could be free of the responsibilities of parenthood. The fathers are less likely to express these misgivings and their willingness to do so is not associated with the number of children they have. Considering the fact that studies of time use show that most of the time spent on child care is contributed by the mothers rather than the fathers, this finding seems readily understandable.

Having a child promises both positive and negative experiences. Carrying the first baby home from the hospital may be a moment of high euphoria, but it is followed by many moments of a different character as the child puts insistent demands on its parents. As we will see in Chapter 12, the early years of child-raising are a time of stress for both parents and they put pressure on the marriage. But most parents weather this period and when they finally win through to the "empty nest," when the children have left home, their satisfaction with their marriage and their appraisal of their relationships with their spouse are at the highest point in their married life. They are now very likely to say that being a parent has always been enjoyable and to deny that they had ever wished to be free of the responsibilities of being a parent. Father and mother are both very positive at this stage of life, a father a little more so than the mother. If they have not forgotten the harassment they endured, they appear to have forgiven it.

The psychological and economic costs of raising a large family are apparently a charge which American families are increasingly reluctant to pay. The declining birthrate, resulting largely from the elimination of third and later parity children, is convincing evidence that people in the childbearing years are assigning different values to the costs and benefits of having children than they did during the 1950s. The experience of parenthood and the deferred gratification of having grown children in their later years are sufficient motives to lead most young couples to have one child or two, but the psychology of diminishing returns appears to make subsequent births less likely.

Conclusions

The institution of marriage appears to exist throughout the world and so far as we know throughout time. It has played an indispensable role in the preservation of the human species, and it plays a preeminent role in the lives of individual women and men. Within the last decade or so there has been a certain amount of criticism of the American pattern of marriage (much of it growing out of changing concepts of women's roles), some experimentation with alternative forms of intimate interpersonal relationships, and some outright rejection of marriage as a tolerable life-style.

Despite this continuing controversy and despite the large number of marriages which prove unsuccessful, there is very little indication that the human need for the kind of intimate and supportive relationship which marriage has historically provided has diminished. Alternative life-styles may be devised which will fill this need for some or many people but the need itself seems very persistent. It remains to be seen how much and in what ways modifications of the conventional marriage pattern will enhance or detract from the subjective values which people look for in their marital relationships.

When people in this country are asked what they consider the most important elements of a good life, they place "a happy marriage" and "good health" at the top of their list of alternatives. And the national surveys tell us that among the domains of life that give us the best prediction of whether people are living happy and contented lives or not, marriage and family life rank very high. We have deferred consideration of those people who never marry or whose marriages are broken by death or divorce until a later chapter, but we will find there that none of these groups is as positive in its general sense of well-being as people who are married and some of them are very negative indeed. If we judge the importance of the marriage experience by the characteristics associated with its absence we are compelled to conclude that, flawed and inadequate an arrangement as it may be, for most people a good marriage is a good deal better than any of its alternatives.

Repeated surveys over the years have found that most married people say they are "very happy" or "completely satisfied" with their marriage. We do not know what kind of standard they use in making this judgment; since there is no common example that everyone could accept as "perfect," different people must use different points of reference. Whatever basis of comparison they use, most people judge their marriage favorably; a small minority do not. We have not been very successful in explaining what it is that is responsible for this difference.

If we turn to economic status as a probable associate of marital satisfaction, we find very little; people at different income levels do not differ significantly in the degree of satisfaction they report from their marriage. As we saw in Chapter 5, economic affluence does not gratify the need for relating. Other important aspects of the individual's characteristics and circumstances also prove disappointing—education, occupation, church preference—none of these tells us much. Even such a plausible hypothesis that children of broken homes are less likely to experience successful marriages than children who grew up with both parents is found to have only limited support. All these "objective" facts about an individual's life account for a very small part, perhaps 5 percent, of whatever it is that makes one marriage satisfying and another not.

The major part of what it is that determines the quality of a marriage appears to lie not in the conditions in which an individual lives but in the characteristics of the individual and of the person he or she marries. Some people are simply better prospects for a successful marriage than others. They have personal qualities which make it possible for them to live amiably with another person in an intimate relationship. Some people are so lacking in these qualities that they are unable to develop a relationship that might lead to marriage; they remain single. Others marry but with poor prospects for success, unless they are fortunate enough to marry a person whose characteristics complement their own in a positive way. Of course many people do not marry primarily because of the "luck of the draw"; they have the personal qualities necessary for a successful marriage but the right opportunity never presents itself.

We do not know how people acquire the traits that predispose to a satisfying or a dissatisfying marriage; perhaps through the germ plasm, perhaps through childhood experience, perhaps through living together, probably through all of these. But we can be sure that they are not associated in any significant way with whether a person is rich or poor, poorly or well-educated, a farmer or a banker, or a member of this or that church. These important attributes of social position have significant association with some other aspects of life experience but not with the uniquely personal experience of marriage.

7

Having Family and Friends

Of people 18 years and older in this country, about one out of three are not married. But the fact that they do not have a spouse does not mean that they are without close personal relationships. They nearly all have living relatives and friends who are not relatives. These associations add to the total pattern of psychological support which married people experience, and they provide a major source of such support to people who are not married.

We need not assume that everyone's need for relating to other people is equally demanding; indeed, some misanthropic types appear to prefer a life with as little human contact as possible. But this is surely exceptional; commonplace observation would tell us that most people value their family and friends, and their lives would be much poorer without them. Indeed there is reason to believe that the absence of such supportive relationships is associated not only with psychological distress but also with some susceptibility to physiological trauma.

Some gregarious people are surrounded by a complicated network of friends and relatives. They see them regularly; they depend on them for advice and count on them for help in case of trouble. The average person may have fewer associates of this kind, but they may be equally important. It is not easy to describe these networks without an elaborate sociometric map, and we will confine this presentation to a counting of the number of relatives and friends a person claims to have and an estimation of how close in a psychological sense these associations are. We will then ask how much a person's sense of well-being depends on these relationships and will discover that most people have both family associations and close friends and that those who do not lose something in the quality of their lives.

Closeness of Family Members

In some parts of the world the word "family" implies an extended pattern of kinship on both mother's and father's side with appropriate names and behaviors for each level of relationship. In this country, as we have moved from a primarily rural society to one which is largely urban, the family has increasingly come to mean those persons living together in a common household, usually the parents and their children. Beyond this nuclear family there are the grandparents and the brothers and sisters of the parents. Cousins are more remote and in many cases, especially where large distances intervene, they are scarcely known. In this discussion of family relationships we will stop short of the cousins, considering in order the parents, siblings, and children.

Approximately four adults in ten in this country still have two living parents; about one in three have lost both parents. The mother is more likely to have survived than the father, both because she is likely to have been younger than he and because women live about eight years longer than men on the average. People are generally reluctant to admit that they do not feel close to their parents. When asked, "Would you say that you feel closer to your parents than most people of your age do, that you are about average, or that you feel less close than most?" fewer than one person in ten whose parents are both living would say that he or she felt less close than most, while more than one in three felt they were closer to their parents than most people. Feeling closer than average is considerably more common among daughters than sons, another indication of the kind we saw earlier that women are more expressive of feeling than men are.

Of the two parents it is the mother to whom the children are more likely to feel close. Somewhat over half of the people who have living parents say they feel equally close to both, but if they make a distinction, it is three times more likely to favor the mother than the father. This may simply reflect the objective fact that in many homes the parenting role is taken primarily by the mother, with the father sometimes a rather remote figure. Or it may be that some people find the phrase "feeling close" easier to associate with a female relative rather than a male.

Nine adults out of ten have a living brother or sister, and most of them have more than one. People are not quite as likely to describe themselves as feeling closer than average to their siblings as to their parents but they do not often (12 percent) admit being less close. Here again women are clearly more likely than men to claim closer than average feelings for their brothers and sisters.

Nine married couples out of ten in the general population have at least one child, and of the remaining 10 percent some younger couples are still likely to have children. Despite the falling birthrate and some indication of changing values regarding marriage and family formation, there is as yet little evidence of a significant increase in the number of "child-free" marriages in this country. There has been without doubt a decline in the number of children people say they want and actually have, but national surveys still show a very small proportion of women and men who say they would prefer to have no children. As women continue to enter the job market and particularly as they are concerned about careers rather than intermittent jobs, this proportion may increase.

No one needs to be told that the emotional bonds between parents and children are typically very strong. But parenthood is not a totally positive experience, and children can be the source of great frustration and misery. When asked, however, most parents (four out of five) insist that being a mother or father has always or nearly always been enjoyable. Almost as many say they have never wished they could be free of the responsibilities of being a parent. About three parents out of four describe their children as having given them no problems or only a few problems. These statements may be a little embellished by parents who may not want to remember or admit some of the seamier moments of their relationships with their children, but one cannot be surprised at the generally positive tone of the images of their children.

Nor is it surprising to find that people's feelings about the role of parenting change rather substantially as they move through the life cycle. Young parents are on the average relatively unlikely to complain that their children make problems for them; this proportion increases quite noticeably for parents in their 30's and 40's and then declines again among older parents. The same pattern emerges when they are asked how much of the time they "enjoy being parents," the greatest enjoyment being reported by those whose children are now adults. Older people are also very unlikely to admit that they ever wished to be "free from the responsibilities of being a parent." This admission is most common among younger parents and diminishes progressively in the older age groups. The problems children create, particularly while in their school years (6 to 17), are clearly more real to parents who still have school-age children in their home than they are to older people who appear to remember their experiences as parents with a favorable bias.

The generally favorable descriptions parents give of their children and their experiences as parents cover up rather substantial differences which exist within the total population of parents. It is clear, for example, that mothers do not feel quite the same as fathers about enjoying their experience as parents and wishing to be free of it. Men seem to be about equally positive about their role as parents whatever the age of their children. Women, however, are much less positive when they have a child under school age than they are when their children are older, and mothers of preschool children are much less positive than fathers of children at that age.

These differences between men and women obviously reflect the different roles mothers and fathers typically play in the raising of children. In most American families the mother of a preschool child has virtually a 24-hour responsibility for its well-being. The father may be an interested spectator, but only in the most "liberated" households does he carry anything close to an equal share of the burden of child care. After the child has reached 18 years, the pressure is reduced for the parents, and mothers and fathers are equally positive in describing the experiences of parenting. The father, who is more removed from the problems of child-raising from the beginning, seems to find the experience about equally pleasant all the way through. The mother starts with a heavy responsibility which gradually lightens. Her attitudes are least positive during the early years of child care and gradually brighten as the burden is lifted.

This pattern was apparent in both the 1971 and 1978 surveys, but it became more pronounced as the decade passed. When we compare the attitudes of parents of different ages in 1971 and 1978, we find that there was no change whatever during those years in the generally positive tone with which fathers described their enjoyment of their children and their feelings about being a parent. There was a clear change, however, among the mothers of preschool and school-age children. They were less willing in 1978 than they had been in 1971 to say they always enjoyed being a parent or that they never wished they could be free of the responsibilities of parenthood. Mothers of adult children, like the fathers of these children, did not change between 1971 and 1978.

What was there about the decade of the 1970s that produced these different effects in male and female parents? There was a good deal of turmoil associated with changes in the "youth culture"—widespread use of drugs, increased teenage pregnancy, teenage crime, the substitution of cohabitation for marriage among some young people—developments that might well disturb parents who found, or feared they might find, their children involved. It does not seem likely, however, that these problems would be exclusively disturbing to mothers. It seems more probable that the diminishing pleasure women found in their role as parents reflected other changes in their life situations. Many mothers of young children went into the job market during the 1970s, and there is no doubt that this additional responsibility increased the burden these women carried. Their husbands, as we know from studies of use of time, characteristically make very little effort to share the duties of child care when the wives go to work. Many women, especially young mothers of small children, must have come to question traditional concepts of women's roles during this period and to ask themselves whether the demands being put on them were reasonable. We will see other indications in later pages of the ways in which the situation of American women is changing; their diminishing satisfaction with the experiences of mothering young children appears to be a consequence of these changes.

Satisfaction with Family Life

Among married people, those who claim to be completely satisfied with their marriage are also very likely to say they are completely satisfied with their family life. No other domain of life is so often described as fully satisfying as these two areas of marriage and family life. The importance of a satisfying marriage to an individual's family life can scarcely be doubted, and it can be dramatically demonstrated by comparing people who are married to those who have not married or are no longer married.

Survey data from 1971 and 1978 show us that a large majority of all married men and women express a high level of satisfaction when asked, "All things considered, how satisfied are you with your family life—the time you spend and the things you do with members of your family?" On the other hand, men and women who are separated or divorced are substantially less likely to see their family life so favorably; those who are separated are especially negative. Widowed people present a quite different pattern; they are nearly as positive about their family life as people of their age who are still married. That small portion of the population who has never married resemble people who are divorced, clearly less satisfied than people of their age who are married.

These differences between people living in different family patterns will engage our attention at greater length in Chapter 12 when we consider changes in perceived well-being at succeeding stages of the life cycle. At this point, we simply note the unsurprising fact that people who have been able to sustain a marriage are more satisfied with their family life than those who have not. We also observe that widowed men and women, despite their loss, find a good deal of contentment in their relations with other family members, and we will encounter additional evidence at later points that their situation is less damaging to feelings of well-being than that of people whose marriage has ended in separation or divorce.

The possession of living parents or brothers and sisters has much less meaning for feelings of satisfaction with family life than does the possession of a spouse. Having parents or a parent to whom one feels close, or siblings who are felt to be close, relates in a positive way to the quality of one's family life, but the association is very modest and it is clearly possible for a married person to be fully satisfied with family life in the absence of either parents or siblings.

Most married people have children, and it might be reasonably assumed that those who do would have a fuller sense of satisfaction with family life than those who do not. Children are so closely identified with family life that married couples without children are commonly said not to have a family. But these childless couples are no more ready to admit dissatisfaction with their family life than are couples with children. They may define family life differently than other people do, but in their perception parenthood is not essential to a sense of family or to their sense of satisfaction with this aspect of their lives.

But if people do have children, it makes a difference to their feelings about their family life whether their experiences with those children have been positive or negative. Since a large majority of parents insist that their children have given them no difficulty and have been virtually a constant joy, we have to look to the small number of parents who admit negative relationships with their children to find the impact children can have. And we discover that it can be substantial; those parents who have problems with their children, who enjoy them only sometimes, or who occasionally wish they could be free of the responsibilities of parenthood are not likely to describe themselves as fully satisfied with their family life.

If we compare the relative importance of these four elements of the family structure—spouse, parents, siblings, and children—in accounting for differences in how satisfied people are with their family life, it is undoubtedly the spouse that carries the greatest weight. Children also make a significant contribution when they are present; parents and siblings are less important. In individual cases this ordering might be quite different, but for the average family it is the spouse and the children who count most.

It can be argued that merely counting the number of family associations a person has is a poor way of assessing that person's family support, since he or she may be so out of touch with these relatives that they scarcely exist psychologically. One of the common criticisms of contemporary American life is that families are fragmented, the protective and supportive qualities of the extended family have been lost, and individual members confine their concerns to their immediate household. This image of the changing American family enjoys considerable currency at the present time, but it may underestimate the actual amount of interpersonal contact one finds among family members who do not live together.

In the 1978 Institute for Social Research survey the following question was asked, "Besides the people living right here with you, how many other members of your family—parents, grown children, relatives, and in-laws—do you have living within a couple of hours driving time from here?" Only one person in eight reported having no relatives (outside their own household) living within that rather restricted geographical range, and half of the population claim to have at least five households of relatives at this near distance. Despite the extraordinary amount of moving about that Americans do, they apparently do not often move beyond easy access to other members of their family.

Those persons who claimed at least one nearby household of relatives (nearly 90 percent of the population) were asked, "About how often do you see any of these grown children or other relatives either in their home or yours? Would you say almost every day, once a week or more, once a month or more, less than once a month, or less than once a year?" Twenty percent of these people said they saw one or another of these relatives almost every day and another 40 percent said they saw such a person once a week or more. Fewer than one person in five saw such a relative less often than once a month. In other words most people in this country are not only within reach of their relatives, they in fact see them frequently.

If we put together those people who have no relatives nearby with those who see nearby relatives less than once a month, we have about 30 percent of the population who appear to have very little personal contact with any family member except those with whom they live. They may of course be in touch by letter or telephone, and they may occasionally see other relatives who live at greater distances. It is quite likely that this proportion (30 percent) is relatively high compared with other countries which are smaller and less mobile. We doubt if Americans find it any more or less difficult to get along with their relatives than other nationalities do, but they are probably more likely to move to distant locations than other people are. Even so, it is apparent that the typical individual in this country maintains rather frequent face-to-face contact with other members of the extended family. The development of the nuclear family may have reduced these contacts, but they still remain a common aspect of American family life.

The presence of these relatives with whom one is in frequent contact appears to add marginally to the degree of satisfaction people feel with their family life. The simple number of nearby relatives is not the critical factor; many or few is not important unless some one or more of them are in close personal contact. Those people who see such a relative almost every day speak more positively of their family life than do those who have no such relative or see such a person only infrequently. Since most people live with at least one other family member and this relationship is undoubtedly the core of their feelings about family, it could not be expected that contact with other relatives would make a major contribution to these feelings. But these relationships are not insignificant; people are more likely to feel well-satisfied with their family life if they have them than if they do not.

* * * *

When people are asked how they feel about "the time they spend and the things they do with their family," most of them say they are very well-satisfied. But some are much less satisfied, and this number increased somewhat between 1971 and 1978. We learn virtually nothing about why one person is satisfied with family life and another is not from a knowledge of his or her *sex*, *race*, *income*, *education*, *religion*, or *place of residence*. These aspects of a person's life situation, which have important implications in other domains, have no influence on a person's satisfaction with family life. What does matter is the family situation the person lives in. Those people who are currently living with a wife or husband speak much more favorably of their family relationships than those who do not. The only exception to this generalization are widowed people, who, despite their loss, appear to feel as positively about their family life as people who are still married. As we will see again later, the memory of a successful marriage which has ended by death has quite different implications than that of a marriage which has failed or of no marriage at all.

Friends

Friendship is a quality of life which has been extolled in the world's literature. "The worst solitude is to have no true friendship," wrote Francis Bacon, and many authors before and since have elaborated the same theme. To have the psychological support of an intimate circle of friends is a goal to which most people aspire but which not everyone achieves.

To have a friend may mean much or little. Perhaps the least restrictive definition of a friend is a person whom one knows by name and with whom one has some personal association. One form of such a friend may be the people who live in one's surrounding neighborhood. In 1978 the Institute for Social Research national survey asked people, "Of the ten families that live closest to you here, how many would you say you know by name?" It then asked, "Of these ten families how many have you visited with, either in their homes or in yours?" The average American says he or she knows seven of the nearest ten neighbors by name and has visited with an average of four. About 5 percent of the population say they do not know a single one of their neighbors by name, and 9 percent say they have never visited with any of them. Since about 20 percent of the families in this country move their residence during the course of a year, it is not surprising that some families are not in close contact with the people who live near them. And, as one might expect, the number of neighbors one knows and visits varies according to the size of the place one lives in. We will see in Chapter 10 that this figure is lowest in the metropolitan centers, increases through the smaller places, and is highest in the rural counties.

We must assume that some of these people down the block whose name one knows are not really friends in any intimate sense, and we would come closer to a proper definition of friend if we spoke of those people whom one can turn to in times of distress and who can be counted on to give aid even at the cost of some personal sacrifice. Most Americans feel they have at least one such friend other than relatives, someone they "can call on for advice or help in time of trouble." Some few people say they have as many as fifty such friends, but the average is more nearly four or five. About one person in twenty says he or she has no such friend.

There is no one segment of the population which is notably lacking in friends of this kind, but people are more likely to report having such a friend if they are white, well-off financially, well-educated, and living outside the metropolitan centers. Perhaps it is not surprising to find that people who enjoy higher than average income and education are not without friends. Their average number of friends is not much larger than that of people of less achievement, but they are less than half as likely to have no friends at all. Place of residence shows a similar pattern, with people in the metropolitan centers quite clearly reporting fewer friends than people in the rural counties. Some of this difference may be attributed to the fact that black people make up a much larger proportion of the population of the metropolitan centers than they do of any other geographical stratum of the country, and black people, wherever they live, are less likely to claim to have many friends than are white people in the same area.

Surveys by the Institute for Social Research have repeatedly found that black people as a whole are much less willing than white people to agree with the statements "Most people can be trusted," "Most of the time people try to be helpful," and "Most people try to be fair." Poor people of both races are generally more cautious in answering these questions than affluent people but black people at all income levels are less trusting than white people at the same levels. Considering the experiences black people have lived through in this country over the last 300 years, it is surely not surprising to find that their faith in the goodwill of people in general is somewhat limited. Perhaps it is this attitude of caution that explains the fact that black people appear to have fewer friends than white people do.

There is surprisingly little difference between young people and old people in the number of friends they "can call on—in time of trouble." The popular image of sociable youth and abandoned, lonely old people would have suggested greater differences than we find. People of retirement age are in fact a little more likely to say they have no such friend, but the number of such isolated people is very small at all age levels, and on the average old people and young people claim about the same number of friends.

The circumstances in which people live undoubtedly tell us something about their friendship pattern, but they do not explain a very large part of the substantial differences we see among individual Americans in their number of friends. The greater part of these differences must depend on the personalities of the individuals themselves. Commonplace observation tells us that some people are simply more friendly than others and that friendly and unfriendly people are found in all walks of life. Some of these walks are more conducive to friendly relationships than others, but none of them makes them impossible or guarantees they will happen.

Confidantes

We see from the foregoing that most people have relatives near at hand and friends who are not relatives. Among these relatives and friends, there is usually at least one individual who might be called a "confidante," a person from whom one has no secrets. The 1978 survey asked the following question, "Not counting those who live here with you, do you have any friends or relatives so close that you would feel comfortable discussing just about any private problem you might have, no matter how personal it might be?" Five people out of six say they indeed do have such a close friend or relative, a somewhat smaller number than the number who say they have a friend they could "call on for advice or help."

People do not have as many confidantes as they have friends and some people who do not have many friends have one friend whom they consider a confidential friend. Income level does not seem to play much of a role in whether or not a person has such a friend, but educational level does make a difference. People with a college education are somewhat more likely than people of more limited education to say they have no confidential friend or no more than one. In view of the fact that they are more likely than other people to say they have friends they can turn to in time of trouble, it is perplexing that these college people appear less likely to claim a friend or relative with whom they can discuss anything. It may be that college-educated people are less forthcoming about their private affairs than people of less education, less willing to confide in people outside their immediate family.

The relatively high number of friendless people we saw in the metropolitan centers appears again in the number of confidantes; one person in five in the large cities says he or she has no such close friend. This proportion is not accounted for by the presence of proportionally larger numbers of black people in the cities, since black people are as likely to claim to have a confidential friend as white people are. They do not have as many such friends, but they are as likely to have at least one.

Young people appear to have different friendship patterns than older people do or at least they describe their friendships differently. We have seen earlier that young people do not differ much from older people in number of "friends other than relatives they can turn to," but we now find that they claim to have more friends of a confidential kind than older people do. People of retirement years are twice as likely to say they have no confidential friend than people in their early twenties, and those who have such a friend have fewer friends than younger people do. Perhaps older people tend to be more reserved in their relationships with other people; young people may be more open in their sharing of confidences, less willing to make a distinction between a friend and an intimate friend. The fact that the number of people who say they have no confidential friend with whom they would feel "comfortable discussing just about any private problem" increases gradually through the life span suggests that on the average people become more discriminating as they grow older, either in their willingness to confide confidential matters "no matter how personal" to someone or in their willingness to admit they have such a confidential friend.

Here again it is prudent to recognize the possibility that this apparent change through the life span may result from generational differences which persist through time. It may be that people now in their later years learned discriminating and reserved attitudes toward friendships when they were young and these attitudes still appear in contemporary surveys. Younger generations may have been exposed to less formal patterns of interpersonal relationships, a greater openness in relations with friends. It seems likely that something of this kind has been happening over the last few generations, but it also seems probable that every generation changes as it grows older, becomes more discriminating, less open to easy confidences.

Satisfaction with Friendships

Most people seem to have little complaint about their friendships. There are certainly more people who feel they would like to have more friends (20 percent) than fewer (2 percent), but for the most part they consider their number of friends "about right." In order to pursue these feelings in somewhat more detail, the 1978 survey asked, "Is there any way your friendship situation could be better so that it would be absolutely ideal for you?" Despite the fact that this question would seem to invite all manner of suggestion for improvements of one kind or another, nearly two people out of three in the study could think of no way their friendship relations could be made more nearly ideal. And those who volunteered some suggestion were for the most part interested in spending more time with their friends rather than finding new friends or a different kind of friend.

In contrast to this general complacency about friendship patterns, there are at least two segments of the population who appear much less satisfied than the average. One of these are the college graduates; over half of them said in the 1978 survey they felt there were ways their friendship situation could be made better. This proportion declined gradually to about one in four in the lowest educational category, people with no high school. There was a similar trend among people of different incomes but much less pronounced. There was also a modest tendency for people living in the large cities to feel their friendship relationships were not ideal; rural people were somewhat less ready to find fault.

The second segment of the population who find a great deal of room for improvement in their friendship patterns are young people; half the men and women under 25 have some suggestions to make their situation more nearly ideal; only 20 percent of those 65 or over have such suggestions. Despite the fact that these older people have fewer friends and relatives they regard as confidants than young people do, they are clearly less ready to suggest that their situation is less than ideal.

This indirect question regarding improvements in friendship relations produces very similar responses as a direct question regarding degree of satisfaction: "All things considered, how satisfied are you with your friendships—with the time you spend with friends, the things you do together, the number of friends you have, as well as the particular people who are your friends?" As we have seen in Appendix Table 2, satisfaction with friendships is relatively high compared with that in other domains of life; fewer than 10 percent of the population described themselves as dissatisfied in any degree in either 1971 or 1978.

Again we find that satisfaction with one's friends is related to both education and age; it is the people with no more than a grammar school education and those in their retirement years who are the most likely to describe themselves as completely satisfied and the least likely to express any kind of dissatisfaction. Since both of these groups contain a larger than average number of people who say they have no close or intimate friends and have fewer friends altogether than other people, it is apparent that for them at least satisfaction with friendship is not a simple reflection of number of friends. Satisfaction with the various domains of life seems never to be fully determined by the objective characteristics of those domains. Even in as "objective" a domain as standard of living, satisfaction is only moderately related to income level. Aspirations, expectations, perceived standards and value, personality traits all enter into the way an individual perceives and evaluates the world, and they influence the experience of satisfaction or dissatisfaction he or she may feel.

We have seen earlier that people with limited education express relatively high levels of satisfaction in a number of life domains, clearly higher than one might expect from knowing only their physical and economic circumstances. These people apparently compare the conditions of their lives to a very modest standard; their lack of education appears to limit their range of experience and to hold down their levels of aspiration. People of greater educational achievement are generally more sophisticated; they are more aware of the possible range of options and more sensitive to the unattained possibilities in life. In those domains of life in which their achievements are clearly superior to the average, standard of living and education, for example, their expressed satisfaction is relatively high, but in those domains in which they have no obvious advantage, such as friendship, they are seldom more satisfied than the rest of the population and, in some cases, less.

Age is a different story. There are, of course, people of all educational levels in every age cohort, although there are more college graduates in the younger cohorts than there are in the older. As we have seen, people in their 20's express relatively high dissatisfaction with their lives in general and with many of the major domains of life. People in the later decades of life express increasingly greater satisfaction, and there appears to be a general life cycle change toward a more positive appraisal of one's life. It is possible, to be sure, that successive generations have entered the adult population with increasingly negative outlooks on life; this appears to have happened in some degree to the post-World War II generation of young people, as we will see in Chapter 12. But this can only be a partial explanation, and we are inclined to accept the more general proposition that people tend to change as they grow older, accommodating themselves to the realities of life and becoming more satisfied as they adjust their youthful aspirations downward toward a closer match with their actual status in life. Older people get along with less in many areas of their lives, but they appear able to adjust their needs to these deprivations, to resign themselves to what they cannot change, and to put forward the appearance at least of being well-satisfied with their lives. The alternative, after all, is not very attractive.

* * * *

Not very many Americans are disturbed about their friendships. Four out of five of them feel they have at least an average number of "very good friends," and less than one in ten say they are dissatisfied with the quality of their friendships. Reasonably enough, those who have no friend with whom they are in close touch are less likely than other people to be satisfied with this domain of their lives. The fact that people of retirement age express more satisfaction with their friendships than younger people appears to be an example of what we have called the satisfaction of accommodation. The high satisfaction levels of people with limited education would appear to represent an example of satisfaction based on undeveloped aspirations.

Social Isolation and Social Support

We see from the preceding pages that most people in this country are surrounded by a network of relatives and friends whom they see frequently and who provide for them feelings of satisfaction with family and friendships which we know to be important to the individual's sense of well-being. But not everyone is so well supplied with social support of this kind, and when it is absent the consequences for the psychological quality of the person's life are apparent.

The closest form of social contact for most people is the person with whom they live, usually a spouse. If there is no such person, a significant source of social support is removed. In this country, one person in eight reports living by themselves; they may have minor children in their household, but they have no adult companion. Living alone is considerably more common among women than men, largely because of the fact that widows outnumber men so heavily. It is also more common among black people than white, in the large cities than in smaller places, and among people with low incomes than among the more affluent. Of course a large proportion of these people are separated, divorced, or never married.

People who live alone do not describe their lives as favorably as that much larger part of the population who are living with another adult. Both in affect and in satisfaction they are generally less positive. Of course this deficit in their feelings of well-being cannot be attributed exclusively to their aloneness, since many of these people, being either never married or the survivors of broken marriages, have other problems that may have contributed to their feelings of ill-being. We may assume that being alone is an unfavorable condition for most people, but the event that led to their aloneness may have had an influence of its own.

We come closer to an uncontaminated test of the impact of social isolation if we compare those people who live alone but have at least one intimate friend, a confidante with whom they "would feel comfortable discussing just about any private problem," with people living alone who have no such confidential friend. This latter group is very small, only 2 percent of the total population, but they resemble the larger group of living-alone people in age, sex, income, location, marital status, and other characteristics. They are not, however, either as happy or as satisfied with their lives as people who live alone but claim to have a confidential friend.

It is not possible to assign exact values to the relative importance of these two attributes of a person's social relationships, spouse and friend, but both have meaning for feelings of well-being. Most people are living with a spouse or companion and have at least one intimate friend. Their affect and satisfaction is on the average more positive than that of those people who are living with another adult but do not have an intimate friend. Since the objective circumstances in which these two groups live differ only slightly, the absence of the close friend would appear to be significant.

People who live with another person and have a friend whom they regard as a confidante are the most favored of these four segments of the population in descriptions of their lives, and those who have neither a companion nor a confidential friend are the least. Both aspects of social support appear to make an independent contribution to the quality of people's lives. These relationships do not tell us, however, why it is that some people have both a living companion and a confidential friend and other people have neither. The answer to this question must lie for the most part in the traits of personality that distinguish one individual from another. Some people find it easier to establish and maintain close personal relationships than others do. On the average they will also find their lives more pleasant and rewarding than those people who do not achieve this kind of companionship.

Conclusions

Americans have been called a nation of people living among strangers, and the picture of the ordinary city dweller jostling his or her way through crowds of unknown people can easily give this impression. Strangers there are in great numbers, but the image of the lonely American has certainly been overdrawn. Most people in this country have neighbors whom they know and socialize with; they typically have a number of relatives in the near vicinity, and they nearly all have at least one friend to whom they could turn in time of trouble. In 1978 the proportion of the population who admitted to having no such close friend or relative was only one in twenty.

The presence of these relationships is obviously important to how people evaluate their lives. Marriage, family, and friends make up the social support on which people depend; of these, marriage undoubtedly has the strongest influence. But for those widowed, divorced, and never married people who do not have this resource, family and friends provide something of the same experience of intimate human contact.

Marriage, family, and friends are among the major contributors to the satisfaction of people's need for relating, and we find that satisfaction in these domains of life is affected very little by considerations of income, education, or other aspects of status. This kind of advantage, significant as it is, simply does not make it more likely that an individual will be satisfied with these interpersonal relationships. Satisfaction in these domains depends on the social context in which people live and on their personal qualities but only marginally on their economic status.

It is not impossible for a person to live a happy and contented life without a marriage partner, and there are a good many people who have apparently decided they are happier unmarried than married. And there are people without close relatives or friends who describe their lives very favorably. But it has been believed since biblical times that it is not good for man or woman to be alone, and most people today find this to be true.

8
Having a Job

About four adult men out of five in this country are employed, most of them full-time. The number of employed women has been growing steadily since the Second World War and has now passed the 50 percent mark. Most of the men who are not employed have retired for reasons of age; the others are either unemployed, disabled, or students. The largest proportion of the women who are not employed are homemakers, although women are also unemployed, retired, disabled, and students.

The significance which work has in the lives of these people no doubt varies from one person to another, but we clearly cannot assess the level of well-being in this country without considering the contribution made to it by one's experience on the job. For some people work is an obsession, absorbing their energies, filling their waking hours. For these "workaholics" the quality of their work experience must determine in large part the quality of their lives. But there are others for whom work is more peripheral, an on-and-off obligation undertaken for short-term purposes and having no substantial importance in the individual's pattern of life. Probably the bulk of the working population fall between these extremes.

The situation of working men has historically been so different from that of working women that we cannot consider them in this chapter as a single work force. Men are the largest segment of the work force, and we will begin by examining their work experience and the way in which it contributes to their sense of well-being. This will require a comparison of men who are currently employed, those who are unemployed, and those who are retired. We will consider the somewhat different situation of women in the following chapter.

Men at Work

For most men the decision to go to work is not a fully voluntary one. Society expects a man to be employed, to be a wage earner, and to be self-supporting. The work-or-starve philosophy which characterized this country during its early days has been considerably softened in recent years, but society still makes it clear through both legal and social pressures that it has no respect and little patience for an able-bodied man who does not work. Of course it has little difficulty tolerating those few "idle rich" who do not become a public charge, but it even has some reservation about them.

Men work because they feel they are expected to, because it is necessary to "make a living," and because work is intrinsically rewarding. Whatever the motivation, most men expect to be employed in some full-time occupation from their late teens or early twenties into their late sixties. In the age cohort of 18 through 24 a certain proportion of men are still students and some are unemployed, but the large majority are employed. This proportion rises to over 90 percent in the subsequent decade of life as the number of students declines, and it remains high until the late 50's when it begins a sharp decline. In the age bracket of 65 to 74, one man in four is still employed, and about one in 10 of those 75 or older is still working. All but a small fraction of these men work full-time, which on the average means 40 hours a week. About 10 percent of these employed men are "moonlighting"; they report holding two jobs, and their total hours of work per week total considerably over 40 hours.

The Experience of Work

These men work in jobs of every description. They bring to their work a great range of skills and talents and they differ greatly in their aspirations, expectations, and attitudes toward their jobs. Since very few people are prepared to work without pay (except for voluntary activities which are usually part-time), it is generally assumed that the monetary reward is the major motivating force which impels people to take a job. It is not, however, the only such force, as we discover when we ask men who are employed, "If you were to get enough money to live as comfortably as you would like for the rest of your life, would you continue to work?" No doubt this is an "iffy" question and not a very realistic possibility, but three-quarters of these men answered by saying they would want to continue working. Not all of them would choose to stay at their present job by any means; nearly half of those who would continue working would prefer to change their job. These proportions changed only slightly between 1971 and 1978.

What are the attributes of a job that make it seem attractive or unattractive, that would make a person want to stay with it or seek a new job? A job may seem pleasant because it pays well; has agreeable associates; is secure, clean, and convenient; is interesting and challenging. A job may seem unpleasant because it is noisy, dirty, physically difficult, monotonous, and fatiguing. Many researchers have sought to describe the qualities which working people see in their jobs, and it has been established that from these numerous attributes four major dimensions emerge. They are (1) challenge—those aspects of a job that give stimulation and the opportunity to exercise personal skills, (2) financial reward—including rate of pay and job security, (3) coworker relations—the presence of friends and help among other people on the job, and (4) working conditions—pleasant surroundings, convenient commuting, and lack of time pressure. The way a worker sees these four attributes of the job determines in large part the way he or she evaluates the job.

Different jobs have different profiles. In the accompanying table we have arrayed the major working groups (including both men and women) and have shown how they describe their jobs in terms of the four basic attributes. It is immediately apparent that none of the job categories has an entirely positive or negative pattern. The professional, managerial, and proprietorial workers all find their jobs very challenging, but they do not consider their working conditions to be especially impressive. Proprietors clearly see their work as more "friendly" than professional or managerial people do. Operatives and service workers are least likely to describe their work as challenging; operatives feel much more positive about their pay than service workers do. Perhaps the most interesting pattern is that of farmers who rate their work very high in terms of challenge (exceeded only by the proprietors) and in the pleasant conditions of

	Challenge	Financial reward	Coworker relations	Working conditions
Professional, technical	Much above average	Average	Average	Average
Managerial	Much above average	Above average	Average	Below average
Proprietors	Much above average	Above average	Much above average	Average
Clerical, sales	Below average	Average	Average	Above average
Skilled workers, foremen	Above average	Average	Average	Below average
Operatives	Much below average	Average	Average	Average
Service workers	Much below average	Much below average	Below average	Average
Farmers	Much above average	Much below average	Much below average	Much above average

their work. Understandably, however, they see their work as well below average in sociability, and their evaluation of its financial rewards is the most negative of all the occupational groups. As a group farmers appear to value very highly the kind of work they are doing, but they see it as very poorly paid.

If we set aside farmers as rather different from the other occupational groups, we see that the attribute which is most clearly associated with the prestige order of the job is challenge, and, as we will see, it is also the most closely associated with the individual's general satisfaction with his or her job. Perceptions of financial rewards also tend to follow the same pattern, although the differences between occupations are not as sharp. Working people seem very sensitive to whether or not a job is interesting and whether it gives them a chance to develop and exercise their abilities. If one were to order the different occupations in terms of the amount of challenge they appear to offer, this ordering would conform very well to the evaluations given by the people who are actually in the occupations.

These job profiles changed very little between 1971 and 1978. The professional people seemed a little less favorably impressed with their financial rewards in the latter year; farmers were a little less negative than they had been. One might have thought that the entry of so many women into the work force during the 1970s might have changed some of these occupational profiles, but the fact is that women differ very little from men in their perceptions of these attributes of their work, except in the case of working conditions, which women on the average find more pleasant than men do.

Satisfaction with Work

It is a bit of common folklore that a person who is unhappy with his or her job is likely to be unhappy with life in general. This is a generality which no doubt has many exceptions, but, as we saw in Chapter 4, satisfaction with work is indeed one of the more important contributors to an individual's satisfaction with life in general.

In light of the numerous tracts that have been written over the years describing the "mindless, hateful, numbing" character of work in this country, one would hardly be surprised to find most American working men in a state of sullen rebellion against their jobs. The fact is that no careful survey that undertook to describe the nation's work force has ever failed to find an impressive majority who say they are satisfied with their jobs. In 1978, four out of five employed men across the country told the Institute for Social Research's interviewers that they were satisfied in some degree with their jobs. One out of three described themselves as "completely satisfied." This does not mean that they have no criticisms of their jobs and, as we have seen, a good many of them would prefer a different job from the one they have. But for the most part they do not find their work so objectionable that they say they are dissatisfied with it. This perhaps surprisingly high level of satisfaction with the job declined slightly among male workers from 1971 to 1978, but it still remained very high.

One might imagine, if one took the economic aspects of life to be the main determiners of feelings of well-being, that the most important influence on a worker's evaluation of his job would be how well it pays. Indeed there is a modest tendency for people with higher incomes to feel more satisfied with their work, but the relationship is very weak, largely because so many people with low incomes seem very well pleased with their jobs. If we consider instead of actual income whether or not the person thinks his "pay is good," we find that the relationship is somewhat stronger, but it is still not the aspect of the job which contributes most to his feelings of satisfaction. That distinction goes to whether or not he thinks his job is "interesting"; those men who say it is "very true" that their work is interesting are quite substantially more likely to describe themselves as satisfied with their job than those who say it is "not very true" or "not true at all."

As we have seen, the likelihood that a worker will find his work interesting or challenging varies a good deal from one occupation to another, and so we would expect degree of satisfaction with one's work to vary between occupations in the same manner. This is indeed the pattern we find, with the professional and managerial employees more satisfied than average and the operatives and service workers less satisfied. But there are a good many people who do not fit the pattern: unskilled workers who describe their work as very interesting and professional workers who do not, and the result is that the differences in the levels of satisfaction with work expressed by people in different occupations are not as great as one might have expected.

Part of the explanation of the high proportions of satisfied workers we find in all these occupations suggests itself when we compare the degree of job satisfaction expressed by men with much or little schooling. Our expectations in this case might be influenced by our knowledge that the dirtiest, noisiest, most physically tiring, least well-paid jobs are generally held by people with the least education and that these aspects of the job become less common among people with more educational background. But the surprising fact is that working men with the least education are most likely to describe themselves as satisfied with their job. The lowest average level of job satisfaction is given by men who have attended college but did not complete a degree. College graduates are more satisfied than college dropouts, but they are not as high as those people who did not even go to high school.

We take this curious pattern to mean that many men who leave school early go into whatever job is available with no greater aspiration than to have full-time employment. They stay in this job or one not very different from it with no strong sense of an upwardly mobile work career. They are satisfied with their work partly because they see the alternative as no work at all and partly because they do not have the option of a better job. If they happen to be in a work situation which pays relatively well, their satisfaction may be determined primarily by their feeling of being well-paid. Basically their work satisfaction reflects their undeveloped aspirations.

Those men with somewhat higher education are not so willing to say they are fully satisfied with their work, and this is especially true of men who have a partial college education. They have been exposed to a long period of formal education which must have broadened their perceptions of occupational options and raised their job aspirations. Relatively few of these men will be able to enter the professions or other prestigious occupations, however, and this is likely to leave them in the situation of achieving considerably less than they aspire to. The college graduates do enter these professional and other high-level positions. They aspire high and they attain high. They are not as unquestionably accepting of their jobs as the less-than-high-school people appear to be, but, having a good deal to be satisfied with, they seem relatively content with their achievement.

The distinctive quality of the value patterns of college graduates as compared with those people with less formal education, which we noted in Chapter 5, appears again in their attitudes toward work. An Institute for Social Research study of young employed men in 1971 asked these men to choose those "things about a job you would most prefer." All the educational levels below college graduate gave their first preference to either "a steady income" or "a high income." Very few of the college graduate men selected either of these choices, the greater majority giving their preference to work that is "important, gives a feeling of accomplishment." When asked which attributes of a new job might tempt them to change jobs, they showed the same pattern. The less-than-college men emphasized "a higher income"; the college graduates gave preference to a job where the "work was more important." It is significant that the some-college men gave very much the same preferences as the high school graduate; it is the college graduates who are distinctive. Their evaluation of their work is clearly less dominated by purely economic considerations than that of men at lower educational levels.

Job satisfaction, like satisfaction with other domains of life, is also influenced by a person's age. Young men under 25 are clearly least satisfied with their jobs; only one in five say they are completely satisfied with the work they are doing. But in the older decades the level of satisfaction rises, and of those men who are employed after the age of 65, two out of three say they are completely satisfied with their work. It is not hard to understand why a young man getting started in a work career may be impatient to get ahead and may perceive a wide gap between where he is and where he aspires to be. Later he may close this gap and feel satisfaction with the progress he has made. Or he may not achieve as much as he had hoped for but gradually comes to terms with reality, bringing his aspirations into close relation to his achievements. The satisfaction he expresses results from this accommodation. This adjustment to the realities of life appears to occur rather broadly in the total experience of growing older.

Being Unemployed

As we have seen, most employed men say they would rather work than not work, even if money were not a consideration. There also are some men who are not working who would very much prefer to be working. They are unemployed, and we get an additional insight into the meaning of work when we examine the way these men evaluate their life experience.

The proportion of employed men who describe themselves as "very happy" is about the same as that of the population at large. Among unemployed men this proportion sinks to one of the lowest levels of any of the groups we will consider in this book, 12 percent in 1971, 10 percent in 1978. Reports of recent positive and negative experiences show the same discrepancy. Unemployed men are particularly prone to remember affective experiences of a negative kind—feeling lonely and being bored, depressed, or upset by criticism.

This same pattern appears when employed and unemployed men are compared in their satisfactions with life. Unemployment is associated with low levels of satisfaction, not only with life in general but also with the specific domains of life. It is easy to understand that so many of these men are discontent with their family income and their standard of living. The interesting fact is that they are less satisfied than employed men with many of the other domains of their lives—their neighborhood, their housing, their health, their level of education. They are not less satisfied with their marriage, however, despite the pressures being unemployed might be expected to put on a marriage. And they are not less likely to say they are satisfied with themselves "as a person." We will see later that these men are much more likely than employed men to feel their lives are controlled by outside forces rather than by themselves; this attribution may serve to protect them from whatever damage the condition of being unemployed might have done to their feelings of self-regard.

Although most unemployment is relatively short-term, interspersed between periods of working, men who are unemployed not only find their lives "these days" relatively negative, they also tend to feel they have been shortchanged in their lives as a whole. When asked if they feel they have had all the happiness they could reasonably expect in their lives "up to now," nearly half of them say they have had less than their share. This is over twice the proportion found among employed men, and it is one of the most extreme expressions of discontent found in these surveys.

As one might expect, unemployment is also associated with feelings of strain. Men without jobs are much more concerned than employed men about meeting their bills, more often worried or frightened about something that might happen to them or their families, and twice as likely to say they sometimes worry about having a nervous breakdown. Despite the fact that they do not have the responsibilities of a job, they do not describe their lives as "easy." They are somewhat more likely than employed men to speak of life as "hard."

Not every unemployed man describes his life in these negative terms. There is even a small fraction who insist that they are "very happy." But it is clear that for most men unemployment is not an easy condition to feel good about. There are no doubt some individuals living a carefree life despite their unemployment, but on the average the facts of being without a job clearly diminishes feelings of well-being about life in general and about the specific domains of life. The whole range of measures we have considered is remorselessly negative; for most people being unemployed is a disagreeable way of life, not only in financial terms but in the quality of psychological life.

This dismal picture of the unemployed male was substantially the same in 1978, when the economy had still not recovered from the severe recession of 1974–75, as it had been in 1971 while the postwar cycle of prosperity was still in full flower. It would be reasonable to assume that the miseries these men feel depend fundamentally on financial difficulties to which their joblessness exposes them. But in fact, if we compare unemployed people at different levels of income, we find very little difference in their average levels of well-being. It is evidently not the low income that depresses these men; it is the psychological trauma of having no work and the diminished sense of controlling one's life that accompanies it.

Being Retired

The second large group of men without employment in this country are those who have retired. In most bureaucratic settings, retirement has been mandatory, usually at age 65. These policies were originally based on the presumption that by this age a man's health would have deteriorated to the point that he could no longer fulfill the demands of a full-time job. With the significant increase in longevity and the shift from industrial and agricultural work to the lighter service occupations, however, this rationale has become less convincing and resistance to compulsory retirement has begun to attract legislative attention.

It is not true, however, that most men resist retirement or are unhappy in this status when they attain it. The ardor with which an older man will cling to his job depends obviously on how attractive his job situation is as compared with the circumstances he will find himself in once he retires. In some cases the job seems to be so unrewarding that retirement seems the clear choice. Studies of blue-collar workers in the automobile industry find a large majority choosing to retire after 30 years on the job and feeling well-satisfied with their decision after they have made it. Other men, working in more rewarding jobs, resist the prospect of giving up their occupation and the financial penalty it implies. When retired men at large are asked whether they are glad they retired when they did, some two out of three say they are and of the others far more wish they had retired earlier than later than they actually did.

When we consider retired men as a whole, we discover that in their professed happiness and contentment with life they compare closely with those younger men who are still employed. They resemble working men in describing themselves as happy or unhappy and in their expressions of satisfaction with life. They are not quite as likely to report pleasant experiences in the recent past, but they are clearly less likely to remember unpleasant experiences. Their satisfaction with the specific domains of life is very similar to that of employed men except in the domain of health, where as older people they have a good deal to complain about. They are no more or less likely than men still working to feel that they have had their full share of happiness in life.

Retired men report less strain in their lives than men who are still working. They are far less likely to describe their lives as hard rather than easy, or tied down rather than free. They are less likely to express fear or worry about events in their lives, and they have relatively little concern about the possibility of a "nervous breakdown." Despite their generally low incomes, they are less likely than men still working to say they worry about meeting their bills. Retirement appears to have something of the quality of serenity it is supposed to have.

Of course men who are retired are considerably older on the average than men who are still working; seven out of ten are over 65, and this age differential is undoubtedly responsible in large degree for the way retired men evaluate their lives. Their dissatisfaction with their health, for example, must depend less on their retirement than on the fact that they are in the age bracket when health is a common problem. Their relatively high levels of satisfaction in other domains of life reflect the tendency we have commented upon earlier of older people to accommodate themselves to the realities of life and to content themselves with what they have. Their freedom from strain, however, must derive in part at least from the unpressured situation they find themselves in as retired people. The contrast we see between retired and unemployed men in this regard reveals something of the psychological quality of these two life situations. Both groups of men tend to find more free time on their hands "than they know what to do with," but among the unemployed this is associated with far greater than average feelings of pressure, uncertainty, and worry. Retired men are also without an occupation, but they find their lives easy and free of strain.

For the average man retirement is a profoundly different situation from unemployment. Typically the person who retires has had a long time to anticipate leaving his job, and he has made some provision for his retirement income, even if it is no more than Social Security. He is playing the role society expects him to play, and he has no reason to feel guilt or shame at not working. He has reached an age at which his major family responsibilities have passed, and he can relax into a slower-paced style of life. Some men undoubtedly find this change from their work life an unwelcome shunting aside from the active world of affairs; they feel unwanted. But for the most part men in retirement do not find their lives to be unhappy or unsatisfying; their outlook on life is as positive as that of men who are still working. This is in striking contrast to the men who are unemployed—who are involuntarily and often unexpectedly removed from the payroll, their capacity to support themselves and their families thrown into question, their self-respect impugned by the public opprobrium they feel, and their sense of security and self-confidence shaken by their inability to find work. For most men being retired seems to be a rather benign condition of life; being unemployed is a disturbing and often degrading experience.

Free Time

Employment for pay implies an obligation to perform specified functions for an agreed-upon number of hours per week. The remaining hours of the week are used up in a great variety of activities which can be combined into the categories of housework, child care, travel, personal care including sleeping, eating, dressing, and bathing, and the residual category of free time. Leisure-time activities take place within these hours of free time.

Leisure is a highly positive word in the current vocabulary. We associate it with the short workweek, annual vacations, sports activities, labor-saving devices, and other attributes of contemporary life which contrast with the bad old days of sweatshops, 12-hour days, and household drudgery. This contrast is so great and our sense of progress so strong that we are easily led to the assumption that the individual's sense of well-being must rise as leisure time increases and that the national quality of life will be enhanced as we find ways to increase the amount of free time the population can command.

People obviously differ very greatly in the amount of free time at their disposal, from the small businessman who keeps his shop open at all hours of the week to the retired teacher who has no work requirements or other obligations to fill the time. Some segments of the population have considerably more free time than others, but those who have much are not always more positive in their feelings of well-being than those who have less. Studies of the American population show, for example, that homemakers have more hours of free time on the average (40 hours a week) than employed men (33 hours), and employed men in turn have more free time than employed women (28 hours). But none of these groups describes itself as happier or more satisfied with life than any of the others. Employed women are somewhat more likely to report feelings of strain than homemakers are, but even this difference is smaller than might have been expected. Homemakers are clearly less likely to see themselves as rushed for time than either employed men or women, a reflection no doubt of their greater freedom of movement and their greater number of free hours.

An additional example of the different meaning free time has to people in different circumstances comes from the comparison we have just seen of retired people and unemployed people. Both of these segments of the population have far more than an average amount of free time, but they differ dramatically in their sense of well-being. The availability of many hours of free time does not seem to brighten the lives of people who cannot find a job nor to burden the lives of older people who are retired.

Most people say they are satisfied with the way they spend their free time, but they differ a good deal in how they feel about the amount of free time they have. When asked directly, about a quarter of the population say they "always feel rushed," while about one in ten say they are never rushed and often have time on their hands "they don't know what to do with." It is the people in between, who only occasionally feel rushed and only now and then have time on their hands, who are the most satisfied with their free time. The always-rushed people are somewhat less satisfied than the population in general with their use of free time and the often-have-time-on-their-hands people are very much further below the average.

The same pattern reveals itself when we compare these people's expressions of general well-being. The most positive expressions of affect and satisfaction come from those people who do not feel themselves either overly rushed or with too much time on their hands. And of course, these people are less likely to report other experiences of strain in their lives—worries, fears, and sense of pressure.

Free time turns out not to be the unlimited good that it is often thought to be. It is possible to have far too much free time, and those people who do are not happy with it or with their lives in general. Unemployed people represent a dramatic case in point. More commonly people have too little time and feel overly rushed; their sense of well-being also seems to suffer, although not as acutely as that of those who have too much time on their hands. For people in their preretirement years it seems clearly better to be too busy than to be idle.

Conclusions

For the man who is employed, the hours at the job and in job-related travel make up nearly half of the total waking hours of a week. If work had no more meaning than simply filling one's time, it would be an important part of a man's life. Of course the psychological implications of work go far beyond the mere filling of time, providing rewards and frustrations which contribute substantially to the individual's sense of well-being. For most people the income the job provides is essential for the fulfillment of their need for the material necessities of life. But the fact that a large majority of employed men and women believe they would prefer to continue to work even if their economic needs were taken care of demonstrates that for most of them work has a broader meaning than just its financial return. Variety of experience, personal challenge, sense of achievement, pleasure in exercising skills, recognition, sociability—these values are all served in some degree by a person's work. The different occupations differ substantially in the degree to which they are seen to have these qualities, but for many people the work experience makes a significant contribution to their need for social relationships and their sense of being fulfilled.

Most men say they are satisfied with their work, including those working at jobs which would appear to have very little intrinsic interest. This contrasts rather sharply with the way some theorists feel workers ought to feel about their jobs, and they take this sense of satisfaction as an example of "false consciousness," a misperception of the real world. Of course people respond to the world as they perceive it, and they evaluate their jobs in relation to the options they see and the aspirations they have. Working people often find fault with their working conditions, their pay, their changes for promotion, or other specific aspects of their job, and only about one-third of them say they are "completely satisfied" with their work, but most of the rest find their jobs more satisfying than dissatisfying.

People obviously expect different things from their jobs, and those who work only for the economic return can find a very routine job satisfying if it meets their economic aspirations. Others who look for personal challenge and fulfillment in a job may find intolerable a job that pays well but does not meet these needs. Most people seem to find in their jobs at least a moderately satisfying supply of what they are asking from the job.

During the early 1970s it was commonly heard in this country that the traditional work ethic, on which American productivity was presumably based, was fading away; that absenteeism, apathy, and insubordination had become standard behavior in the workplace; and that the younger generation was turned off by the rigidities of work life and was taking to farming, arts and crafts, and other nonbureaucratic occupations. None of these evidences of alienation reveals itself in the data of national surveys. Comparable studies done by the Institute for Social Research in 1971 and 1978 showed no significant changes in level of job satisfaction or in satisfaction with its major facets—challenge, working conditions, financial rewards, or relations with coworkers. Nor has there been any notable change in the proportion of male workers who would prefer to stop working if their economic needs were taken care of. Young workers are even more likely than those of middle age or older to say they would prefer to go on working. Granting the presence of numerous individual exceptions, the degree of work orientation of the average American does not seem to have diminished.

The time people spend at work diminishes the time they have free. There have been continuing efforts on the part of labor unions and other organizations to reduce the length of the workweek, and there is an increasing proportion of the work force who work fewer than 40 hours a week. But at the same time there is an increasing proportion who are working more than 40 hours, and the average workweek in this country remains virtually unchanged. Free time obviously has greater value to some parts of the work force than it does to others. It seems probable that as time passes those people working in occupations which are not intrinsically rewarding will work a shorter week, perhaps a four-day week. But it is not likely that this pattern will cover the entire work force; there will continue to be many people who will work a longer week. Free time, and the leisure activities it makes possible, may be virtually universal values, but work also has value, both instrumental and intrinsic. Most people would want to continue working even if there were no economic need to do so; they do not want all their time to be free. The trade-off they are prepared to make between hours on the job and hours of free time is no doubt affected by the kind of work they do, but it is also influenced by the circumstances they live in and the kind of person they are.

9

Being a Working Woman

Women in this country do not live the same lives men do. They grow up in different cultures, develop different expectations, learn different roles, and hold different values. Their experiences as children and adults differ in many ways. All of this is changing and the lives of men and women now have more in common than was formerly the case, but substantial differences remain.

There is a good deal of traditional folklore about sex differences, much of it intended to describe and explain the inferiority of the "weaker" sex. This has little scientific merit, but it has historically had a great deal of influence on the roles societies specify for women and on the way women and men live their lives. In recent years scholars have begun to ask what the impact of these prescribed roles is on the mental health of women. It has been argued that the lives of women in this country are "more frustrating and less rewarding than those of men" and that this condition explains the fact that women outnumber men in some categories of admissions to mental hospitals. The role of the housewife has been described as "pathogenic," and it has been proposed that increased participation in the labor force would have "benign effects on the wife."

We will be primarily concerned in this chapter with comparing the life experiences of married women who are not employed outside the home (homemakers) with married women who are so employed (working wives). But first we will look at the evidence of the national surveys to find what broad differences exist in the way women and men describe their lives. In what ways, if any, are the lives of women more or less pleasant, satisfying, and free of strain than those of men?

When our original question concerning how happy your life is "these days" was first asked of a national sample in 1957, there was no difference in the answers given by women and men. This question has been asked numerous times since, most recently in 1978, always with the same result. When the questions of the Positive Affect Scale were first asked in 1965, there was no gender difference; women were just as likely as men to say they felt excited, proud, pleased, on top of the world, and feeling things were going their way. When the Institute for Social Research asked the same question in 1978, there was still no difference between men and women. Clearly in these perceptions of the positive qualities of life, men and women do not differ.

It is intriguing, however, that in both 1965 and 1978 women were somewhat more likely than men to remember negative experiences in their recent past—feeling restless, lonely, bored, depressed, or upset. These differences were not great, but they seem to have persisted over this 15-year period. Women also more often report being worried about money problems, being frightened that something might happen to them or their families, and being worried that they might have a nervous breakdown. These evidences of strain were no more or less frequent in 1978 than they had been in 1971, but they contribute to the pattern of negative affect that appears to be somewhat stronger among women than men.

Men and women differ very little in their satisfaction with life as a whole. They are equally content with their housing, neighborhood, and community, although women are much more likely to believe it is not safe to go out walking at night. They are equally satisfied with their education, jobs, and financial situation. They differ very little in their satisfaction with friendships and family life, but they express a little less satisfaction with their marriages than men do. In both 1971 and 1978 women were also a little less satisfied with their health, especially after the age of 45. In 1978 women were slightly less willing to express satisfaction with themselves "as a person." Finally, "considering everything up to now," a majority of both men and women feel they have had all the happiness a person can reasonably expect in life, but women are a little more likely than men to say they have had less than their share.

These various indicators of the several aspects of well-being lead to one major conclusion—when we compare men and women as a whole, we do not find major differences in their feelings of well-being. In positive affect and most aspects of satisfaction men and women seem very similar. There is a persistently greater inclination among women, however, to report negative experiences—feeling depressed, worried, or frightened. This is not a large difference, but it keeps reappearing in national surveys, and it must be attributed either to differences in the physiological makeup of men and women, to differences in the psychological circumstances in which men and women live, or to differences in the sensitivity and expectations with which men and women perceive and evaluate their circumstances.

There are obviously great differences in the situations in which women of different status live, and these are obscured when we consider the population of women as a whole. Women are single or married, divorced or widowed, with children or without children, and we will see in Chapter 12 how these different women feel about their lives. Women are also divided into those married women who do not work outside the home and those who are employed. Much current speculation revolves around the meaning these two roles, homemaking and employment, have to women, the possible conflict between them, and their impact on marriage. We will discover in this chapter that most women still value their role in the home, but attitudes and choices are changing.

Women at Home and at Work

One of the major changes in the American pattern of life since World War II has been the great increase in the number of married women who are employed outside the home. Single women have been employed in large numbers in this country for the last 100 years, but married women traditionally stayed in the home. In 1890 only three percent of married white women were recorded as employed, as compared with a much larger proportion of black women (23 percent). The two World Wars brought many women out of the home, and in 1951 about one in four married white women were employed, 36 percent of black women. During the ensuing years these numbers have steadily increased until the proportions for both white and black married women are now somewhat over 50 percent.

Despite these rising numbers, women are not in quite the same relationship to the job market as men are. Boys are brought up in this country with a certain expectation that after they leave school, they will find a job and work until they retire. Until recently girls grew up with almost as firm an assumption that sometime rather soon they would marry and raise children. They might ultimately also work outside the home, but that was a secondary expectation. Their main role was to be a homemaker. This pattern characterized the lives of white girls more clearly than it did of black, black women having historically had a greater expectation of working. It is a pattern that is changing, partly as the result of the great increase in the number of women with education beyond high school and partly because of a general change in societal attitudes toward the roles of women. Most women still have a place in the home, but an increasing number of them also have a place in the work force.

We will not be concerned in this chapter with single women. They account for about 35 percent of all adult women, and they are made up of three quite different groups—women who have never married (mostly under 30), women who are separated or divorced, and widows (mostly over 65). Each of these groups will be considered separately in Chapter 12.

In 1971 the Institute for Social Research asked a national sample of homemakers the following question: "Different people feel differently about taking care of a home. I don't mean taking care of children, but things like cooking, sewing, and keeping house. Some women look on these things as just a job that has to be done; other women really enjoy them. How do you feel about it?" Six out of ten of these women said without reservation that they enjoyed taking care of their home. One in ten said they regarded housework as just a job that had to be done and three women in a hundred expressed unqualified dislike for it. Whatever the shortcomings of housework might have been, there were far more homemakers who found it enjoyable than found it disagreeable.

The ensuing years brought a good deal of derogatory comment regarding the "housewife's trauma," and one would not have been surprised if during this period women became somewhat disenchanted with the role of homemaker. When this same question was asked again of women in this role in 1978, the proportion who described themselves as liking their housework without qualification was slightly lower than it had been in

1971 (57 percent as compared with 60 percent), and the proportion who unreservedly disliked it had risen slightly (from 3 percent to 6 percent). Although one might have thought that the events of the 1970s would have led many women to view housework in a different light than they had before, in fact the majority of women in the homemaker's role still spoke of their housework as enjoyable, and very few of them appeared to find it totally objectionable.

Women not only tend to view their housework favorably, they tend also to say they are satisfied with being a homemaker. When homemakers were asked in 1971, "Overall, how satisfied are you with being a homemaker—I don't mean with your family life, but with housework?" about half of them professed to be completely satisfied. In 1978 the proportion was 44 percent. One homemaker out of six described herself as feeling neutral or dissatisfied with her role in 1971, but in 1978 this ratio had gone up to one in four.

Employed wives also do housework and take care of children, but their evaluation of this role is not as favorable as that of wives who are not employed. We may presume that some of these women took a job in order to get away from a household role they found unsatisfying. It may also be true that homemakers who take a job find their housework more burdensome than it had been before they became employed, and they are now less favorably disposed toward it. The attitudes of employed wives toward the homemaker's role are still generally positive, but the proportion who were neutral or dissatisfied, which was one in four in 1971, had gone up to slightly over one in three in 1978.

It is not surprising that we find sizable differences in degree of satisfaction with being a homemaker when we compare young women with older women, college graduates with women of low educational achievement, or urban women with rural women. The young, the educated, and the urban are the segments of society which are most receptive to change from traditional attitudes and values; as one might expect, they have been the most ready to question the conventional definition of women's role. But they are not the only women who have increasing reservations about the role of homemaker; between 1971 and 1978 there was a general decline in satisfaction with this role throughout the female population, even among those parts of the population who are most favorably disposed toward the role.

Being Employed

The question of why some women take jobs and some do not is not easy to answer. Among young women who have completed their schooling and are not yet married, taking a job has come to have almost the same imperative quality that it has for men. Not very many young women stayed home waiting for Prince Charming in the 1970s; they were mostly employed. After they marry, they are likely to continue their work until the first child arrives. Historically this is the point at which the average white woman's employment career ended. Black women commonly went back to work, but white women did not. The great change in women's employment in the postwar period has been the increase in the number of married women, most of them with children, who have chosen to take employment outside the home.

The most commonly given explanation for this spectacular increase is an economic one; the family needs money to meet its consumer aspirations, and the wife goes to work to add to the family income. This is plausible and obviously has merit, but like so many economic explanations of human motivation it is incomplete and fits some parts of the population much better than others. It does not, for example, explain the fact that it is not the women in the poorest families, where the financial pressure to work might be thought to be greatest, who are the most likely to take jobs; it is those in the more advantaged families. The more formal education a married woman has, the more likely she is to be employed. Despite the economic pressures that poorly educated and low-income women feel, they are the most likely to remain in their home with their family. Perhaps the traditional ethic of the full-time mother is stronger at this social level; perhaps the husbands are more likely to feel it is a reflection on them if their wife works; or perhaps the home obligations of these women are heavier than those at more affluent levels—more children, more extended family, fewer labor-saving devices, less sharing from the husband. The decisions women make are clearly influenced by considerations that have little to do with how much money they are offered.

It is true of course that when homemakers who think they might take a job sometime in the future are asked "the main reason" they would have for taking a job, a majority gave some kind of economic answer. The others talk about the personal satisfaction they would get out of working, the sense of independence, the chance to be out of the house and with other people, or the feeling that idleness is immoral or improper. It is women in the lower part of the income distribution who are most likely to give economic reasons for working; black women are more likely to do so than white. Most college-graduate women emphasize the personal satisfaction they would expect to get from a job. Certainly very few women enter employment without some thought regarding the compensation, but it is a far more preeminent consideration for some women than for others.

A different indication of motivation can be obtained by asking women the same question that was asked men, "If you were to get enough money to live as comfortably as you'd like for the rest of your life, would you continue to work?" As we have seen, about three out of four working men answered this speculative question by saying they would want to go on working, and this proportion did not change between 1971 and 1978. In 1971 working women were clearly less interested in continuing to work than men were (60 percent compared with 75 percent), but in 1978 this gap had been largely closed. In 1971 it was the college women who were most likely to be employed and the most likely to say they would want to continue to work. This was also true in 1978, but there had been a general increase in the employment of women at all educational levels and greater interest in all these levels in continuing to work.

These differences in attitudes toward employment among women of different educational achievement must have both economic and psychological bases. The high employment rates among college graduates certainly are influenced by the fact that these women go into the most attractive jobs, professional or technical for the most part, where both the pay and the conditions of work are considerably above average. These women are also, as the result of their education and family background, more liberated from conventional views of women's roles, more open to alternatives to the traditional role of homemaker. They also of course have made a considerable investment in their college training and are likely to feel some motivation to put their skills into practice. Lying behind all this is the more sophisticated attitude of these educated women toward childbearing. Family planning has been a characteristic of educated families for many years, with the result that the number of children born and the number of years spent in child-raising is smaller among these families than in the rest of the population. A woman who has completed college is more in control of the way she balances her interests in work, marriage, and children than she was some years ago or than other women of her own generation are.

In contrast women who go into the job market with limited educational credentials find themselves channeled into those low-pay, low-status, low-challenging jobs which American business and industry seem to have reserved especially for women. Their lack of highly valued skills makes it very difficult for them to rise occupationally or to think of progressing through a work career. They are certainly more likely than a college graduate to be married to a man who prefers that his wife not work outside the home, and, of course, they are more likely to marry early, bear children, and devote a good many years to the demands these children put on them. They are more likely to have been raised believing that "woman's place is in the home," and it is not surprising that so many of them find this role preferable to that of working at the kind of job that is available to them.

Despite the fact that the role of homemaker has been subjected to a certain amount of derogation from women's groups in recent years, there remains a sizable proportion of married women in this country who for the time being at least appear to prefer the responsibilities of homemaking to the rewards of outside employment. When married women not employed outside the home were asked in 1971, "If you could have someone to take care of things here at home, would you like to take an outside job right now, or are you happy enough to be at home?" approximately one in five said they would like to take a job. In 1978 the number of homemakers had declined, but the proportion of those remaining who wanted to "take an outside job right now" was still about one in five. A somewhat larger number of housewives say they expect to take a job at some time in the future, but the majority, three out of four, are not interested in taking a job either now or in the future. This preference for the home is especially strong among women with limited education, but it is present at all educational levels, including college graduates.

Of course many young women of every social class are engaged in planning their lives so that their concerns with the values of employment and homemaking can both be satisfied. They begin their employment as single women and continue to work during the early years of marriage.

When the first child is born, they leave the labor force and devote themselves to their home during the years of child-raising. At a time when their full-time commitment to the home no longer seems so imperative, they again take up their work career. This pattern is increasingly replacing the earlier pattern in which the employed married woman gave up her job when her children were born and did not return to the work force.

As we see, most employed women prefer to remain employed, and most homemakers prefer to remain in the home. Since married women are for the most part not under the kind of compulsion to work that men are, we must assume that these women have chosen the role which seems best to them. We are currently in a period of change in attitudes toward women's roles, and it may well be that these options will look different to women as time passes. There is not much likelihood of change in the choices of college women since most of them have already chosen the employment path and seem very well satisfied with it. It is the women of lesser educational achievement whose situation is likely to change. They will become increasingly subject to liberated ideas of the roles and potentialities of women. With the seemingly insatiable American appetite for consumer goods, they will be under increasing pressure to contribute to the family income. They have already begun to reduce their number of children and the number of years spent in child-raising, and this trend is not likely to be reversed. Other deterrents to their employment remain, however, and their recruitment into the job market may proceed slowly.

The Sense of Well-Being of Homemakers and Working Wives

Which of these situations, homemaker or employed wife, provides the greatest sense of well-being to present-day women? The flow of married women into the work force would suggest that the homemaking role fails to satisfy the needs of many women and that the role of working wife is somehow more rewarding. In fact, however, the survey evidence does not show that those women who are still homemakers see their lives any less positively than do married women who are employed. They are just as likely to say they are very happy and completely satisfied with their lives. They differ very little in their answers to the positive and negative affect questions and, if anything, homemakers are a little less likely to describe their lives as stressful, not altogether surprising in view of the fact that most employed wives still retain a substantial part of their responsibilities in the home.

Not only do these two groups of women resemble each other rather closely in these various measures of well-being, this similarity has persisted throughout the 20 years these measures have been taken. In 1957, well before the women's movement had reached its present prominence and when a much smaller proportion of women were employed than at present, homemakers and employed wives gave almost identical answers to the question, "How happy are you?" This resemblance appeared again in 1971 and yet again in 1978. The proportion of married women who were homemakers declined steadily, but they did not fall behind employed wives in their perceived happiness. The resemblance in answers to the question regarding satisfaction with life which was seen in 1971 was present again in 1978. The same was true of the measures of strain. In 1971 the homemakers were much more likely than employed wives to describe their lives as "easy" rather than "hard," just as they were later in 1978.

There is no striking difference between these groups in these general measures of well-being, and there is none in their satisfaction with the specific domains of their lives. It is particularly interesting that the proportions who say they are very satisfied with their marriage and family life do not differ significantly. In answering the four questions regarding their relations with their spouse, their responses are similar. Homemakers are no more or less likely than married women who are employed to say they understand their husbands, that their husbands understand them, that they never disagree about money, or that they share many companionable activities. Moreover it is of interest that the husbands of employed women do not evaluate their marriages any more or less positively than do the husbands of women who are not employed. There are undoubtedly individual husbands who are unhappy about the fact that their wife works or does not work, but on the average the quality of the marriage as the husband sees it is not related one way or the other to the fact that the wife works outside the home.

We can carry this comparison one step further by dividing these groups of women into groups with more or less education. Despite the fact that this results in comparing women of very different occupations and incomes, the pattern remains similar to that of the total population.

Homemakers and employed married women resemble each other in these various measures of well-being at all educational levels. In 1971, married college women who worked seemed more positive about their lives and their marriages than college-graduate homemakers did. In 1978 this difference had disappeared. The proportion of married college graduates who were employed had increased from 57 percent to 73 percent, and those who remained in the home now seemed no less positive in their feelings of well-being than those who worked. One might speculate that those college women who were dissatisfied as housewives in 1971 had taken jobs in 1978 and those who remained preferred to be housewives and were satisfied with their lives as such, although without longitudinal data this hypothesis remains a speculative one.

Of course we cannot conclude from these comparisons that homemaking and paid employment are equally attractive to all women. On the contrary, there is obviously a great deal of self-selection underlying the present sorting of women into employed wives and homemakers. In 1978 close to half of all married women were not employed, and most of them preferred to remain so. For whatever reasons they had made the decision not to take a job. The other half were employed, probably motivated in part by economic concerns but preferring to continue working even if income were not a consideration. In either case most women seem to be in the role they prefer, and those who have chosen homemaking are as satisfied with their lives as those who have made the other choice.

Satisfaction with Work

It is curious that women workers as a whole describe their jobs in much the same terms as male workers do. Considering the fact that most women go into low-status occupations and are paid on the average about 60 percent as much as men, it would not be surprising to find them describing their work rather negatively. The fact that they do not must mean that women do not have the same expectations from their jobs as men do and evaluate them on a different basis. Women differ a good deal among themselves, however, in their perceptions of their jobs, particularly regarding the attributes of challenge and financial reward. Women of low educational achievement (less than a high school diploma) are much less likely than women with more formal education to describe their jobs as interesting, giving them an opportunity to develop their skills, or giving them a chance to do what they do best. They are also less likely than men of the same limited education to see these attributes in their jobs. Women of high education (college graduates) on the other hand are much more likely than other women to say their jobs have these challenging characteristics and are indeed a little more likely than male college graduates to do so. Women who attended college but did not graduate hold an anomalous position. They find less evidence of challenge in their jobs than high school graduates and of course much less than college graduates. Male workers with some college education do not show this pattern.

The evaluations by male and female workers of the financial rewards of their jobs follow very much the same pattern. Low-income women are less likely than low-education men to say their pay and chances for promotion are good. College graduates are considerably more likely to speak favorably of their pay and promotion prospects than less educated women, but they are somewhat less likely than male college graduates to say their chances for promotion are good. Women with some college education are again very negative about these aspects of their job, especially their rate of pay.

All of this seems sensible and would appear to demonstrate that women's subjective evaluations of their jobs reflect objective reality. The situation of the women with an incomplete college education is particularly interesting. In contrast to college-graduate women, very few of these women go into professional, managerial, or self-employed occupations. Their lack of a diploma effectively screens them out of most of these jobs. As a consequence, their choice of jobs is very similar to that of high school graduates, about two-thirds of them going into clerical and sales jobs, and their pay levels do not differ greatly. It is easy to imagine that these women develop occupational aspirations during their period in college which are not fulfilled when they go into the job market, with the result that they are more likely to feel they have fallen short of their goals than either high school graduates, who do not aspire as high, or college graduates who achieve more. An Institute for Social Research study of white, married working women in 1969 found 76 percent of those with some college saying they had more education than their job required, compared with only 21 percent of high school graduates and 29 percent of college graduates. The woman with some college has high aspirations and low achievement—the formula for frustration—lowered self-esteem, and negative affect.

Women's evaluations of job attributes seem to be much more influenced by educational level than those of men. In general women of limited education are lower in these evaluations than men of that level, and the job evaluations of college-graduate women are higher than those of college men. Men with incomplete college do not show the negative pattern that women at that level do. It is probable that women with some college are more handicapped in the job market by the lack of a diploma than men are; only half as large a proportion of such women find their way into professional, managerial, and self-employed positions as is true of men with some college. It is also probably true that men in the occupations requiring less formal education are more likely to go into employment which is strongly unionized and has substantially higher wages than women who go into white-collar jobs which are poorly organized and poorly paid. This leaves unexplained why these men find more challenge in their jobs than low-education women do and leaves one wondering whether the jobs which are available to these women are not uniquely lacking in interest and stimulation.

Women, despite their occupational disadvantages, are on the average as satisfied with their jobs as men, although when workers of different educational levels are compared, women with some college but not a diploma fall short of all other educational groups, men or women, in their satisfactions with their jobs. None of these differences is very impressive, however, and it is clearly difficult to predict from a knowledge of the kind of job a person has how satisfied that person will be with it.

The proportion of married women who are employed rose substantially during the 1970s, from near 40 percent in 1971 to slightly over 50 percent in 1978. Married women went into the full range of jobs but primarily into the traditional female occupations and the greatly expanded sector of low-level white-collar work. Their perceptions of these jobs and their evaluations of them were on the average about the same in 1978 as they had been in 1971. In both years they were very similar to those of men. Objectively their jobs would appear to be less rewarding than those of men, but women do not describe them as such. It is an interesting and perhaps related fact that relatively few women feel they suffer from discrimination in the job market; one working woman in six does, and this proportion did not change during the 1970s. Most women appear to enter the work force with a basically undemanding attitude, accepting the wage and other differentials that exist between them and the male employees, and expressing satisfaction with the conditions of the job as they find it. And despite the federal affirmative-action programs and much aggressive advocacy of women's rights, this pattern changed very little between 1971 and 1978.

Being Unemployed or Retired

Although the term "unemployed" usually evokes the image of a man, as female employment increases there is inevitably an increasing number of unemployed women. Just as men without jobs show low levels of satisfaction, low positive affect, and high perceived strain compared with men who are employed, so do unemployed women show the same pattern compared with both working women and homemakers. In 1971 unemployment did not appear to be as negative a condition for women as it was for men; the pattern was the same, but the differences were not as sharp. By 1978 this distinction had been completely erased; women without jobs were as negative in every respect as unemployed men. The contrast between their evaluation of their lives and that of employed women was just as great as that between the evaluations of employed and unemployed men.

This substantial shift in the outlook of unemployed women during the decade of the 1970s provides an additional piece of evidence of the change occurring during that period in the relation of women to the job market. Not only were more women seeking employment, they were taking a different attitude toward the jobs they entered. Where earlier, some women may have regarded their jobs as temporary engagements which they could easily leave to return to their role as homemakers, this attitude now seems to be much less common. As we have seen, many women still prefer to remain in the home rather than take an outside job, but if they do take a job, involuntary unemployment seems to have much the same meaning to them as it does to working men. For these women the fact that they can return to 40 or more hours of employment at home does not protect them from the sense of ill-being that is associated with unemployment.

There are not a great many retired women, and the situation of those who did have work careers and are now retired is often complicated by the fact that they are also widowed. We will consider the lives of widowed women and men in Chapter 12, where we will see that they seem neither very positive nor entirely negative.

Conclusions

There have been two significant movements toward equality in American society in the last 20 years, one by blacks and one by women. In the case of women, it has meant throwing off a tradition of subordination that goes back into antiquity and seeking to find a new definition of women's rights and a new pattern of women's roles.

In contrast to black people who, despite their recent gains, still find the quality of their lives less positive than white people do, women find their lives no less pleasant and satisfying than men do. They are somewhat more likely to report experiences of negative affect than men are and show more evidence of perceived strain, reflecting perhaps a greater sensitivity to the disagreeable and stressful aspects of life than men have. But considering the countless inequities that women encounter in American life, the impressive fact is how closely their feelings of well-being resemble those of men rather than how they differ in some specific respects.

One of the most dramatic aspects of the changing life-styles of women since the Second World War is the increasing number of employed women, especially married women. It has been argued in recent years that homemaking is an unfulfilling role for most women and that their lives would be enhanced if they were employed. Millions of homemakers have indeed moved into the job market and become working wives, and the proportion of married women who are employed is virtually double what it was in 1950. But this transition, significant as it was for the lives of these women and for the national economy, was not associated with an increase in reported well-being among married women during this period. Nor do we find that working wives are more happy and contented with their lives than women who are still homemakers.

Of course the increase in the number of wives who are in the work force was not made up entirely of women who found homemaking unsatisfying and took a job in order to escape its tedium. It must also have included women who would have preferred to stay at home but went to work because of economic pressure. And these movements into the work force were undoubtedly partially offset by women who left their jobs because they preferred the life of the homemaker. The only way to ascertain precisely what the effect of taking a job is on the feelings of well-being of a woman who has been a homemaker is to follow a sample of such women as they make this transition and record their feelings before and after. Unfortunately no longitudinal evidence of this kind is available, and we are not able to dissect out the different components of the change in ratio of homemakers to working wives.

The image of a massive escape of unhappy women from the prison of homemaking is probably not a very realistic picture. Most women speak favorably of their homemaking role and a very small percent seem totally dissatisfied with it. Most of this small percent have taken a job but so also have a great many other women who do not find homemaking disagreeable but, for a variety of reasons, have chosen the alternative of working.

Although the decade of the 1970s was a period of great excitement and activity in the movement to liberate women from their subordinate position in society, it was not characterized by a great change in the way American women talk about homemaking. Women were obviously making decisions that affected their role as homemakers, reducing their number of children and taking outside employment, but there was little evidence that they had been generally "turned off" on homemaking. There was a decrease, however, between 1971 and 1978 in the number of women who described themselves as satisfied with "being a homemaker" and this may be a step in a trend.

10
Where You Live

The physical surroundings in which people live differ so profoundly from one family to another that we could reasonably expect them to have a major influence on how these families evaluate their lives. The contrast in the circumstances of the ghetto slum dweller, the affluent suburbanite, and the rural farmer are impressive. Architects, city planners, and a growing number of people who call themselves "environmentalists" have urged increasingly that the physical conditions in which people live are important contributors to the quality of their lives and that these conditions have been deteriorating as the country has become more industrialized, more densely populated, and more affluent.

People live in a region of the country, a community, a neighborhood, and a dwelling unit. They may be more or less satisfied with these layers of their environment, and this satisfaction or dissatisfaction may have much or little impact on their feelings of well-being. We will begin this chapter by comparing people who live in the largest of the areal divisions, the four major regions of the country, and move to the smallest, the dwelling unit. We will discover that where we live makes a difference in our lives, but not always as much difference as one might have expected.

The Four Regions

The United States (excluding Alaska and Hawaii) can be divided naturally into four geographical regions, differing in climate, history, and, in a degree, culture—the Northeast, the Central area, the South, and the West. Although there has been a general trend toward increasing homogeneity throughout the country over the years, these major regions still maintain some of the economic and social differences which developed during the nineteenth century. The Southern states specifically are still the least affluent of the 48, and their educational and health standards reflect this economic disadvantage. The other regions do not differ greatly in their average economic conditions. A comprehensive study of the 50 states in 1970 brought together a number of objective indicators (economic, educational, medical, and employment) and ranked the states in order of their "quality of life." Of the ten highest states in this ranking, seven were in the West; all of the ten lowest states were in the South. By these standards the differences between the four regions were substantial.

But when the people who live in these regions are asked to describe their lives, the pattern is quite different. Instead of standing at the bottom of the regional ranking, the South stands at least as high as the others, and this is true for both white and black people. White people in the South are a little more willing than white people in the other three regions to say they are "very happy" and "very satisfied" with their lives. Otherwise white people in the four regions do not differ in any significant degree, either in their reports of positive or negative affective experiences or in their satisfaction with the specific domains of their lives. Feelings of strain also seem equally common throughout the country.

There is some indication of a more personal quality in social relationships in the Southern states than elsewhere. White Southerners are more likely to describe their lives as friendly rather than lonely, they are more likely to claim to have many good friends, and they apparently visit with their neighbors more often than other people do. This pattern fits the common stereotype of the Southern way of life, but the difference between regions is only one of degree. All parts of the country are generally sociable; the South is a little more so than the rest.

Black people in this country are neither as happy nor as satisfied with their lives as white people; there are interesting differences, however, between black people who live in the South and those who live in the North. Black Southerners differ very little from black Northerners in any of the measures of affect—happiness, the Bradburn Index of Positive and Negative Affect, feelings of strain—but they are consistently more likely to describe themselves as satisfied with their lives, not only with life in general but with the various domains of life. Black people in the South are particularly more likely to express high satisfaction with their community, the city they live in, their neighborhood, and the country at large. They are more satisfied with their jobs and, even though their incomes are clearly lower than those of black people elsewhere in the country, they are somewhat more likely to express satisfaction with their standard of living. Northern black people have a clearly greater inclination to the expression of discontent than black people in the South.

Before we conclude that the South is somehow a more benign location for black people than the North, we must take account of the fact that black people in the southern states are on the average older, less well educated, and more likely to live in a small town or rural area than black people in the North. All of these attributes are associated with a less demanding view of life and they undoubtedly account for some of the regional differences we see. Whether there is something beyond these influences, something in the situation of Northern black people which raises their aspirations and creates a greater sense of discrepancy and deprivation, is a question the survey findings do not answer. It seems likely that there is.

It is intriguing that these subjective indicators of quality of life in the different regions depart so dramatically from what we learn from comparison of their objective characteristics. It might not have been surprising, for example, to find regional differences in feelings of well-being associated with simple differences in climate. If climate were the determining factor the West would be the clear favorite, since a larger proportion of the residents of those states regard their climate as "very good" than is true in any of the other regions. The South stands well ahead of the Northeastern and Central states in this regard, and of these two regions the Central area seems least attractive climatically in the eyes of the people who live there. If we were to plot the actual distribution of temperatures over a year in these different regions we would have to conclude that these subjective evaluations of the climate reflect rather accurately the extent to which the temperature departs from the range of comfort. Temperature ranges relate rather poorly, however, to the way people evaluate their lives.

We have seen earlier that when measures of subjective well-being are compared in countries which differ in level of economic affluence, the more positive evaluations tend to be found in the more affluent countries. We have also seen that within these countries, individual affluence tends to go with high sense of well-being. Within the regions of the United States there is a dependable relationship between personal affluence and sense of well-being, but there is not a similar relationship between regional economic status and regional sense of well-being. It may be that we fail to find this relationship because the economic differences between the regions of the country are too small to produce the regional differences in well-being we might have expected. Perhaps there are cultural differences between the regions which would produce even greater differences in well-being if they were not dampened by the offsetting influence of the economic difference. However that may be, the surveys demonstrate that the differences in perceived well-being in the major regions of the country are modest at best, and such differences as there are cannot be explained by the economic and related characteristics of the regions.

It seems likely that if we were able to select smaller areas of the four large regions, we might find localities where the beauty of the surrounding environment was so unusual that the people there might feel generally pleased with their lives because of it. Or there may be places that are so miserable that they depress the feelings of the unfortunate people who live there. National surveys do not permit the comparison of small local areas, and regional comparisons cover up local differences which may be substantial. The quality of the environment undoubtedly has great importance in the lives of many ecosensitive individuals, and, under unusual circumstances, it may also influence the sense of well-being of whole communities.

City, Town, and Open Country

City life has suffered a bad reputation among social critics for many years. When the 13 colonies came together 200 years ago to form a union of states, they were all heavily rural, and the Founding Fathers, especially Jefferson, were apprehensive of the consequences of the growth of the cities. As nations all over the world have become increasingly urban, the iniquities of the cities have become a popular theme, with the anonymity and stress of the large urban centers compared unfavorably with the human, neighborly quality of the small communities.

Despite these widely proclaimed failings of urban life, Americans have stubbornly persisted in migrating from the rural areas into the nation's towns and cities. Where 60 percent of the population lived in the open country in 1900, only one in four lived there in 1970. Some of this movement was into relatively small towns located in rural areas, but a substantial part of it was into the larger cities. This movement was especially striking among black people, who in 1900 were very heavily a farm and small town population; in 1970 blacks had become largely urban, with over half living within the central cities.

The motivation which led to these moves can only be guessed; perhaps in some cases it was the lure of the city lights and the excitement which life in the city promised. More probably it was basically economic. People went to the cities because that is where the jobs were. Had they had their choice, they might have preferred to remain in their rural setting, but the exigencies of making a living compelled them to move to the city.

If we order the localities within which people live from the largest metropolitan places to the most rural, we find that there are indeed predictable differences in the way these people describe their lives. It is surely true that the large cities are less sociable than the rural communities. Nearly a quarter of the white people in the metropolitan centers say they have never visited in the home of any of their close neighbors; in the rural counties this figure is near 5 percent. Nearly one in ten of the white metropolitan residents do not know the name of any of their closest neighbors; in the rural areas hardly more than 1 percent. City people are less likely than rural people to feel they have a number of close friends or to describe their lives as generally friendly. The sense of living among strangers clearly increases with the size of the community in which one lives.

The large cities are also plainly more dangerous than the small places. Over a third of the white metropolitan residents feel it is not safe to walk around their neighborhood at night. In the rural areas this figure is close to one in ten. Three-quarters of the metropolitan people say it is "very important" to lock the doors when leaving the house; only a third of the rural people feel this is necessary. One white person in five in the metropolitan centers reports having been attacked or robbed during the preceding five years. This figure diminishes in the smaller places and is less than 5 percent in the rural counties. The large cities have a reputation for violence which is apparently well-deserved.

It is also clear that residents of the large cities recognize that they live in polluted environments. Two-thirds of the white people in the metropolitan centers describe their air as either "somewhat" or "very" polluted, a figure which gradually diminishes to 10 percent in the rural areas. The pattern for polluted water is similar but not quite as dramatic. No doubt people in these polluted areas become accustomed to these conditions, but they do not lose awareness of them.

As we might expect, the larger the community a person lives in, the less likely he or she is to say it is "a good place to live." Only a third of the white people in the major cities say this is "a very good" place to live, but this proportion rises to over half in the rural areas. City dwellers are several times more likely to describe their city as "not very good" or "not good at all" as a place to live than are people who live outside the large cities.

In light of these comparisons it is rather surprising to find how little people in these communities of varying size differ in their expressions of positive affect. With regard to geographic location, there is virtually no difference in the proportions of white people who say they are very happy or who report having positive experiences in the recent past. City dwellers are a little more likely, however, to say they have felt restless, lonely, depressed, bored and upset (experiences with negative affect) than people in the smaller places. City life is apparently more likely to expose a person to disagreeable experiences than life in the smaller or rural places is, but it does not diminish the quality of happiness and positive affect.

There is, however, a persistent inclination of white people living in the major cities to feel less satisfaction with various aspects of their lives than other people do. This is particularly marked in their evaluation of the city itself and of the neighborhood in which they live; rural people are clearly more satisfied with their surrounding community. The same pattern is present, not so sharply, in other domains of life and in satisfaction with life as a whole. Metropolitan people are also most inclined to believe that they have not had their full share of happiness in life. These differences suggest either that life in the metropolitan centers is more frustrating than life in the smaller places or that the people who live there are particularly given to finding fault. It is intriguing to find that the proportion of white people who are ready to consider leaving the United States and settling in another country is almost twice as large in the metropolitan centers as it is in the small towns and rural places.

Black people in this country were originally a highly rural and Southern population, but by the 1970s half of them were living in the Northern states and most of these were urban residents. It is not possible to make as fine-grained a comparison of blacks in communities of different size as we can of whites (because of the sample size), but if we compare black people in cities of over 100,000 with those in smaller places or in rural areas, we find a pattern which is similar to that of whites. Black people as a whole are generally less positive in describing their lives than white people, less happy, have less positive affect, are less satisfied, and especially less likely to believe they have had their full share of happiness in life. But like white people, those blacks who live in the cities are less likely to visit with their neighbors, more critical of pollution in their environment, more apprehensive of danger in the streets, and more likely to have been robbed or assaulted. They do not differ greatly from blacks in smaller places in their perceived happiness and positive affect, but they do express greater dissatisfaction with their community, their neighborhood, life in the United States in general, and with their life as a whole. It seems very likely that a larger-scale study which would make it possible to isolate blacks in the metropolitan centers would find sharper differences.

These findings confirm what we would have intuitively guessed: both whites and blacks are less satisfied with life in the urban centers than they are elsewhere. The large cities appear to have lost something of the quality of a human community which the smaller places have retained. Whether it is the sheer size of these places with the associated impersonality of relationships, the heterogeneity of subcultures that develops in large cities, the frequent moves from place to place, or other related phenomena, metropolitan life has special qualities which diminish the attractiveness of these communities in the eyes of the people who live there.

Of course there are many people who would consider it unthinkable to live anywhere but in the metropolitan centers. The variety, the excitement, the entertainment, the artistic and cultural activities, the access to economic and political power—for them these attractions far outweigh the negative characteristics of big city life. The populations of the large cities are not generally dissatisfied with their environment; they are simply less satisfied on the average than people who live in other places. Among those other places are the metropolitan suburbs to which in the last two decades a great many metropolitan residents have moved. These communities of less than a hundred thousand population consist almost entirely of white people, and the average income in these places is visibly above the national mean. People apparently move to these suburban places looking for a more agreeable way of life than they had in the metropolis, and on the average they find it. They are more satisfied with their communities and their neighborhoods than the people in the metropolitan centers. They have a greater sense of security and are less likely to have been the victim of street crime. They also more commonly believe their communities are free of air and water pollution. They are more likely to think their suburban communities are a good place to live than people in the metropolitan centers are, and they are more generally positive in their feelings of well-being.

The most generally favorable evaluations of the surrounding environment do not come from these suburban towns, however; they come from the rural areas—the people living in counties which have no town as large as 50,000 or in towns with less than 2,500 population or in the open country. Only a small part of these people are engaged in farming, but they live a very rural life. And their view of their communities and neighborhoods is substantially more positive than the one we saw among residents of the metropolitan centers. They are much more likely to socialize with their neighbors, they are far less concerned with pollution, and they are much freer of fear of crime. They are also generally more satisfied with their lives and with the various domains of their lives.

The rural areas are not a Thoreauvian paradise. The people living there do not differ greatly from other people in their feelings of well-being. But they do live in a situation which is certainly closer to the natural environment than that of city folk—less polluted, less noisy, less crowded, and less dangerous. Rural people appear to appreciate these qualities of their surroundings.

Within the decade of the 1970s, a quiet turnaround has occurred in the migration pattern of this country which may, if it continues, lead to significant consequences. The "flight to the suburbs" and the associated decline in the population of the large cities are well-documented; less well-recognized has been a reversal of the long-time flow of people from the rural areas into the cities. This movement is not large and it may not continue, but it is a startling and largely unpredicted break with the past. As yet we do not know who the people who make up this movement are, or why they are leaving the cities. They may be retired people who are looking for a quiet, safe place and lower costs, young people who are turned off by the material values of the "rat race," or parents of young children searching for a community setting which is supportive of family life. In many cases they must be making this decision risking some economic sacrifice, since the opportunities to achieve affluence are lower in the countryside than they are in the large cities. They may be seeking the community feeling which rural and small-town society have historically enjoyed, and the surveys indicate that in some degree at least, they will find it.

Satisfaction with Community

As we have seen, the larger the community in which people live, the less likely they are to describe themselves as satisfied with it. There is apparently a great deal to be dissatisfied with in the large cities. The public schools are the object of much criticism, much more than in the smaller communities. So also are the local taxes, which are thought to be very high by metropolitan residents. The condition of the streets and roads, the collection of garbage, police protection, police-community relations, and adequacy of parks and playgrounds are all less well-regarded by people in the large cities than by people in the smaller towns. Those people living within the city limits of the nation's 12 largest cities are especially critical of these aspects of their communities; only in their general satisfaction with their public transportation systems are they more positive than other people. People living in the most rural counties generally resemble people in the smaller towns and cities, but they think much less well of their public transportation and they are not quite as well-satisfied with their police protection. In view of the widespread deterioration of public transportation in the rural areas throughout the country and the generally thin coverage of county police departments, their dissatisfaction would appear to reflect a realistic recognition of the limitations of these services.

Recent surveys have asked people living throughout the country where they would choose to live if they could have their preference. If these people all lived where they say they would like to live, the large cities would lose half their population and the rural areas would more than double. Fewer than one in ten of the people living in the towns or rural areas would prefer to live in the cities or the urban suburbs. Four out of ten of the people living in the cities say they would prefer a small town or rural area. These preferences conform to the pattern of well-being and community satisfaction we have seen. The Great White Way which may have seemed attractive to small-town and rural people in earlier generations seems to have lost a good deal of its glitter.

Satisfaction with Neighborhood

In general people tend to express greater satisfaction with their neighborhood than they do with the larger community in which they live, although if they are satisfied with one, they are likely to be satisfied with the other. Not surprisingly, the larger the community in which people live, the less likely they are to be fully satisfied with their immediate neighborhood.

There are undoubtedly many objective attributes of a neighborhood that make it seem attractive or unattractive to the people who live there: the flow of traffic, the noise level, the amount of open space, the presence of trees, the standard of upkeep of the buildings. Taking the latter of these as an indicator of general physical quality, it is clear that the poorer the condition of the buildings, the lower the satisfaction with the neighborhood. This is what one might expect; more surprising is the large number of people living in physically deteriorated areas who declare themselves entirely satisfied with their neighborhood.

A second objective characteristic of a neighborhood, social rather than physical, is its racial composition. Well over half of the white families in this country live in neighborhoods that are entirely white; a much smaller proportion of black families live in a neighborhood that is all black. There has been a gradual decline since World War II in the proportion of white people who live in exclusively white neighborhoods, and this trend continued during the 1970s. In 1964, the year of the passage of the Civil Rights Act, eight white people out of ten told the Institute for Social Research interviewers that the neighborhoods in which they lived were entirely white. This proportion declined gradually to 75 percent in 1968, to seven out of ten in 1971, and to six out of ten in 1978. There were offsetting increases in the number of neighborhoods that were described as "mostly white." During the same period, however, there was a drop and then a rise in the number of black people who described their neighborhoods as entirely black. In 1964 one black person in three across the country reported living in an entirely black neighborhood. This proportion fell to about one in five in 1970 and held near that point through 1974. In 1976 it had risen again to one in four and in 1978 to three in ten. These apparently conflicting trends are probably accounted for by an increasing scattering of black middle-class families in previously all-white neighborhoods and the movement of white families out of neighborhoods which have gradually become all black.

Various studies have shown that when people, white or black, are asked if they would prefer to live in a neighborhood that is all their own race or one that is mixed, the majority choose a neighborhood that is mixed but at least half of their own race. In fact, however, among white people, satisfaction with neighborhood is highest among those who live in an all-white area, and it declines steadily through mostly white, half-and-half, to mostly black. Whether because of the economic differences in these different neighborhoods or for reasons associated with race, white people are clearly more satisfied with their surrounding area when fewer black people live there.

Among black people satisfaction with the neighborhood does not have this relationship to racial composition. Black people who live in a neighborhood they describe as all-black are no more or less satisfied with it than blacks who live in mixed neighborhoods. Since these all-black neighborhoods tend to be at a low economic level, the people who live there must find advantages of a noneconomic character that make them attractive; no doubt for some of them, it is the experience of being surrounded by their own race.

Of course a basic attribute of a neighborhood is its neighborliness, the extent people living geographically near each other know and associate with each other. As we have seen, some people find their neighborhoods inhabited entirely by strangers (Appendix Table 7). They not only do not socialize with the people who live around them, they do not even know their names. And the larger the community they live in, the more likely this is to be the case. We have seen in Chapter 7 that people who live in the large cities are no less likely to claim a network of family and friends than people in the rural counties, but it is clear that these friendly contacts are less likely to be among their immediate neighbors. Social networks in the cities appear to depend more on work-related and other associations than those in the smaller places, which are more dependent on geographical proximity.

Socializing with one's neighbors is not entirely a matter of where one lives; it is also influenced by how long one has lived there. Part of the relatively distant relationships between neighbors in the urban centers reflects the fact that people change addresses more often there than they do elsewhere. Generally speaking, the longer a person has lived in the same residence, the more likely he or she is to be on visiting terms with the people next door. And this in turn relates to the person's family status. The large cities, and especially the metropolitan centers, have many more single-person households than the small towns and rural areas have. They have more never-married, separated, and divorced people who are more mobile and less settled than families with children and who are less likely, we may guess, to know their neighbors.

Reasonably enough, people who do not know their neighbors are not as likely to express satisfaction with their neighborhood as people who do. The relationship is not precise; nearly a fourth of the people who seem to be totally out of touch with the people who live around them say they are completely satisfied with their neighborhood. Apparently their evaluation of the area in which they live is based more on considerations of location and physical characteristics than it is on their relationships with their neighbors.

As we have noted earlier, people's feelings of satisfaction depend less on their objective surroundings than on their perception of these surroundings. The two are seldom unrelated of course; the objective facts influence the perception and the perception influences the sense of satisfaction. Satisfaction with neighborhood is most strongly determined by the individual's perception of the condition of the neighborhood housing, of the friendliness of its residents, of its security from criminals, and of the convenience to work and shopping. Most Americans are generally satisfied with the neighborhood they live in; two out of five say they are completely satisfied. But about 10 percent describe themselves as dissatisfied in some degree, and they are likely to perceive their neighborhoods as lacking in these important qualities.

Satisfaction with Housing

While the community and the neighborhood compose the broader environment within which people live, they are most immediately enclosed by their dwelling unit. Housing units differ enormously in this country, ranging from palatial to the truly miserable, and so also does the degree of satisfaction of the people who live in them.

To a significant degree satisfaction with the three stages of environment—community, neighborhood, and housing—tends to be held in common. People who are satisfied with their community tend to be satisfied with their neighborhood, and those satisfied with their neighborhood tend to be satisfied with their housing. Half of the people who find their community unsatisfactory are also dissatisfied with their housing; of those who are completely satisfied with their community, only one in seven find their housing unsatisfactory.

In light of the fact that about one American family in five changes its address during the course of each year, one might be led to conclude that a great many people are dissatisfied with their housing. But in fact, as we saw earlier, only about one in ten say they are dissatisfied in some degree; an equal number say they are neither satisfied nor dissatisfied. Apparently some people are prepared to move out of residences with which they are moderately well-satisfied since in both 1971 and 1978 something over a quarter of the population said they would prefer to move to a different house or apartment rather than stay where they were. People move for a great many different reasons—changes in family size, economic gains or setbacks, changes in employment, changes in neighborhood quality—but, as we will see, one of the major reasons is their perception of shortcomings in their present housing.

There are certainly many nonmaterial aspects of one's housing that contribute to one's feeling about that house. A dwelling which has been lived in for many years, in which great events in one's life have taken place, will very likely have taken on connotations which depend very little on the physical characteristics of the structure itself. One's home is not only a dwelling, it is a refuge, a place of privacy, a family gathering place, an object of pride. There is much that is subjective and psychological in the way people see their dwelling place.

Nevertheless people are clearly more satisfied with some kinds of dwelling than with others. More than with any other nationality the ultimate goal of Americans is to live in a detached single-family house which they own, and nearly two American families out of three achieve this objective, with an additional few percent owning an apartment or attached house. Not surprisingly, the owners of detached single-family homes are more satisfied with their housing than people living in any other type of structure. Whether it is pride of ownership, sense of security, feeling of status, or some other psychological need that is fulfilled by the fact of owning one's home, there is no doubt that owners are more satisfied than renters, both in this country and elsewhere. Even trailer dwellers, who have a miniature kind of single-family residence, also rank high in their satisfaction level. It is the apartment renters who are least likely to consider their housing to be fully satisfactory.

Part of this pattern of satisfaction derives without doubt from the simple fact that houses are typically larger than apartments. Two out of five of those people who live in dwellings which provide them one room or less per person are not satisfied with their housing; for those people who enjoy the luxury of as many as three rooms per person this figure is only 12 percent. The comfort and privacy provided by adequate space appears to be important to these people. Trailer dwellers must respond to a different pattern of values since they seem quite well-satisfied with what in ordinary terms would be regarded as very restricted space.

It is surprisingly true that those people who pay a relatively high rent are not significantly more satisfied with their housing than those who pay considerably less. People who own relatively expensive homes are somewhat more ready to express satisfaction with their housing than owners of more modest places, but here again the difference is not substantial. This failure to find the relationship we might have anticipated depends not so much on a lack of satisfaction among the more affluent renters and owners but on an unexpectedly high level of satisfaction among those whose housing is least expensive. Tracing this finding back a step, we discover that many of these low-income owners are older people and, as we know, many older people, especially retired people who own their own homes, live in residences which are considerably more pretentious than their incomes. Even with the influence of these older people removed, however, the relationship of income to level of satisfaction with housing is much lower than the equivalent relationship of income to satisfaction with general standard of living.

Housing is not a domain of life to which people are indifferent; it is a significant contributor to one's general sense of satisfaction with life. The objective characteristics of their housing clearly influence the way people evaluate their dwelling units and how satisfied they are with them, but people seem to have an extraordinary capacity to adjust themselves to substandard housing. Although they may criticize the construction and the heating and other inadequacies, they seem reluctant to admit to being generally dissatisfied with the place in which they live.

Conclusions

Everyone occupies a location in space, a location which has physical, social, and psychological characteristics. A person who has moved from Minnesota because he or she cannot tolerate the winter weather or has moved to San Francisco in order to enjoy the bay view can be said to be giving the physical environment a high priority. A family that has moved out of a large city to find an undisturbed school system for its children or a farmer who moves into town in order to be near friends and relatives is seeking a more congenial social location. The upwardly mobile executive who moves from one residence to another more elegant one is moving in psychological as well as physical space.

There are occasions when the physical surroundings become an important determiner of behavior, when we hope to enhance our lives by changing our physical circumstances. But it is also true that we have a remarkable ability to adapt to the peculiarities of our environment and that most of us can learn to live with the situation we find ourselves in. We not only live with it, we can be satisfied with it. Despite the shortcomings that can be found in almost every situation, most of us are at least moderately satisfied with our communities, our neighborhoods, and our dwelling units, and we change our locations only with reluctance and under pressure of circumstances.

Americans have become accustomed to polluted air, chlorinated water, background noise, and other indignities and have endured them because we have assumed that these are the inevitable costs of modern life. We have also submitted to various assaults on the natural environment in the form of multilane highways, shopping centers, industrial construction, high-rise developments—many of which make very little concession to the sensibilities of the human beings who may come in contact with them. For many years as the country has grown larger and more complex, the environment has steadily deteriorated.

In the absence of survey data, we do not know how sensitive Americans have been to these changes over the last 100 years and in what degree the subjective quality of their lives has in fact been diminished by them. In all probability they were accepted by most people without much notice. Perhaps in the last two decades or so the general public has become more sensitive to the quality of the environment, and this may be a trend which will become increasingly apparent in future surveys. At the present time the environmentalist movement probably draws most of its support from a rather narrow economically and educationally advantaged segment of the population. If their views become more widely accepted, the quality of the environment will become a more significant contributor to the public's sense of well-being than it appears to be at present.

Life in the large cities is undoubtedly regarded by a great many people as less attractive than life in the smaller places. Whether this distaste for the cities is a reaction to their physical characteristics—noise, traffic, crowding, lack of open space—or to their social and psychological qualities—crime, impersonality, racial and ethnic diversity—cannot be precisely estimated, but it almost certainly partakes of both. The major cities have been losing population steadily during the postwar years for what would appear to be quality of life reasons. The cities attracted people for reasons which were largely economic; they are now losing them for reasons which appear to be largely noneconomic.

There is now some inclination in American cities to try to find ways to ameliorate the physical conditions of city life. Building restrictions, restraints on offensive advertising, greenery and miniparks, an occasional piece of outdoor art—cities are becoming self-conscious about the more obvious aspects of urban blight. How much these efforts lift the spirits of city dwellers is problematic. A far more impressive change in the physical environment of the American population is in the upgrading of their housing. The proportion of households with full amenities in this country has grown dramatically since the Second World War, and the per-room occupancy rate has improved in the same fashion. But there are still areas in every large city which are a noisome eyesore, and there are a great many people who do not appear to be greatly disturbed that their housing falls below the national standard. Most houses are homes, and people seem to evaluate their homes at least as much on the basis of psychological considerations as of physical. People living in poor housing do not appear to be as dissatisfied with it as they reasonably ought to be.

George Orwell reports a conversation with a British coal miner whom he asked, "When did you first decide your housing was unsatisfactory?" The miner responded, "When somebody told me it was." The housing didn't change, but the miner's perception of it did. Many Americans live in substandard housing, but apparently no one has convinced them that it is unsatisfactory.

There is very little evidence of change in the public's satisfaction with its environmental surroundings during the 1970s. There was a modest rise in the number of people who felt it would be safe to walk about in their neighborhood at night, perhaps reflecting the declining incidence of street crime reported in the latter part of the decade. But in general, levels of satisfaction with community, neighborhood, and housing stood in 1978 very nearly where they were in 1971 with no visible trend one way or the other.

11
Living in America

The physical characteristics of the communities and neighborhoods in which people live define the quality of their immediate environment; the nation provides a different kind of environment which has the potential to enhance or diminish the life of every citizen.

People are made aware of their national identity in two different ways. They are in the first place privileged to act as citizens, to vote and to participate in "politics." Many people take this as a serious obligation and they undertake to inform themselves, to communicate with others, and to act out their citizen roles. A sizable part of the population, however, does none of these things. National politics seems too remote to hold their attention, and they do not concern themselves with it.

But even these politically apathetic people are reminded of their identity as Americans by the intrusion of national events into their daily lives. They know that when they pay their income tax, apply for a driver's license, or collect a Social Security check they are in touch with "the government," and they may find these experiences pleasant, disagreeable, or infuriating. They also are likely to have some feeling that the nation's affairs are going well or badly, that conditions are improving, or that "things aren't like they used to be." These feelings may be based on very little information or they may be associated with a well-developed ideology, a system of ideas about the nation and its proper functioning.

We will not be concerned in this book with the way people play their political roles, but we will examine the way people perceive American life and how satisfied they are with it. We have already seen in Chapter 4 that assessments of "life in the United States today" do not tell us much about how people feel about their lives in general. Their feelings of well-being are more dependent on those aspects of their lives which are more personal and immediate—family and marriage, work, standard of living, self-evaluation. This is true for the population at large, but it is not true for everyone; there are some individuals for whom the quality of national life has high priority. Some of them develop a pattern of grievances and a sense of dissatisfaction which leads them in the extreme to want to reject their national identity, to emigrate to another country.

The decade of the 1970s was not this country's finest hour. It began with campus violence, racial confrontations, street demonstrations, and the final stages of the Vietnam war. It moved through the period of Watergate and a presidential resignation. It saw the worst recession since World War II in 1974 and 1975. In the latter half of the decade the violence and tension appeared to moderate, leaving the seemingly intractable problems of unemployment and inflation as a preoccupation of national life. The surveys taken in 1971 and 1978 make it possible to compare the perceptions people had of conditions in the United States at the beginning and end of the decade and to examine the factors which contributed to their degree of satisfaction with life in this country.

Perceptions of Life in the United States

The impressions people have of the conditions of life in the country where they live must come through many sources. We may tend to assume that the news of national affairs that is carried by the media plays a major role in this impression-formation, but there are also countless personal experiences which may in fact be at least as important. A person who is offended by obstreperous young people in a theater, poor service in a restaurant, or ineffective and expensive repairs in a garage may conclude that the country is "going to the dogs," and if that person is unfortunate enough to be held up or mugged, he or she may have little doubt of it. It is not possible to trace the influence of these various kinds of input into the public's image of the United States, but it is possible to see what the profile of this image was over the decade of the 1970s.

In 1971 there was only one person in eight in this country who could not think of any way "in which life in the United States is getting worse" when specifically asked if there were such. Nearly two out of five could not think of any way in which life in this country was "getting better." When they were asked, "All things considered, do you think things are getting better, or worse, or that they are staying the same, or what?" the balance was worse over better, 36 percent to 17 percent, the rest seeing things about the same or some things better and some worse. Although we do not know what the comparable balance of perceptions would be in other countries, this record does not impress one as a very glowing testimonial to the American way of life in the early 1970s.

The components of these images, especially the negative ones, were not drawn from vague generalities about long-term trends; they reflected the immediate events and issues of the time. Crime, drug abuse, deteriorating moral standards, protest movements, the behavior of young people, and other social phenomena were cited along with inflation, taxation, pollution, and other economic and ecological concerns. The positive aspects of the image tended to be less specific, referring to improvements in education, science and technology, better health care, better housing and economic conditions, with much less reference to the attitudes or behavior of individuals in social situations. About one white person in twenty-five offered improvement in the racial situation as evidence of a way the country is getting better, and one out of five black people made a similar reference.

There was no Vietnam war in 1978, the racial confrontations were much cooler, Watergate had passed, and the worst of the economic recession was over. But the memory seemed to linger on. Americans were no more favorably impressed about the trend of "life in the United States" than they had been in 1971. The agenda of criticisms had changed somewhat; inflation had displaced crime as the major grievance, but the proportion believing things were getting worse was still twice as large as the number thinking they were improving. Just as in 1971, this perception of a state of decline was not located in any particular part of the population; it was not disgruntled old people or dissatisfied metropolitan dwellers or hard-to-please college graduates who especially held this view. It was everywhere. And it was not a single issue; it was a time when the American people found much to criticize in the state of the nation.

Earlier surveys, asking somewhat different questions, record a time in recent American history when public perceptions of life in this country were far more positive than they were in the 1970s. The evidence is not systematic enough to provide a precise trend line of the changes which followed, but it would appear that the decline began during the 1960s. In the ensuing years criticism and distrust of American institutions became widespread, and this mood persisted through the 1970s.

Trust in Government

One important aspect of this loss of confidence is well-documented through a series of measures between 1958 and 1978 of the public's trust in the federal government. At several points during these 30 years, the Institute for Social Research asked samples of the national population the following five questions:

Do you think that people in the government in Washington waste a lot of the money we pay in taxes, waste most of it, or don't waste very much of it?

How much of the time do you think you can trust the government in Washington to do what is right—just about always, most of the time, or only some of the time?

Would you say the government is pretty much run by a few big interests looking out for themselves or that it is run for the benefit of all the people?

Do you feel that almost all the people running the government are smart people, or do you think that quite a few of them don't seem to know what they're doing?

Do you think that quite a few of the people running the government are crooked, not very many are, or do you think hardly any of them are crooked?

When these questions were first asked in the latter years of the Eisenhower administration, the prevailing attitude toward the national government was one of substantial trust (see Appendix Table 8). In retrospect the decade of the 1950s appears to have been an age of innocence before the great disillusionment that was to come. During the Johnson administration the level of public trust began to drop; it declined steadily during the Vietnam period and reached its lowest point during the ordeal of Richard Nixon. It was not only a striking change in the public's perception of its government, it was a change that was felt almost universally throughout the population, among young and old, educated and uneducated, black and white, and it occurred about equally at all levels of the population.

Despite the fact that a new administration had occupied the White House for nearly two years when this series of questions was asked in 1978, there was no revival of public confidence from the low level of the Watergate period. According to the newspaper polls, the public was willing to give the new President high marks for personal integrity, but it is apparent that their disillusionment of the preceding 10 or 15 years had not been lifted. The mood of the people was critical and distrusting in 1971, and it remained so in 1978.

Fairness and Freedom

Two fundamental aspects of the individual's perception of the consequences of his or her citizenship are the sense of being fairly or unfairly treated by government officials and the feeling of being free, or not free, to live the kind of life one wants. The person who feels unfairly treated or that "there isn't as much freedom in this country as there ought to be" is not likely to be entirely satisfied with life in the United States.

In 1971 about one American in five said they felt public officials generally treated them "not very fairly" or "not fairly at all." In 1978 this proportion had risen slightly to about one person in four. Black people were a little more critical than white, men more than women, young people more than older people, and metropolitan residents more than small town people. It is significant, however, that there was no difference among people of high and low incomes. It would not be surprising to find that people of low economic status receive less careful attention from public officials than people of higher status. If they do, they apparently do not perceive it as such, and their sense of fair treatment is no less than that of other people.

In 1971 when people in this country were asked, "How free do you feel to live the kind of life you want to?" 90 percent said they felt "very free" or at least "free enough," and again in 1978 the proportion was very much the same. This sense of personal freedom is strong in all social groups, but it is visibly weaker among urban black people than among the rest of the population. Of the many complaints voiced by the 10 percent who feel themselves less than "free enough," the most common referred to governmental regulations or requirements that were regarded as burdensome. Financial restraints were more frequently mentioned in 1978 than they had been in 1971, and the number of references to racial discrimination had declined.

It would be helpful to know how these attributes of fairness and freedom are seen by the citizens of countries with which we compare ourselves. It would be particularly interesting to know whether these perceptions differ as democratic theory might predict in those countries which have more or less citizen participation in political decisions. Unfortunately these data are not available, and in the absence of international comparisons we can only say that most Americans appear to be positive in their evaluation of the fairness of the treatment they receive from public officials and the degree of freedom they feel to live their lives as they wish.

It may be objected that a government whose officials treat its citizens in such a way that a quarter of them feel unfairly dealt with has little to be pleased about. And even 10 percent may seem too high a proportion of people who feel "not very free" in a society with democratic aspirations and values. There is obviously no passing grade to which these figures can be compared, but future readings can document their trend and demonstrate whether the public's feelings of fairness and freedom are moving upward or dropping back.

Satisfaction with Life in the United States

Despite the many aspects of American life that people found to criticize during the 1970s and the fact that one person in three believed that, everything considered, things were getting worse, it is an impressive fact that 80 percent of the population said they were satisfied with life in the United States. Most of them have some reservation, and the number who are completely satisfied is smaller than it is for most other domains of life, but the proportion who classify themselves as dissatisfied is less than 10 percent. There was no change in this proportion between 1971 and 1978.

Here again we are handicapped in our evaluation of these findings by the lack of comparable data from other countries or from earlier periods in this country. We know that Americans are considerably less willing to consider emigrating to another country than the citizens of some European countries are, and this may indicate that satisfaction levels are higher here than they are elsewhere. It may be on the other hand that people in this country are particularly responsive to patriotic impulses and find it unacceptable to describe themselves as dissatisfied with the nation with which they identify. Their sense of loyalty may not inhibit their expressions of criticism of particular trends in American life, but it may make it difficult for them to go so far as to say they are dissatisfied with their country.

Of course some people do go this far, and they can be found in all parts of the population. Urban black people, young people under 30, and college-educated people are the most grudging in their expressions of satisfaction with life in the United States. None of these groups records high levels of dissatisfaction, but they are all more unwilling than other groups of the population to say they are completely satisfied.

As we have seen earlier, satisfaction with life in the United States contributes only modestly to the determination of a person's general satisfaction with life. For many people, the nation appears to be a very marginal concern. Their lives are absorbed in much more personal domains of life—family, work, marriage, making a living. During the 1970s, relatively few people had any complaint about their role as citizens, and this role had relatively little influence on their general feelings of well-being.

Disaffection

That small fraction of the population who feel unfairly treated by public officials, or who do not feel free to live as they wish to, or who are generally dissatisfied with life in this country may all be said to be disaffected in some degree from the society in which they live. As might be expected, a common thread runs through these three measures. Those people who express dissatisfaction in response to one question are likely to do so in response to others. This relationship makes it possible to combine answers to the questions concerning fairness, freedom, and general satisfaction and create a scale which may be used to identify those parts of the population which are most and least critical of Ameican life. In 1971 two percent of the population placed themselves at the negative extreme of this scale, complaining of being unfairly treated, not free enough, and dissatisfied with life in this country. A much larger proportion classified themselves at the positive extreme of the scale. An impressive demonstration of the breadth of difference in the attitudes of these two extreme groups is revealed when they are asked about their willingness to emigrate.

Perhaps the most critical test of how people feel about the country in which they live is their degree of willingness to leave it. Not very many Americans respond favorably to the suggestion that they might like to "settle down for good in some other country." About one in ten accept the idea outright and half as many more think they might be willing to leave under some circumstances. This includes a good many people whose reasons for leaving do not reflect serious discontent or dissatisfaction but merely an interest in seeing new places, getting a fresh start, or in some cases returning to the land of their birth. But willingness to leave the country, whatever the motivation, surely implies a certain lack of attachment at the least and resentment and rejection at the most.

The number of people who accepted the suggestion of leaving the country in 1978 was virtually the same as it had been in 1971, and the reasons they gave for leaving remained unchanged. Some thought of leaving for essentially benign reasons of the kind mentioned above; others expressed a dislike for some aspect of American society—its form of government, its racial problems, its violence and crime. No overriding issue or social problem seemed to be motivating any large proportion of these people to think of emigration, but it is clear that the potential emigrants were much more likely to be found among those people at the negative extreme of the disaffection scale than among those with no grievances. Of the two percent of the population who were the most disaffected in 1971, nearly two out of five pronounced themselves interested in emigrating; the corresponding figure among the least disaffected was only two percent. The same pattern appeared in 1978.

Disaffection is concentrated in those parts of the population which we have seen earlier to be least satisfied wtih their surrounding community. As the accompanying figures show, the contrast in the proportions of young, black, metropolitan, and college-educated people among the most and least disaffected groups was substantial in 1971. The difference was still present in 1978, but it appears to have declined somewhat from the level of the earlier year.

It is noteworthy that in neither 1971 nor 1978 was the disaffection pattern found to be especially frequent among people with low family incomes. People in working-class occupations were somewhat less posi-

Of those people most disaffected			Of those people least disaffected	
In 1971	In 1978		In 1971	In 1978
62%	39%	Were under 35 years old	25%	21%
50%	43%	Had attended college	22%	30%
30%	26%	Were black	4%	10%
26%	15%	Lived in metropolitan centers	4%	5%

tive than people in other occupations, but professional people were more negative than other white-collar workers, while farmers were the most positive of all. It is not possible to give a simple social-class explanation of the differences in the way these people perceive their society and in their satisfaction with it. Considerations of age, race, and urban residence are more important in this regard than where a person stands on the occupational or income ladder. Unemployment, however, is a different matter; the average level of disaffection in this small fraction of the population was higher than that of any of the other occupational, racial, age, or residential groups.

One would hardly expect to find people who are so out of joint with the society they live in as the people at the extreme of this disaffection scale apparently are to be very upbeat in their more general feelings about their lives. Some of them clearly are, despite their grievances, but on the average they are much less likely to describe their lives in positive terms than those people who are the least disaffected. The accompanying comparisons demonstrate that these disaffected people display a full syndrome of negative perceptions and feelings regarding life in general, and this pattern did not change between 1971 and 1978.

We may well ask at this point, which comes first for these people, the disaffection or the depressed feelings of well-being? Following the argument that specific grievances add up to more general unhappiness, we could imagine that an individual who begins to feel badly treated, hemmed in by government regulations, and aggravated with other aspects of national life will not only become dissatisfied with the national scene but will in due course develop negative feelings about life in general. Our discussion of the 1957–1972 decline in levels of expressed happiness which we saw in Chapter 3 follows this interpretation; the decline was assumed to follow from grievances growing out of the social and political

Of those people most disaffected			Of those people least disaffected	
In 1971	In 1978		In 1971	In 1978
17%	17%	Said they were "very happy"	51%	51%
10%	12%	Expressed complete satisfaction with life	44%	52%
*	*	Expressed high average domain satisfaction	41%	46%
11%	5%	Perceived low level of strain	47%	41%
19%	11%	Had strong sense of personal control	46%	49%
39%	47%	Expressed willingness to emigrate	2%	7%

* Less than 1 percent.

events of the time. No doubt there were individuals who were unhappy before they were disaffected, but the sequence would appear to be more commonly in the other direction.

The particular combination of questions which was used to identify "disaffected" people in these surveys was of course quite arbitrary, and a different choice might have produced a larger or smaller number of people in this category. It is probable, however, that it would have found them in the same parts of the population—young, unmarried, metropolitan, better than average education, and black. It seems very likely that these are the seed conditions for political disaffection, not only in this country but elsewhere as well.

Conclusions

Of the various domains of life we are considering in these chapters, the one which is most remote from the personal life of the individual is surely the country at large. We know from a long series of studies that a sizable portion of the population pays very little attention to what is going on in the national scene and is very poorly informed about it. The low voting turnout in American elections is a convincing demonstration of how little some people are engaged by it. While there are occasions such as wars and national catastrophes when national identity becomes salient, for many people national affairs take place in a different world from the one they live in. Of course some people are intensely involved, but they are a small proportion of the population, and it is not surprising to find that for the public at large, satisfaction with the state of the nation has relatively little influence on their general feelings of well-being.

The 20-year series of measurements of trust in government is one of the few indicators we have of trends in public attitudes toward this country and its institutions. The shape of this trend line strongly suggests that if people had been asked during the Eisenhower period whether they felt things in this country were getting better or worse, their response would have been different than it was in the 1970s. Their impressions would certainly have been more positive, and there is little doubt that the events of the Johnson and Nixon periods led to the widespread criticism of life in this country which was apparent during the 1970s.

The decline in public trust in government from its high point in the late 1950s to the low point in the early 1970s paralleled the drop in public happiness recorded in national surveys during this same period. Can one believe these simultaneous movements were no more than coincidental? On the contrary, it seems very probable that the decline in confidence in government contributed to the more general decline in expressed happiness. Even though satisfaction with life in this country is not strongly related to happiness, or to the other components of well-being, the drop in political trust was so precipitous that it seems unlikely that it had no relation to general feelings of well-being. Trust in government did not rise in the later 1970s; happiness and positive affect did, we must assume under the influence of other perceptions and experiences.

The early years of the 1970s brought to a close a period of public disorder and conflict which led many observers to believe that disaffection and alienation were rife and that even more serious disturbances were inevitable. The daily concentration of the media, and especially television, on the drama of protest and confrontation created an impression which subsequent events have proved to be exaggerated. Despite the fact that they filled the television screens, the actual proportion of disaffected people in this country was much smaller than it was thought to be.

It is probably a general law that public involvement in current issues is always less than it appears to be. The level of disaffection expressed in

1971 is less surprising than the fact that it was virtually unchanged in 1978. Although the circumstances had changed, the expression of discontent and low morale remained the same. One is left with the impression that once a spirit of disillusionment and cynicism is created, it may be very difficult to overcome.

12
Through the Life Span

Nothing is more obvious in human society than the fact that people's roles, relationships, and behavior change as they grow older. Whatever other circumstances people may experience in life, they inexorably move from one age to the next, each "in his time plays many parts."

Youth and Age

There are many literary allusions to the quality of life at different stages of the life cycle, usually comparing the high-spirited, careless rapture of youth with the cautious contentment of old age, and commonplace observation would lead us to expect that if we compared people at different ages, we would find differences in their expressions of well-being. When our first questions about happiness were asked over 20 years ago, Gurin and his associates did indeed find that young people were clearly more likely to describe themselves as "very happy" than older people, and the least happy of all were the people over 60.

When the happiness question was asked in the 1970s, this age difference had greatly diminished (see Appendix Table 9). People in their 20's and 30's who in 1957 had been so much more positive than people over 60 were no longer so in 1978. The older people had moved up marginally over the two decades in their estimates of their happiness, and the young people had declined quite substantially in theirs.

In 1965 Bradburn found that young people reported both more positive experiences and more negative experiences than older people, with the incidence of these affective experiences declining consistently through the life span. He also reported that when these two measures were combined into a single scale, the Affect Balance Scale, this decline with age persisted, although it was not very pronounced. On balance young people were slightly more positive than older people. In 1978 the decline in reported positive and negative experiences through the life span was still present, but when the two were combined, the young people were less positive than any of the older generations except the very old. The pattern is similar to that given in answer to the question regarding happiness; the lives of young people lost something in general affective quality during the 1960s and 1970s.

While youth is generally thought of in our society as a period of fun and good times, it is also a period of psychological strain. People under 30 are more likely than people of older ages to describe their lives as hard rather than easy, to feel themselves tied down rather than free, to worry about financial and other difficulties, and to be concerned that they might have a nervous breakdown. In all these respects, people over 65 are more serene and less worried than any of the generations younger than themselves, and this pattern was as strong in 1978 as it had been in 1971.

We saw in Chapter 5 that the decline in professed happiness which took place among the American people during the 1960s was concentrated primarily among the educationally and economically advantaged segments of the population, and we see now that it was most prominent in the younger generations. This pattern of movement invites either of two explanations. We might propose on the one hand that contemporary events that tend to depress feelings of well-being will have their greatest impact on those parts of the population whose sense of well-being is highest, not because these events have any peculiar relevance to them but simply because they have more room to move downward. People at the lower levels of well-being may be there for reasons which are more or less chronic—health, family, and financial—and they are not moved further by passing events.

What is more probably true is that the groups that move—affluent, educated, young—are the most aware of the flow of current events, positive and negative, and the most sensitive to their implications for them.

They tend to lead opinion change in many areas of national life—women's liberation, civil rights, conservation, consumer protest—and their feelings of well-being may be expected to be more responsive to the influence of political and economic trends than those of the rest of the population.

It may also happen that the well-being of a particular segment of the population may change because some important event of that period of time has particular meaning to them. This could well have been the case with people in their 20's during the 1960s and 1970s. People of that age in 1957 were busy "making it," getting married, having babies, and riding the economic boom upward. The generation that followed them was selected by an unkind fate to fight an unpopular war; they found it a bitter time. One is not surprised that their feelings of well-being were more negative than the generation which had preceded them. It is impressive, however, that those young people who are taking their place in the later 1970s do not appear to see their lives more positively than they did. Those people under 30 in 1978, most of whom were below adult age in 1971, were no more inclined to call themselves "very happy" than young people in the early 1970s. Despite the fact that Vietnam was receding into history, the cloud which depressed the affect of young people in the 1960s did not appear to have lifted.

Young people in the 1970s did not describe their time of life as an especially happy one, and neither did they not find it a period of great satisfaction with life. In all but one of the domains of life the Institute for Social Research surveys inquired about, people under 30 were less satisfied with their situation than older people—less satisfied with their education and their work, their marriage, their family life and friendships, their standard of living, savings, and housing, their community and neighborhood, and the country as a whole. Only in their satisfaction with their health were they substantially more positive than people in the older generations. This pattern was present in 1971, and it had not changed in 1978.

Satisfaction with health, as we will see, reflects the objective facts of health; people who have health problems are less satisfied with their health than people who do not, and the more severe the problem, the greater the dissatisfaction. Health is obviously related to age. The increasing proportion of people who say they are dissatisfied with their health through the life cycle simply reflects the increasing number of physical problems people at the older ages have.

It is not so clear why young people are less satisfied with the other domains of their lives—their jobs, housing, standard of living, education, and so on, or why they are the most likely of the successive age groups to believe they have had less than their share of the happiness they might reasonably have expected in life. Is this a peculiarity of the 1970s? Was this a time when young people had higher expectations than their parents and grandparents had when they were young and now perceived greater discrepancies between what they had and what they hoped for? Or do older people express more satisfaction because they have more to be satisfied with? In the material domains of life—standard of living, savings, housing, work—we might expect greater contentment as people move into their period of highest income and status; people in their 50's are generally better off than people in their 20's. But this is not true of other domains of life—education, marriage, family life, friendships—and yet satisfaction levels increase with age in these domains as well. Even in their evaluation of the climate in which they live, older people are more favorable than younger. The proportion who describe their climate as "very good" is clearly higher among older people than younger in all four of the major regions of the country.

There is still the third possibility that this is a phenomenon of the life cycle, that every coming-of-age generation begins its adult life with high hopes and expectations, which it later learns to modify as it encounters the realities of life. The increasing expressions of satisfaction we see in succeeding decades of life reflect an accommodation and a resignation to what must be accepted. This may be a life-cycle pattern which characterizes the experiences of every generation as it grows older.

These are questions we cannot answer unequivocally without following successive generations through their life cycles. But the progressive increase in professed satisfaction from the 20's into the later years which is characteristic of these different domains of life suggests that this is a pattern which is not peculiar to our time or to the specific experience of any particular generation. There appears to be a general narrowing of the discrepancies between aspirations and achievements as people grow older, partly because achievements tend to rise and partly because aspirations tend to fall. Only in the case of health, where physical well-being persistently declines, is this pattern reversed.

One wonders in the face of this evidence why the popular stereotype of American youth is so persistent. Perhaps the external image of energetic, healthy, physically attractive young people creates a "halo effect" which makes them appear happy and content as well. In fact, of course, it is well known that the years of early adulthood are a time of many trials, much uncertainty, and many crises and changes. The passage from parental home to one's own place, from school to work, from one job to another, from single life to marriage, from nonparent to parent, from one location to another—these are critical transition events in a person's life, and they often produce problems of identity, attachment, and self-esteem. The appearance of youth is often more positive than the psychological realities that accompany it.

There are also common stereotypes about older people which are not supported by the evidence of these surveys. Old age is not given great respect in our society; it is indeed frequently the object of ridicule. American culture is often described as "youth-oriented," and it tends to regard age as an unfortunate time of life. Of course surveys do not include those individuals whose mental or physical infirmities have removed them from the general population to the care of relatives or nursing homes, but those older people who are living in their own households seem to be a remarkably satisfied and undisturbed group of people.

Life expectancy has been increasing in this country and elsewhere for the last hundred years, and the number of people who are over 65 is now at an all-time high. If we divide these people of retirement age into those between 65 and 74 and those 75 or older, we will be able to compare expressions of well-being and ill-being in these later years. We must keep in mind that we are looking at the survivors, people who are still in sufficiently good health to be living in a private residence and able to be interviewed. We are obviously missing a good many people, especially in the over-75 group, who are institutionalized or have died. Among these older people whom the Institute for Social Research interviewed in 1978, there is surprisingly little difference in the responses given by those in the two age groups. The people over 75, predictably, more often say they have health problems which restrict their activities. They are a little more likely to report having time on their hands they do not know what to do with, but in general they are at least as satisfied with their lives and the various domains of life as people in the 65 to 74 group; both groups report less strain than the rest of the population. It is only in the area of positive affect, the incidence of pleasant experiences, that the people over 75 seem less favorable. They do not so often report being excited or interested in something, proud or pleased, being on top of the world, and they more often say they have felt lonely. Old age seems to be a time of contentment, but not a time of great enjoyment.

A study of people over 65 in England has shown that older people in that country who live alone are more likely to describe their lives as unhappy, miserable, lonely, and unsatisfying than people of similar age who live with someone. We have seen in Chapter 7 that having a living companion seems to make a positive contribution to the lives of people in the general population, and now we find that this is also true of people in the older age categories.

Somewhat over one in four of the over-65 people in this country who live in private households do in fact live alone. One older man in eight lives alone, two older women in five. In all the measures of affect, those men and women living with another person are more positive than those living alone. They are less likely to report feeling "lonely," especially the men. These differences are not remarkably large, but they are consistent and in the same direction as the findings in England. Older Americans do not differ, however, when divided into those living alone or with someone, in their sense of satisfaction with life or with the specific domains of life. We know that these older people have generally high levels of satisfaction, higher than the population at large, and while living with someone is associated with a more pleasant life, it is not associated with greater satisfaction with life.

The problems of older people have become an increasing concern in this country in the last decade or so, and federal and state programs have been initiated which are intended to enhance the quality of these people's lives. Aside from the difficulties associated with their accumulating problems of health, however, these older people are not a lost generation; they have come to terms with life. Perhaps if those people now in their middle years develop greater expectations of life than their predecessors did and carry them into their retirement years, old age may lose some of the serenity it now appears to have.

The Life Cycle

Much interest has been invested in recent years in attempts to develop "sociopsychological conceptions of the life course and its various developmental periods." Theories of the life cycle have plotted a series of transition points during the adult years, associated with specific ages in the individual's life—leaving the family, getting into the adult world, becoming one's own person, facing a midlife transition, and moving through a late adult transition into old age. The studies on which these theories are based have tended to depend on very long biographical interviews with a small number of respondents.

These descriptions of life-cycle development have not concerned themselves primarily with levels of psychological well-being at these successive stages of life, and it is not clear what the underlying theory would predict. Since the most important points of transition are closely linked with specific age bands, however, it is possible to examine the Institute for Social Research surveys to find if these age cohorts have characteristic patterns of well-being or ill-being. For example, Daniel Levinson and his associates emphasize the importance of the midlife transition (called the midlife crisis by some), which they believe occurs among men between the ages of 40 and 45. When we look at the men at this age in the national samples, we find no indication that their feelings of affect or satisfaction with life or the domains of life are in any way unique to that five-year period. Neither is there any unusual pattern of responses to the survey questions in the early 30's when the young man is making his transition into the adult world. No doubt points of transition similar to those Levinson describes occur in the lives of most men and women in American society, but they are either not linked as closely to specific ages as he believes or they do not create the kind of affective or evaluative response that would be recorded by the kind of questions our surveys ask.

Most of the interest in life-span research seems to have focused on men, but it may be noted that our surveys also fail to find any age-bound crises of psychological well-being among women. There are long-term trends through the life span, just as there are with men, but the changes in well-being we find in women's lives are not associated with passing a particular birthday but in passing from one life role to another.

Sociologists have for some years relied on a concept of the life pattern which emphasizes the major changes in social roles which succeed each other during the adult years. We begin life as single persons, we are married, we become parents, we may be separated and divorced and perhaps remarried, the children grow up and leave, and finally we are widowed and again single. We grow older as we pass through this sequence, and our circumstances change as we move from one stage to the next. So also does our sense of well-being.

The life cycle, so defined, has six major stages through which most people pass and several nonconforming situations in which smaller numbers of people find themselves at some time during their lives.

1. Early unmarried adulthood. Most people are still unmarried when they reach adult status at age 18, and some of them remain unmarried throughout their 20's.

2. Early childless marriage. The average age of marriage in this country is now in the early 20's. Many of these first marriages are followed immediately by the birth of the first child, but most are not and there is a period in the lives of most women and men before they reach 30 when they are married but still childless.

3. Married with preschool child. Most married couples will have children, and for some period of time they will have a child in the house who has not reached school age. If they have several children, this period may extend over a substantial number of years.

4. Married with school-age children. Small children eventually reach school age and there ensues a stage in the parents' lives when they have one or more school-age children (six through seventeen) in the house but no child under six.

5. Married with youngest child over 17. In time the youngest child will attain its 18th birthday and in most cases will shortly thereafter leave the parental home. The parents now find themselves in the "empty nest," living alone after their youngest child has departed.

6. Widowhood. Inevitably one member of the married couple will die and the survivor will enter the stage of widowhood. This does not usually occur until the couple are in their 60's or older; the survivor may or may not remarry. This final stage may last a very short or a very long time and in most cases it is the wife who survives rather than the husband.

These are the six basic stages of the life cycle through which Americans typically pass. Most men do not reach the final stage because they predecease their wives, but they move through the earlier stages just as women do. It is necessary, however, to take account of those people who, through choice or accident, do not conform to this pattern. There are four discrepant groups which, though not large, are significant in number.

1. Over 30 years old, never married. Most people who marry will marry before they reach their 30th birthday. Those who do not may prefer not to marry or may not have had what they consider an attractive opportunity. They may marry later, but at this stage they are outside the typical life-cycle pattern.

2. Over 30 years old, married with no children. Some 10 percent of married couples remain childless, some through choice, some through physiological infertility. Most couples will have their first child before they reach age 30, although the incidence of later-born first children is increasing as more women defer marriage and motherhood because of a work career or other reasons.

3. Separated and divorced. More than one-third of the marriages which were entered into in this country in the last decade have ended or will end in divorce. Most of these people later remarry, but for a period they are single after a failed marriage.

4. Unmarried parents.

There is one additional nonconforming group—parents who have never married and who are living in a household with their minor child or children but not with a companionate spouse. They make up less than one percent of the population, and they are nearly all women. Of course there have always been mothers without husbands, but with the rising incidence of illegitimate births in this country, their number has been increasing. Because of their unusual circumstances, we will include this group in our review of life-cycle stages even though it is much smaller than the other groups.

We have seen that the various measures of well-being indicate that changes appear to occur progressively as people grow older. We will now find as we look more closely that people in the same age cohorts may see their lives quite differently if they are in different stages of the life cycle.

Early Unmarried Adulthood

This is the stage of life which is often regarded as the halcyon period of youth, the time of carefree adventure, new experience, and happy times. But as we have seen, surveys in the 1970s have shown young people under 30 to be no more inclined to see their lives in such positive terms than older people are, and they are clearly less satisfied with most domains of their lives and more likely to report symptoms of psychological strain.

Half of the people still under 30 have not yet married. When we isolate this segment of the under-30 cohort, we find that they are consistently less positive in their feelings of well-being than the rest of their age group. They are well above average in their report of positive experiences, feeling excited, proud, pleased, on top of the world, things going their way, but they are also quite high in their negative experiences, feeling restless, lonely, bored, depressed, upset. As we have seen, young people generally appear to experience more such affective episodes than older people do, both positive and negative; their lives might be said to have more bright color than those of older people whose lives seem more bland. In the case of this young, never-married cohort the incidence of these affective events is high, but they balance out to a rather negative total. The men in the group, the carefree bachelors of popular myth, are no more positive than the women.

Their affect balance is low and their satisfaction with life is also low. In satisfaction with their health and education they are higher than people in the later stages of the life cycle, reflecting the advantages they enjoy in these domains of life. But in other domains they are either the least satisfied or near it—work, community, neighborhood, life in the United States, income, standard of living, family life. Women at this stage of the life cycle express more dissatisfaction with the role of homemaker than women at any of the other stages of life.

If any aspect of the traditional image of the carefree young person, unfettered by the responsibilities of marriage, is true to life, we might expect to find it in the measure of perceived strain, especially among the young men. But young never-married men are no less likely than men in general to say they worry about money matters, and they do not think of their lives as especially free or easy. In their worries about life's problems and the possibility of a nervous breakdown they are not very different from other men. They are visibly different, however, from the single women in their age cohort. For women, the period between 18 and 30, if they are not yet married, has more feeling of strain than most periods of the life cycle do.

The exuberance of youth which we might have expected to find in these young unmarried people seems strangely absent. Perhaps it was there at some earlier, simpler time, when expectations were different and youth was a less introspective, self-conscious period of life than it is now. If so, it seems to have faded away, and we find this first stage of single life a rather subdued introduction to the drama of the life cycle which will follow.

Early Childless Marriage

Some of the quality of the lives of the young, single people we have just described no doubt comes from the simple fact of their youth, but some of it is associated with their unmarried state as we now see when we compare them with those people of similar age who are married but do not as yet have children.

The contrast in the feelings of positive affect expressed by these two young groups is remarkable, especially among the women. Where only one young single woman in four considers her life "very happy," fully half of the young married women do, the highest level of any of the life-cycle stages. They are also the highest of the women's groups in their report of positive experiences, with a moderate report of negative experiences and a resulting much higher affect balance than young unmarried women. This is the first of several indications we will see that the years of early marriage, before the first child has arrived, are a particularly favorable time in the lives of women and a positive but not as distinctive a period in the lives of men.

Young women at this stage of life are more ready than any other category of women or men to declare themselves satisfied with their life as a whole, and they are among the least likely of women to show evidence of psychological strain. Young men, married but still not parents, are not so positive. They are somewhat more satisfied with their lives than young single men but not noticeably more satisfied than men or women in general. And they perceive more strain in their lives than those young men who are still not married. The contrast between young men and young women in this respect is intriguing; young women appear to feel less strain in their lives after they marry and young men feel more. Young married women, for example, less frequently say they worry about meeting their bills than young single women do, but young married men are more likely to report such financial worries than young single men. This stage of life obviously feels a little different to a woman than it does to a man.

The general lift in feelings of positive affect which we see associated with early marriage is not uniformly reflected in satisfaction with the individual domains of life. Unmarried young people are well below the average of the population in their satisfaction with these specific areas of experience, and the young married people are not very different from them. In their satisfaction with family life, however, the young people who were married were far more positive than those who were still not married, and this was true of both women and men.

It is intriguing that in spite of their low satisfaction with some of the major domains of life, these young married people are the least inclined of all the life-cycle groups to feel they have had less happiness in life than they might reasonably have expected (11 percent), about half the proportion of those people in their age cohort who have not married (23 percent). At this age being married is apparently an important component of what one expects in life.

Although it would appear from these comparisons that the transition from the unmarried to the married state greatly brightens the lives of young people, especially women, we must keep in mind the possibility that the differences we see may be the result of a selection process which takes the majority of these people into the married state and leaves the others still unmarried. It seems not unlikely that those young people who are most satisfied with life, most positive in their feelings, least subject to strain, would be attractive to other people and would be the first to be married. The kind of longitudinal study that would be necessary to test this hypothesis has not been done, and we can only guess what it would show. Probably some selection of this kind does occur, but it is not likely that it could account for a very large part of the differences in sense of well-being we see at these two stages of the life cycle. If it were merely a matter of selection, we would expect the young married men to be as positive in their outlook as the young married women, and we would surely not expect their feelings of strain to exceed those of the unmarried. The fact of being married obviously changes the circumstances of young people in many important ways; it would appear that for the most part these changes enhance the psychological quality of the person's life. But as we will now see, when this period of marriage without children comes to an end, life takes on a different flavor.

Married with Preschool Child

In due time nine out of ten of these young couples will have a child and will move into a new stage of the life cycle which looks rather different from the one they have left. The early years of their child's life will put demands on the parents' time and energies and will require virtually full-time attention. If there is more than one child, this period may go on for some years until the last six-year-old goes off to school.

However the arrival of the first child is received, with joy, resignation, or resentment, it will certainly change its parents' life-style and the quality of their life experience. The presence of a small child in the home undoubtedly has many rewarding aspects, but the total impact is not entirely positive. Parents of preschool children (who may also have older children) are not more willing to describe their lives as very happy or to report more positive affective experiences than young married people who are not yet parents. On the contrary, they are less likely to do so, especially the young mothers whose euphoric period as childless wives comes to an abrupt end. These young parents are not more or less inclined than other people to express satisfaction with their life in general or with the domains of life. There is a difference, however, in their perception of strain; both men and women express more feeling of strain at this stage than at any other period of their married lives. There is a particularly sharp contrast between the mothers of young children and young, married women who still do not have a child—a greater feeling of being tied down, of finding life hard rather than easy, a greater concern about financial matters, and more frequent fears and worry about having a nervous breakdown. Every parent recognizes these symptoms of the early years of child-raising; they are stressful for both parents.

The period of raising small children also puts strain on the marriage, especially as it is seen by the wife. She is less willing to say her spouse understands her or that she understands him than the under-30 married men and women who are still not parents. She is also more likely to say she and her husband disagree about spending money. Both husband and wife feel they have less companionship at this stage of life than young childless couples do at theirs. And they are both less ready to say they are satisfied with their marriage. In all of this the mother of the preschool child is more negative than her husband and substantially more negative than the young married woman who does not yet have children.

Women are less willing at this stage of their married life to say they "always enjoy" being a parent than parents of older children are, and much less willing than their husbands are. Two out of five of these mothers of small children go so far as to admit they sometimes wish they could be free of the responsibilities of being a parent, a much larger proportion than is found among mothers of older children. Raising a child through the preschool years may enrich a marriage and give it a new quality, but it also puts the parents under stress which is felt by both parents, but especially by the wife.

Of course it is not only the small child that is putting pressure on parents at this stage of life. Most of these people are between 20 and 35 years of age, and these are years of many crises which are not directly associated with parenthood. But the childless couple still in their 20's are going through much the same problems with finding an acceptable job, locating appropriate housing, adjusting to new circumstances, learning to live together; they appear to live through this with relatively little strain. The presence of a preschool child adds a unique quality to the family situation. The joys and rewards of parenthood are undoubtedly great, but there are also costs and, as we will see, the ratio of rewards to costs tends to become more positive as the children grow older.

Married with School-Age Child

By the time the youngest child in the family is in school full-time, the parents have typically passed the age of 35 and their circumstances are quite different from those of the parents of small children. The major wage earner, usually the husband, has settled into his career and is approaching or has reached his highest income level. His wife, who in most cases did not work outside the home while the children were small, is more likely than not to have taken a job. The average income of families at this stage is at a lifetime peak, in part because of the contribution made by the working wife.

Parents find their lives at this stage somewhat more pleasant, more satisfying, and less stressful than parents who are still living with preschool children. This change is not substantial, and it probably cannot be attributed entirely to the presence or absence of small children; the parents are older, better established, more affluent. One might have expected their feelings of well-being to be enhanced as a reflection of these changes alone. But the age of the children undoubtedly makes a difference; how else would one explain the fact that only half as many mothers at this stage of life describe themselves as "tied down" as mothers of children in the preschool years?

After the children have reached school age, their mothers are more willing to say they always enjoy their children and are less likely to say they wish they could be free of the responsibility of being a parent. They appear to find it easier to live with children in the 6 to 17 range than with those still in the preschool years. Parents also find it easier to live with each other at this stage of their married life. They disagree less often about spending money and they feel they understand each other better. But they do not regain the strong sense of companionship, "doing things together," which they had as young couples without children until they reach the next stage of life when the children have grown up.

The period of time in which parents live with one or more children beyond the age of 5 and not yet 18 may take up a substantial proportion of their married life, at least 12 years and perhaps twice that. These are typically the middle years of life, from 35 to 55; they follow the period of early marriage with small children and precede the time when the youngest child has reached adult years. Psychologically it does not appear to be either the best of times or the worst of times for the parents. It is not an especially tranquil time of life, but it is a satisfying one. It ends when the children have grown up and the mother and father are again living alone.

Married with Youngest Child over 17

It is remarkable that this stage of life, often referred to as the "empty nest," should have such a lugubrious reputation when it is in fact for most people the most positive period of their married life. These people are nearly all over 45 years old, and they range into the later years with all the implications for poor health associated with age. They are not especially affluent on the average (fewer of the wives are employed), and some of the older couples live very modestly. But this is a stage of life people find more satisfying and more free of strain than either the years of early marriage or the long period of child-raising. Neither the wives nor the husbands are as ready to describe themselves as "very happy" as the young women in the first years of married life, both positive and negative affect are relatively low at this stage as they are generally for older people, but the affect balance is the highest of all the stages of married life. While these parents may feel some nostalgia for the days when their children were still at home, they do not express any unusual loneliness or any other indication of sadness associated with the "empty nest." It is significant that in all these indications of well-being, the fathers describe their lives more favorably than the mothers do. Most of these women have devoted their lives primarily to their families, and it may not be surprising that the departure of the children has a different meaning to them than it does to the fathers.

The generally high level of satisfaction with life and with the various domains of life which we find associated with this later stage of married life is probably more strongly influenced by the simple fact of growing older than it is by the departure of the children. We have seen earlier that these indications of satisfaction rise gradually as people grow older. The arrival of small children puts a temporary dent in this rising curve, but this period passes and by the time the children have grown up, the parents' feelings of satisfaction have recovered and follow the expected age pattern.

The contrast in the feelings of strain expressed by the parents of grown children compared with parents in the period of school-age children is even sharper than in the feelings of satisfaction of the two groups. This may also be related to the changes in life-style associated with growing older, but it is hard to doubt that being freed from responsibility for their children did contribute to it. With their children no longer an immediate everyday concern, these older parents are more likely to insist that they have always enjoyed their children and have never wished to be freed of parental responsibility. They are now less likely to feel "tied down" or to feel their life is "hard"; they worry less about money problems and about the possibility of having a nervous breakdown. They can now enjoy being parents without the sense of pressure associated with having dependent children in the home.

These later years in the lives of people with children are also the years of greatest harmony in the marriage. Those people who are still married after these years of child-raising (most of whom are still in their first marriage) are more likely than married people at any of the earlier stages of married life to describe themselves as completely satisfied with their marriage and to feel that their relationships with their spouse are amiable, understanding, and compatible. They especially outdistance younger parents in their perception of companionship which, as we have seen, sinks to a low level during the period of preschool children.

There is only one doubtful note in this generally favorable evaluation older parents give of their marriage. During the early years of married life, men and women both have relatively low estimates of the extent to which their spouse understands them. During the "empty nest" years the men have a much more positive estimate of how well they are understood by their wives, but the women's perceptions of their husband's understanding of them remain low. This may mean that over the years women learn to understand their spouse, or at least appear to, and men do not. Or there may be no actual sex differences in degrees of understanding, but the wives at this stage of life may have higher expectations than their husbands do and are less satisfied with what they see.

In general the stage of life when the children are grown and gone and the couple are still living together is a period of contentment and tranquility. These people have come through the years of family formation, child-raising, and career building and have reached a comfortable time of life. Although in most of the families at this stage of life the children have left home, the nest is not really empty. The spouse is still there. For some this period may go on for many years, for others it will be tragically short.

Widowhood

The death of a spouse is recognized throughout the world as an event of great psychological trauma. Usually observed by appropriate forms of speech, dress, and behavior which bespeak the survivor's grief, it is the ultimate point of passage. The deceased person passes from life, and the surviving spouse passes into the last phase of the life cycle.

In the nineteenth century widowhood was not uncommon in what are now regarded as the middle years of life, but with increasing longevity those marriages which have escaped divorce typically go on much longer. In the 1970s over four out of five widowed people in this country were over 55 years of age. There were of course far more widowed women than men, a ratio of five to one.

The clearest demonstration of the unique quality of the life of a widowed person comes from a comparison of widowed men and women with those people of nearly their own age who are still living with their spouse. In their satisfaction with the major domains of life widowed people are the equal of still-married people with grown children, well above average of the population generally. And in their perceptions of strain they seem no more pressured and worried than older people who are still married. In these respects their feelings of well-being seem undiminished by their personal loss. But in their expressions of affect they are strikingly different from older people still living with their spouse. They are less willing to call themselves "very happy" and to report affectively positive episodes in their recent experience. When positive and negative experiences are combined into the measure of affect balance, widowed men and women are far lower than any of the other married groups, with women lower than the men.

In large part the outlook of widowed people seems to be one of resignation. They have sustained a loss they could not avoid and they have had to accommodate to it. Like other older people they are generally content with most domains of life although they have much dissatisfaction with their health. It is in the emotional or affect side of their lives that their loss is most acutely felt. As might be expected, the damage to the widowed person's sense of well-being is most evident in the years immediately following the event, and it gradually lessens thereafter. But even after five years the consequences of the trauma are still clearly evident in the feelings of widowed people.

These are the basic stages of the life cycle through which most Americans pass. Of the others, some marry but do not have children, some never marry, some marry and later separate or divorce, and some have children but do not marry. None of these groups is large, but their circumstances are different from those of most people, and their feelings of well-being and ill-being differ from those of the other life-cycle groups in illuminating ways.

Thirty and Older, Married with No Children

Most married couples will have had a child by the time they reach the age of 30, but approximately one couple in ten who are beyond this age are still childless. Some of the younger of these people may still have children, but since most of these childless couples are over 40 years old, it is not likely that they will become parents. For a sizable number of these people, this is their second or later marriage—a larger proportion than we find in marriages which have produced children.

Our society expects a marriage to have children, and it looks askance at a married couple who have remained childless. In the popular view such a marriage is unfulfilled, and there is a moderate stigma attached to infertility. These traditional views have softened somewhat in recent years, but a young couple is still likely to feel pressure from parents or peers who feel it is "natural" to have children. Most infertility is involuntary, but there is a small number of married people who choose not to have children, and this number has grown somewhat in the last decade.

A childless couple not only find themselves in conflict with cultural norms but if they wished to have children, they may also have experienced a bitter personal disappointment. The very word "childless" conveys a sense of misfortune, and it would not be surprising to discover that married women and men, 30 years old or more, who have no children would have a rather subdued view of life and perhaps some reservations regarding their marriage and family life. But this is not what we find; their pattern of feelings about life is generally positive and in some respects it is very favorable.

Most childless couples over 30 were once childless couples under 30 and their sense of well-being is different from that of the younger couples. Childless men in the early years of marriage do not depart very much from the rest of the population on any of the indicators of well-being. Older married men without children are generally somewhat more favorable than the younger men and than the population in general. Older women without children do not compare so favorably with young childless women. As we have seen, the feelings of well-being of young, married women, still childless, are very high, quite euphoric in their professions of happiness, affect, and satisfaction with life. Those wives who are still childless after age 30 are generally more positive than the population at large, but they do not maintain the extraordinary high feelings of well-being the younger wives experience.

Perhaps a more meaningful way of assessing the feelings associated with childlessness is to compare these childless older people to those parents of older children who no longer have children in the home. These older parents have, on the average, among the highest levels of affect and satisfaction we have seen in these stages of the life cycle. They have fulfilled whatever impulses they may have had to bring children into the world and to raise them to adulthood. The over-30 couples with no children are somewhat younger than the "empty nest" parents, but they are surprisingly similar to them in feelings of well-being, in affect, satisfaction, and lack of strain. Whatever expectations these couples might have had when they married, the absence of children has obviously not blighted their outlook on life.

If there is any area of life in which the absence of children might be expected to create dissatisfaction, it would be in feelings about marriage and family life. There are undoubtedly individuals who find their marriage less than perfect because they do not have children, but for the most part childless couples beyond the age of 30 express as much satisfaction with their marriage and family life as other couples do. They also have very favorable impressions of their relationships with their spouse; compared with other married couples they are less likely to report disagreements about financial matters, more likely to believe their spouse understands them and they understand their spouse, and especially more likely to say they share a great deal of companionship. The only other married group who holds such positive views about their marital relationships are the "empty nest" people, who for the most part are also living without children.

Married people who do not have children may lose something psychologically, but they surely gain economically. The cost of raising children has become a serious concern to many parents and may be one of the contributors to the falling birthrate in this country. The fact that childless people are not paying these costs has obvious consequences in the feelings they have concerning the material areas of their lives. In their satisfaction with their income, savings, and standard of living, they surpass all the other life-cycle groups. Their family incomes are not higher on the average than those of other married couples. The wives are not more inclined to take jobs than other wives (46 percent were employed in 1978). But in relation to their needs their incomes compare very favorably with those of families with children, and it seems quite reasonable that their satisfaction with their material possessions is as high as it is.

One cannot doubt that the lives of these childless couples would have been different if they had had children, but it would not necessarily have been a more enjoyable or more satisfying life. At this stage of the life cycle these people do not have children, but they still have their spouse. After he or she is gone, the significance of childlessness may change. In many societies children are valued because they provide a promise of security in one's old age. This is probably not a very prominent motive in the minds of contemporary Americans contemplating parenthood, but it may later assume a meaning it did not have while they were in their childbearing years and while their spouse was still living.

Thirty and Over, Never Married

About one person in twenty-five in the adult population is a man or a woman, 30 years or older, who has never married. Some of these people have remained single because they have no wish to marry, some because they have not had an appropriate opportunity. Whatever the cause, the person who is single beyond the years in which first marriages are customarily entered into is in as great conflict with societal expectations as the married couple who do not have children. Popular folklore has well-established stereotypes of the older bachelor and the "old maid," usually touched with ridicule and essentially cruel in spirit. American society has historically made very little accommodation for the single individual, especially for those in their middle or later years.

We have seen earlier in this chapter that young people under 30 who have not married describe their lives quite negatively—in satisfactions, in feelings of affect, and, especially among the women, in perceived strain. For those young people who marry, these perceptions change dramatically in a favorable way; for those who remain unmarried into their 30s, the pattern continues to be quite negative, somewhat more negative for men than for women. Single men over 30 are much less likely than men in general to describe themselves as "very happy" or "very satisfied with life." They are the lowest of all the male life-cycle groups in their response to the positive affect questions and lower than most in their expressed satisfaction with specific domains of their lives. Along with divorced men they are the most likely to feel they have had less than a reasonable share of happiness in life. Only in their perceptions of strain are they as favorable in their feelings of well-being as the population at large. In none of these respects are they more positive than single men still under 30 and in some they are clearly less so. Being single appears to be a psychologically negative situation for most men, and they do not appear to find it more positive as they grow older.

In 1971 women who were still single after 30 differed rather little in their reported feelings of happiness and satisfaction from younger single women, but, as with older single men, their feelings of strain were lower than those of the population in general. In 1978 the pattern was similar; their feelings of affect and satisfaction resembled those of the younger women and were less positive than those of women in general. In most of these aspects of well-being, however, they tended to be more positive than single men over 30. The differences are not great and they are not altogether consistent; for example, men at this life-cycle stage are much more satisfied with their health than women are. But these single women more often say they are "very happy," less often report negative affect, and in most domains are more satisfied than the men. They differ very little in their reported symptoms of strain, although this is the only stage of the live cycle in which, in both 1971 and 1978, men more often said they were concerned about having a nervous breakdown than women did. These older single women were more likely than other women to feel they had not had their full share of happiness in life; a high proportion of older single men also make this complaint.

It is apparent that the popular folklore about the carefree bachelor and the forlorn single woman needs a certain amount of revision. Being single is not associated with high feelings of well-being in either sex, either before or after age 30, and it seems a particularly unrewarding condition for men. Anyone who remains single beyond the usual age of marriage in a society which expects everyone to marry has an adjustment to make. Repeated studies have shown that men make this adjustment less well than women, although the differences are not dramatic. We will find in Chapter 13 that these men have a weaker sense of controlling their own lives than any of the other life-cycle groups, weaker than that of women over 30 who have never married. Men appear to suffer more from the absence of a wife than women do from the absence of a husband.

Various explanations can be offered for the fact that the failure to marry appears to have more negative consequences for men than it does for women. It has been argued that a wife serves as a mother substitute to her husband and he suffers a more serious psychological deprivation in the absence of a wife than a woman does in the absence of a husband. It is also possible that in our male-dominated society, it is more damaging to a man's ego to fail to consummate a marriage than it is to the less aggressive woman's. More parsimonious and perhaps more convincing is the explanation that single women are more successful in creating alternative social relationships than single men are. They compensate more adequately for the absence of a spouse by close attachments to parents, other relatives, or friends, often in the kind of nurturant role our society regards as more appropriate for women than for men.

We have seen that the absence of children does not appear to impair the quality of a marriage; we now see that the absence of marriage is strongly associated with feelings of ill-being. We cannot assume that this ill-being is entirely the consequence of being unmarried; some part of the difference we see between married and never-married people is certainly a matter of selection. Being unhappy, discontented, and worried cannot enhance a person's likelihood of being married; these characteristics surely tend to select people out of the state of marriage. We have no way of knowing how important this factor of selection is, but we do not doubt that the psychological circumstances in which single people live makes at least as great a contribution to the low levels of well-being we find at this stage of the life cycle. The fact of being unmarried in a society which almost universally regards marriage as the natural human condition, and develops its institutions around it, puts a single man or woman in a situation he or she cannot ignore. It raises questions of inadequacy and failure to achieve a status which society considers essential to a full life. It is not likely that many single people will be unaffected by the fact that they are a minority within a self-satisfied, uninterested, and sometimes suspicious majority.

The major failing in the single life, one must assume, is the lack of the intimate psychological support which marriage seems uniquely capable of giving. Some single people seem capable of substituting the support of family and friends for that of a marriage partner, but the evidence makes clear that for single people in general this is not a fully successful replacement. The status of the older single man is one of the most negative stages of the male life cycle, paralleled by young single men and by men whose marriages have failed. The older single woman sees her life somewhat more positively than the single men of her age, but, on the average, she is not as happy or as satisfied with life as women of her own age who are married.

Separated or Divorced

This country has for many years had a relatively high rate of divorce, a rate which reached record levels during the 1970s. But as we have seen, most divorced people remarry, in a few cases more than once. At any particular time, however, there exists a scattering of people throughout the population who are at the moment either separated or divorced. In 1978 they made up close to 10 percent of the adult population. Separation is typically a prelude to divorce and extends over a relatively short period of time. Divorce completes the separation and may last for many years. The two circumstances are different, both legally and psychologically; both are painful in the eyes of those who experience them.

It is surely a commonplace observation that divorce and the events leading up to it are a damaging experience for the two people involved, sometimes for one more than the other but typically for both. It is no surprise then to discover in the national surveys that separated and divorced people have on the average the most depressed feelings of well-being of any of the major life-cycle groups. They are much more likely than married people to describe their lives as "not too happy," and they are less likely to report positive experiences and much more likely to report negative ones, especially feeling lonely and depressed. These people with failed or failing marriages are also much less willing than married people to call themselves "very satisfied" with life in general and with the specific domains of life. They feel more strongly than any of the other life-cycle groups that they have not had their full share of happiness in life.

In these respects men and women in this situation resemble each other, men being somewhat less negative than women. In their perceptions of strain, however, they seem quite different. Men who are separated or divorced do not describe themselves as especially burdened, tied down, or worried; they are freer of this kind of feeling than most other men. But separated or divorced women are far more likely than other women (or men) to describe their lives in these terms.

This curious difference in the feelings of strain expressed by these people suggests that they must live in circumstances which put them under different degrees of stress, and one does not have far to seek to find what these circumstances are. Most of these women have children in the home for whom they are responsible; very few divorced men have custody of their children. Most of these women are employed, two out of three. Most of these women are living on substandard incomes; their average income is about half that of the average divorced man and is lower than that of any of the other life-cycle groups except widows. Very few of them, less than 5 percent, hire anyone from outside to help with the housework, not, one may assume, because they do not want to but because they cannot afford to.

It is readily understandable that these women see their situation as stressful and that separated and divorced men who have moved out from under the responsibilities of marriage and parenthood may feel unusually free. A woman who has been left alone with small children, with no recent work experience and modest and often uncertain support from the departed husband, has ample reason to feel harassed and worried. There are also other noneconomic aspects of the single state which are more oppressive to women than to men. Women have traditionally had to cope with the fact that society attaches greater blame and disapproval to a divorced woman than it does to a divorced man. The surveys from which we are drawing do not tell us what the impact of this disparity is on the woman's feelings of guilt and sense of self-esteem, but we cannot doubt that it is real.

Divorced and separated people do not remember their marriages very favorably. These broken marriages are described by the survivors as characterized by disagreements, misunderstandings, and lack of companionship—a striking contrast to the descriptions given by people who are still married. It is a curious fact that separated and divorced women remember their relationship with their former spouse more negatively than the men do. Either the men did not feel these flaws in their marital relationships as acutely as the women did, or they were less willing to admit that the flaws existed.

This pattern of bitter memories is very different from the report given by people whose marriages were ended by a death. Widowed people, mostly women, remember all aspects of their marital relationship very favorably—little disagreement, much mutual understanding, and constant companionship. Perhaps these people tend to adjust their memories of their married life to fit their present attitudes, but their descriptions do not seem unrealistic. Widowed people give a description which is very similar to that given by older married couples still living together, and separated and divorced people describe a relationship which seems programmed for the failure which followed.

For those who enter a successful second marriage, the trauma of a divorce may be short-lived, but for those who do not, the psychological consequences linger on. The contrast in the course of people's feelings after a divorce and death is striking. The pain of being widowed appears to soften as time passes. Among widowed people, the greatest unhappiness, dissatisfaction with life, and feelings of strain are found among those who are most recently widowed. People who have been widowed for some years describe their lives in more positive terms, although their reported happiness does not return to the level of people who are still married. Divorce is followed by a different pattern. While some people who come through a divorce may feel liberated and exhilarated after the event, for the most part divorce is followed by the same kind of negative outlook that follows a death. But the passage of time does not leaven the feelings of those divorced people who do not remarry. Their dissatisfaction with life and feelings of strain remain high even some years after the divorce, and their feelings of positive affect may in fact decline.

Divorce is obviously quite a different experience from being widowed and is followed by different kinds of emotion. While the dominant feeling of a widowed person is likely to be grief, for a divorced person it is more likely to be resentment and anger focused on the former spouse. The widowed person's grief over the departed spouse gradually wanes, and feelings of well-being begin to recover. The divorced person may find it hard to throw off his or her feelings of injury and resentment, especially, one may guess, if the former spouse remains within the orbit of the person's life. Divorce has become a commonplace event in this country in the past two decades, but it seems to be a difficult experience to overcome unless one remarries and, of course, not always then.

We must take account again of the possibility that the people who cannot preserve their marriage brought difficulties into their marriage which contributed to the divorce and to the unhappiness they feel after the divorce. No doubt some people, because of personality problems, are fated to be unhappy whether they are single, married, or divorced, and we do not know how much of the unhappiness we see associated with divorce can be attributed to this source. However much that may be, divorce is an inherently painful experience that appears capable of creating psychological distress for most people who are subject to it. It is a condition of life that is difficult to feel positive about.

Unmarried Mothers

The days of Hester Prynne are long since past, and public attitudes toward the "unwed mother" are surely less censorious than they were in colonial times. Indeed, extramarital parenthood may have acquired a certain chic among some emancipated elements of the population in recent years. It is still not acceptable to the moral code of the country, however, or to a large part of the population. We do not know to what extent unmarried mothers feel themselves the object of social disapproval or are depressed by such a perception, but it is clear that for this or other reasons, they speak very poorly about their lives.

Most of these women are young, half are less than 25 years old. Half of them are employed, mostly in unskilled jobs or household service. Half of them did not finish high school; their income is on the average very low. Some of them live with their mothers or other female relatives.

Their description of their lives is remorselessly negative. They are the least willing of all the life-cycle groups to say they are very happy, some one in twenty. They are lower than average in positive affect and higher in negative affect. They are similar to separated and divorced women in reporting feelings of strain; feeling tied down, worried about money and other problems, nearly half of them express concern about having a nervous breakdown. Their levels of satisfaction are as low as their levels of affect. In virtually every domain of life, they are among the least satisfied. Their sense of deprivation is epitomized by the fact that half of them believe they have had less than the share of happiness they might reasonably expect in life. Among young mothers of their age who are living with a husband, this proportion is about one in five.

These young women undoubtedly live in disadvantaged circumstances—low income, limited education, low level of employment. But it does not appear that these conditions alone could be responsible for more than a part of the very depressed quality of their lives. Most of these women feel they have not been able to satisfy their ambitions in life, and they have a general feeling of being the pawns of a fate they cannot control. They are into a nonconforming life-style that American society tolerates but does not approve. Like people who are unemployed, they are more likely to receive blame and opprobrium from society than understanding and support.

Unmarried mothers are such a small fraction of the population that they had not appeared in significant numbers in national surveys prior to 1978, and there is no indication of whether their situation is changing as time passes. American attitudes regarding the family have moderated in the last two decades, and they may change still further. It is doubtful, however, in the foreseeable future if most women who find themselves in the situation of unmarried mother will find it very positive. Raising a child without a father is a difficult problem for any woman, whether or not she has been married, but raising it outside of wedlock adds additional burdens, both economic and psychological, that are not likely to disappear.

Conclusions

Age is an irresistable force. It moves humankind through the life cycle, changing our appearance, attitudes, roles, values and behavior, and the circumstances of our lives. It also influences our feelings of well-being, sometimes in unexpected ways.

It is difficult to separate the effects of age from those of the life-cycle changes which are associated with age, but there is little doubt that both have their independent impact. The early years of adult life are characterized by strong affective experience; many pleasant and unpleasant events punctuate the lives of young people. As people grow older, these events are less common and less intense; life is more bland. In the 1950s and early 1960s the feelings of young people showed more happiness and other indications of positive affect that those of any of the older generations, but by the end of the 1970s this difference had disappeared, largely because young people no longer saw their world in such positive colors.

Youth was a period of dissatisfaction during the 1970s. As we compare the older cohorts with the younger, we see a consistent increase in the proportion who are satisfied with life in general, with the domains of life, and with their share of happiness in life. It is not an indiscriminate change; older people become increasingly dissatisfied with their health which increasingly gives them problems. But either because their circumstances improve or because their aspirations decline, older people are generally more content with their lives than younger. Although their satisfaction may result largely from their accommodation to conditions they have learned to accept, older people are in fact generally more content than young people, even in areas of life, such as material affluence, in which they are not objectively advantaged. The literary image of the crotchety old person, dissatisfied with everything, is not a very realistic picture of older people.

There are many points of passage during the course of a lifetime at which a person's circumstances change, sometimes with far-reaching implications for feelings of well-being. Although sample surveys are not the instrument of choice for the study of life histories, they are very effective in showing the differences between people located at different points in the life cycle. It is movements into and out of the status of marriage and into and out of the role of parenting that are associated with major contrasts in feelings of well-being. No stage of people's lives in which they are single—never married, separated, divorced, or widowed—is seen to be as pleasant or as satisfying as any of the stages of married life. The termination of a marriage either by divorce or death is typically associated with strong feelings of ill-being, especially in the affective aspects of life. Children are obviously valued by most married people, but they are associated with considerable psychological cost, especially when they are very young and especially to the wife. On the average, being married is more critical to positive feelings of well-being than having children, since married people without children have as positive an outlook on life as married people with children. People with children but without a spouse are generally negative. The uniquely supportive relationship which a successful marriage provides appears to enhance the psychological quality of a person's life, whatever the other circumstances of that person's life may be.

The general pattern of perceived well-being through the life cycle did not change between 1971 and 1978. Perhaps this is not surprising since one would not expect the characteristics of these major stages of life to change very much in the short term. But the decade of the 1970s was not a tranquil period for the American family. Divorces and illegitimate births reached new high levels, the birthrate continued to drop, the number of single-parent households rose, the proportion of married women seeking employment increased dramatically; along with this there was a great controversy over women's roles in marriage, parenting, and work. If differences in well-being had appeared between 1971 and 1978, especially among women in the younger stages of the life span, it would have been tempting to attribute them to reverberations from the "women's movement." But they did not appear. Values and attitudes regarding the family were undoubtedly changing and the situations of many women were also changing, but the net effect of these changes does not appear to have either enhanced or diminished the average levels of affect, satisfaction, or strain of women or men to any significant degree.

13
Personal Characteristics and Sense of Self

We have now examined the major attributes of the circumstances within which people live and have seen that they all contribute in some degree to the ways people perceive and evaluate their lives. There are other attributes, however, that do not reside in the outside world but within the individual, personal characteristics which may contribute very substantially to the individual's sense of well-being. Some of these are physical, including the person's health and physical appearance, and some are psychological, including those characteristics which make up the personality structure.

Related to these characteristics of the self is the individual's perception of self. The way in which the individual perceives himself or herself brings us close to what Allardt calls the need for being, the need for self-actualization. This is a difficult concept and especially difficult to find measures for within the confines of a survey interview. We assume that a person who feels in control of his or her own fate, and who feels satisfied with himself or herself as a person, has more nearly fulfilled the need for being than a person who does not have these self-perceptions. We will see that people who differ in these perceptions of self also differ quite substantially in their sense of well-being.

Health

As we stated in the opening of Chapter 2, our concept of health is not limited by the customary definition of absence of sickness or disability.

Our entire enterprise in this book is based on the conviction that health must be more broadly defined to include subjective health, or, as we have used the term, sense of well-being. Nevertheless, physical health is an important fact of life, and we cannot doubt that it contributes to an individual's subjective health. Measuring the physical health of a single individual can be a difficult task; assessing the physical health of the national population is a prodigious undertaking. Approximations of such an assessment are made annually by the National Center for Health Statistics through its morbidity surveys, utilizing a massive sample and a long, detailed questionnaire.

We will not draw on these morbidity surveys or on other epidemiological surveys in which actual medical examinations have been done. We will depend instead on people's own statements of whether or not they "have any particular problems with their health," and, if so, whether "these problems keep them from doing things they wish they could do." We have no doubt that many people may deny or be unaware of health problems that a medical doctor could readily identify, and these questions must be regarded as permitting only rough sorting of people into those who perceive no problems of physical health and those who see their health as in some degree impaired.

The first fact to be noted from these self-diagnoses is that in 1978 two out of three people in this country said they had no particular health problems. Of those who admitted having problems, about a third said these problems kept them from doing "a lot of things they wished they could do," somewhat less than a third said they were kept from doing "certain things," and the remaining 40 percent said they "could do almost anything they wished." This shorthand indicator of the status of individual health tells us that of the adult population in this country, nearly 20 percent has some significant limitation of activity due to some disabling condition, and this figure is close to that reported by the National Center for Health Statistics. People seem to be quite categorical about the state of their health, and it does not require a detailed interrogation to find out whether or not they think they have a "health problem."

Having "particular problems" with your health obviously implies something more persistent and serious than a bout with the flu or with any of the other short-term miseries. In the absence of comparable data through time or of comparisons across nations, it is difficult to say

whether a record of 19 percent reporting some significant impairment is disgracefully high or remarkably low. There is no doubt, however, that these people with health problems are found much more commonly in some circumstances of life than they are in others.

All studies of physical health show an increase in morbidity and disability with increasing age, and our national surveys show a similar increase in the number of older people who say they have problems which "keep them from doing things they wish they could do." This pattern is very similar for men and women, although at all age levels women are a little more likely than men to say they have health problems. The differences by age are quite substantial: only two or three percent of men and women under 25 say they have a health impairment which prevents them from "doing a lot of things," but this figure rises sharply after age 45 for women, more slowly for men, and among people who are over 75 years old it is about one in three.

As one might expect, people with low incomes are more likely to report health problems than people higher on the income scale. The difference is quite substantial; nearly one person in four of those people in the lowest quartile of the income distribution say they have health problems of a seriously disabling character; in the highest income quartile the proportion is less than one in twenty. Reported disabilities are also quite clearly associated with educational level, with college graduates having the fewest health problems.

We know that income is related to educational level and that age is related to both income and education. These interrelations make it difficult to be sure which of these characteristics is in fact responsible for the presence or absence of health problems. Generally speaking, older people have increasing difficulties with their health, but they are less likely to have these difficulties if they have substantial incomes, which implies that economic status also has a determining influence on health. If we remove the influence of income, we reduce somewhat the differences between the young and old groups, but they still remain substantial. The differences in the incidence of health problems reported by educational groups appear to depend, however, almost entirely on the underlying differences in income. If everyone had the same income, the differences between educational groups would disappear, but older people would still have more health problems than younger people.

Perceived health also varies through the stages of the life cycle, partly because of the underlying factor of age but also for other reasons. We find, for example, that young people (under 30) have very low rates of reported disability, and these rates do not differ between those who have never married but still childless and those who are married. Men and women over 30 who have never married, however, are clearly more likely to report health problems than other people of their age who are married. We do not know whether this means that those over 30 were prevented from marrying because of their health difficulties or that their not having married has somehow been responsible for their disability. People who are separated or divorced report more disability than people of their age who stay married. Here again the question of what came first is not easy to answer. Widowed people have the highest level of reported disability of any of the life-cycle groups. They are also the oldest of these groups on the average, and their health problems may be entirely a consequence of their age, but one wonders if their psychological trauma may not have also contributed to their difficulties. All these groups lack the kind of intimate social support which a continuing marriage provides. Social support has been shown to moderate the effects of major transitions and crises and to reduce the probability of physiological pathologies; its absence in these groups may partially explain the high reported rates of disability.

As we have seen, most of the population reports having no health problems that cause any disability. For these people, good health is a common good which contributes to their general sense of well-being. But people who do have problems with their health do not find their lives to be as happy or as satisfying as those who do not, and this is especially true of those whose problems are serious enough to keep them from "doing a lot of things they wish they could do." These people are most likely to describe themselves as "not too happy," least likely to report positive affective experiences, and most likely to report negative experiences. In all these instances those with no health problems are the most positive.

Health disability is certainly associated with low positive affect. It is not true of course that most people with disabilities find their lives to be miserably unhappy; on the average their view of life is not that unfavorable. But poor health is not a positive condition of life and people with serious health problems are clearly less likely to describe their lives as happy and positive than people who do not have such problems.

Satisfaction with Health

We have seen at earlier points in this book that satisfaction with a domain of life is often only modestly related to the actual objective conditions of that domain. Satisfaction with standard of living, for example, increases as income increases, but the relationship is not very strong. Satisfaction with housing also increases with income, but again there are a surprising number of people who seem very satisfied with very modest housing. Health presents quite a different picture. Over 90 percent of those people who say they have no health problems are satisfied with their health, and most of them are "completely satisfied." One person in three who has a serious disability is willing to describe himself or herself as satisfied with health, and only one in ten is completely satisfied. The more serious the health problem, the more pervasive the feeling of dissatisfaction.

Poor health appears to be a condition of life that is uniquely difficult to accept. Most people seem to have a capacity to live with economic or personal vicissitudes and to develop a degree of satisfaction with their circumstances. People appear to strain toward the positive; if they can find a way to be satisfied with their lives, they seem to want to take it. But poor health is a condition that people find very difficult to feel satisfied with. We find a small number of people who insist that they are completely content with their health even though they have persistent health problems that seriously restrict their freedom of movement, but they are not representative. Poor health appears to have a peculiarly insistent ability to reduce one's sense of well-being, an ability which most people find impossible to resist.

Reasonably enough, poor health is associated with dissatisfaction with health. One might also expect it to be associated with a degree of dissatisfaction in other domains of life, assuming that poor health may make it difficult for a person to hold a job, make a decent living, circulate among family and friends, and otherwise live a "normal" life. People with serious disability are in fact considerably more likely than people with no health problems to express dissatisfaction with their lives, but in many of the specific domains they differ very little, particularly in the areas of interpersonal relations, marriage, family life, and friendships. People with poor health have incomes that are considerably below average, and they are less well-satisfied with their income and savings than people with no health problems. They are also less satisfied with the share of happiness they have had in life "considering everything."

The evidence is surely convincing that poor health is associated with unhappiness and negative affect. The association is even sharper, however, with dissatisfaction with health. As we have seen, some people with serious health disabilities insist that their lives are happy, satisfying, and serene. But if they say they are dissatisfied with their health, the likelihood of their describing their lives in these positive terms is greatly diminished. Not very many people say they are dissatisfied with their health, about one person in ten, but those who do show an impressive pattern of ill-being—not very happy, dissatisfied with life, and high feelings of strain. Dissatisfaction with health has a pervasively negative quality; it is fortunate that the number of people who have health problems and are disturbed by them is no larger than it is. These dissatisfactions might have been more intense if it were not for the fact that a good many of these people with poor health and low incomes are in their later years, years in which we know people tend to describe their lives as satisfying. The accommodative attitudes of age do not seem to be able to overcome the increasing discontent with health, but they appear to prevent the increasing burden of poor health from diminishing satisfaction in other domains of life.

Poor physical health, severe enough to limit a person's activities, might be expected to subject that person to some psychological stress. Such people do not complain that their life is "hard," and they are only slightly more inclined than healthy people to say they feel "tied down." But they do exceed people with no disabilities in their worries—worries about paying their bills, worries about things happening to them or their families, worries about having a nervous breakdown. Women are generally more concerned about a nervous breakdown than men are, and this concern is more clearly associated with health problems among women than it is among men.

In their feelings of strain, people with health problems resemble unemployed people. Both are compelled to accept a quieter kind of life-style than they would ordinarily expect. Neither group finds this life especially rushed for time, tied down, or difficult, but both are subject to the kinds of worries we have noted and to low levels of positive affect. Both are among the least happy of the population groups we have looked at.

Appearance

A person's physical appearance undoubtedly contributes in an important way to his or her self-image, and it would not be unreasonable to expect that it also contributes to the quality of that person's life. In a society as sensitive to personal appearance as ours appears to be, it would not be surprising to discover that the "beautiful people" find their lives more pleasant and satisfying than the average, and those least fortunately endowed should have some of the same low sense of well-being we have seen among people who are handicapped by some chronic health problem.

Judgments of appearance are highly subjective to be sure; beauty, as we have heard so often, is in the eye of the beholder. But we know that standards of physical beauty are not entirely individual and that there is a certain degree of consensus in the population about what kinds of appearance are attractive and which are not.

It might be possible to base an evaluation of appearance on such objective measures as height, weight, posture, complexion, hair color, and the like. The surveys we are drawing from depended instead on a simple rating by the interviewer of the physical attractiveness of the man or woman she was interviewing. This is certainly a minimum kind of measurement, but it is not a totally unreliable one. The same interviewers making separate judgments of the same subjects at an interval of several months were very consistent in their ratings, and the ratings of different interviewers tended also to resemble each other, not as closely as two judgments by the same interviewer but far closer than might be attributed to chance. The different interviewers undoubtedly differed somewhat among themselves in their standards of attractiveness, but they also shared enough in common to make it possible to use their judgments for the purposes that interest us here.

When these ratings were done in the 1971 and 1978 surveys, they distributed themselves according to the familiar bell-shaped curve. The interviewers classified slightly over half of the people they interviewed as "about average" in looks for their age and sex. Only two or three percent impressed them as "strikingly beautiful or handsome" and about an equally small number as "homely." The rest were either "good looking" or "quite plain," more of the former than the latter. They did not find women more or less attractive than men or white people more or less attractive than black. They did, however, tend to restrict their ratings of unusual attractiveness to men and women below the age of 45. In a society which is often described as having a fixation on youth, one cannot be surprised that as people grow older, they are generally seen as less physically attractive. In those societies that are said to revere old age, a lined face, gray hair, and other familiar signs of physical aging may be thought to be attractive, but they clearly are not in modern-day America.

Judgments of physical attractiveness are quite clearly associated with judgments of individual intelligence. The interviewers in these surveys found it very difficult to rate any man or woman as above average in attractiveness if they considered that person low in intelligence. They were almost certainly influenced by a certain "halo effect" in judging these traits; if a person possesses one, he or she is seen as possessing the other. On the other hand one of the early findings of the famous Stanford studies of gifted children was that high intelligence and physical attractiveness do in fact go together in some degree, that the so-called law of compensation operates in reverse. It does not seem unlikely that an air of intelligence may make a person seem attractive, but it may also be that through some quirk of nature the two qualities tend to travel together.

As one might expect, attractive people are found in increasing numbers as one moves up the educational and income ladder. This seems reasonable since attractiveness, with its related intelligence, should make it more probable that a person will achieve success in these areas of life. It is also probable that a person who has the grooming, dress, and manners that are associated with educational and income status will be considered attractive. There is a certain circularity in this relationship. People who achieve high status do so in part because of their personal qualities, including their physical attractiveness. The status they achieve tends to enhance their external appearance, and this in turn makes them appear more attractive.

Do these people whom the interviewers describe as beautiful or good-looking have a stronger sense of well-being than the people they find plain or homely? They do in part. In the affective side of their lives they are clearly more positive; they are more often "very happy" and have more positive experiences and fewer negative ones. But they are not, for the most part, more satisfied with their lives in general or the major domains of life, especially those having to do with interpersonal relationships. Knowing what we know about American society, we might have expected the relationship between attractiveness and positive affect to be stronger among women than among men, but this turns out not to be the case. Being beautiful rather than homely is not a major determiner of subjective well-being in this country for either men or women, but it seems to have the same importance for both.

Although this general relationship is rather modest when we consider the total population, that handful of people who are described as "homely" seem to have a good deal more than their share of disadvantage. Nearly half of them have only a grade school education and over half of them have a health problem of some kind, in most cases one which limits a good many of their activities. Half of them have incomes that fall in the bottom quartile of the income distribution. It would be amazing if these people were able to describe their lives as positively as other people do, and they do not. They are one of those small pockets of people we have seen who live in circumstances which make it difficult to find life pleasant.

Since attractive people are younger, better educated, and more affluent than the general population, one cannot be sure that their positive feelings about life come from their good looks or from their other advantages. If we ask the computer to remove the influence of age, education, and income, we find that age and income make very little difference but taking away educational advantage leaves a very small part of positive affect accounted for by good looks alone.

The Self

We are not surprised to discover that good health and an attractive personal appearance are associated with positive feelings of well-being. These physical qualities surely make it easier for people to live a pleasant life and to develop a favorable evaluation of the self. The Institute for Social Research surveys measure two aspects of this self-evaluation—

the feeling people have that they control the world they live in, or are controlled by it, and their sense of satisfaction with themselves as persons.

Sense of Personal Control

For over 25 years the Institute for Social Research has been interested in the concept of perceived control, the extent to which people feel they are able to control their own lives or see themselves as controlled by outside forces. The quality of this trait can be seen in the context of the six questions which were developed as a measuring instrument.

Have you usually felt pretty sure your life would work out the way you want it to, or have there been times when you haven't been sure about it?

Do you think it's better to plan your life a good way ahead, or would you say life is too much a matter of luck to plan ahead very far?

When you make plans ahead, do you usually get to carry things out the way you expected, or do things usually come up to make you change your plans?

Some people feel they can run their lives pretty much the way they want to; others feel the problems of life are sometimes too big for them. Which one are you most like?

Up to now, have you been able to satisfy most of your ambitions in life, or have you had to settle for less than you had hoped for?

Do you think you have had a fair opportunity to make the most of yourself in life, or have you been held back in some ways?

These items have a strong common element, and they can be combined into a single scale, Sense of Personal Control. Obviously some people stand higher on this scale than others, and we may ask what it is about the lives of these people that contributes to a strong sense of control in one person and not another. It can be argued that these differences between individuals result from genetic factors which influence this aspect of personality or from early socialization that teaches habits and attitudes of self-reliance. Following this theory we would then assume that people who acquire a strong sense of self-confidence through these sources would be influenced by it in the way they live their lives. They would be more likely to achieve economic, occupational, and educational advantage, for example. But it may alternately be true that people's feelings of controlling their lives are the result of advantages they possess as adults—economic status, high education, good health, intelligence, good looks, and the like. Their sense of controlling their fate depends on their experience of having these advantages.

Whatever the weights one attaches to these different factors, it is clear from the accompanying comparisons that advantaged people feel more confident about controlling their lives than people who are not so fortunate.

High-income people College graduates Professional people Healthy people Attractive people Intelligent people	Have a stronger sense of controlling their lives than	Low income people High school dropouts Unskilled workers People with health problems Homely people Less intelligent people

The resources these advantaged people bring to bear on their circumstances evidently enhance their ability to control their lives and their perception that they do in fact control them. Conversely people who have been unsuccessful in some important enterprise in their lives, unemployed and divorced persons, for example, tend to have rather weak feelings of controlling their fate.

All these relationships are in the direction one would expect, but none of them is very strong, and even taking them all together they fall far short of explaining the differences between people in their sense of personal control. Advantaged circumstances are clearly associated with feelings of control, but they are not essential. Many people feel they control their lives even though they have only modest achievements and no outstanding personal attributes.

People who see the control of their lives within themselves are far more likely to describe their life experience positively than those who see themselves controlled by outside forces. They are happier; more likely to report affectively positive experiences; less likely to report negative experiences, worries, and strain; more satisfied with life and the domains of life; and more ready to say that they have had their share or more than their share of happiness in life. Considering the fact that their lives are characterized by more than average advantages and personal resources of various kinds, it is in no way surprising that they find their lives satisfying and pleasant. But these advantages do not explain their feelings of well-being. When the influence of these factors (income, health, attractiveness, apparent intelligence) is removed by statistical methods, the relationship still remains virtually undiminished. The sense of controlling one's fate has an independent association with feelings of well-being.

Satisfaction with One's Self

Being satisfied with one's self implies that one has some more-or-less well-defined self-image and some criterion of excellence against which this image is compared. Some introspective people no doubt give constant attention to their perception of themselves, and some others probably pay it little heed. As we have seen, most people find themselves neither completely satisfying nor dissatisfying, but their evaluation of themselves is a strong contributor to their satisfaction with life in general.

It is curious how little difference in average satisfaction with self there is in the major population groups which differ so consistently in other domains in life. Black people are no more or less satisfied with themselves than white; people with high incomes are no more satisfied than people on the lower rungs of the income ladder. Low-education people have a moderately high evaluation of themselves and so do college graduates. The lowest satisfaction is seen in those who went to college but did not finish. Place of residence is of little significance and differences in age groups are rather minor. Even those groups which seem so negative about other aspects of their lives—unemployed, separated, divorced—are no more willing than other people to express dissatisfaction with themselves as persons.

Satisfaction with self seems to depend rather little on these objective circumstances of one's life. It would appear that the standards by which people judge themselves, when asked to evaluate "yourself as a person," depend on concepts of "being a good person" or "being the kind of person one would like to be" and that these criteria do not relate to income level, education, physical attractiveness, or other such advantages. They do relate, however, to a person's gender; women are less willing to express satisfaction with themselves as a person than men are. The discrepancy is not remarkable, but it is present at every decade of the life span.

One might propose that this difference in readiness to profess satisfaction with oneself is simply an expression of the general personality patterns that distinguish the sexes in American society—the self-confident, aggressive male and the reserved, less assertive female. Men may find it more difficult to admit shortcomings in themselves. It is noteworthy that men are also somewhat more confident than women that they control their own lives. It might be argued that these differences are not a matter of sex-related personal traits but are a realistic reflection of a greater frequency of success experiences in the lives of men. It is not in their feelings of "accomplishments in life," however, that women fall short of men; in answer to this question, they are no less positive than men. More significant is the fact that they are less likely than men to feel they "come close to being the kind of person you would like to be"; in this respect women tend to be more self-critical than men, and their feelings of shortcoming may well carry over into their greater dissatisfaction with themselves as persons.

Satisfaction with self, as we have seen earlier, is strongly related to satisfaction with life in general and, as might be expected, it is also associated, though not so strongly, with positive feelings of affect. Not very many people express even moderate dissatisfaction with themselves (5 percent of men and 7 percent of women), but those who do see their lives in very negative terms. For example, 35 percent of them say they find their lives "not too happy," a proportion several times that given by people "completely satisfied" with themselves. Dissatisfaction with self has a more damaging effect on one's general feeling of well-being than dissatisfaction with any of the other domains of life we have considered.

Satisfaction with Self and Sense of Personal Control

Men and women who are well-satisfied with themselves as persons are clearly more likely than those who are not to see themselves as controlling their own lives. These two aspects of one's self-evaluation obviously have something in common. People who have a strong sense of personal control rarely express lack of satisfaction with themselves as persons, although some people who express high self-satisfaction do not have a strong sense of controlling their lives.

If we isolate that part of the population which expresses both a strong sense of personal control and a high level of satisfaction with self (about 15 percent of the total), we find that we have identified a group of people with extraordinarily positive feelings of well-being. Three out of five of these people describe themselves as "very happy," hardly any of them express themselves as dissatisfied with life in general, very few (4 percent) feel they have not received their reasonable share of happiness in life, and 1 percent say they sometimes worry about having a nervous breakdown. Their strongly positive self-evaluation underlies a highly positive outlook on life.

If these people came very largely from the objectively advantaged parts of the population, we might be inclined to attribute their positive feelings of well-being to these advantages. But in fact, they do not differ greatly from the rest of the population in their economic status, and very little of their positive self-evaluation can be explained in this way. Even those whose family income falls in the lowest quartile of the income distribution have a generally positive profile of well-being which does not differ very much from that of people in the top quartile. They have somehow come, through inherited inclination or environmental influence, to a perception of themselves that makes it possible for them to experience life in a positive way, even if their objective circumstances are not favorable.

Conclusions

The self is far too complex a concept to be considered in any depth in these pages. But we have sought in this chapter to recognize the fact that feelings of well-being depend not only on the circumstances in which a person lives but also on the characteristics of the person.

Physical health is an attribute of the self which has far less salience when it is present than when it is absent. While most Americans say they have no health problems, those who do find them difficult to accept. Older people especially, who appear to accommodate very successfully to most aspects of their lives, are least satisfied with their health. And that proportion of the population which has serious disabilities has a generally negative pattern of well-being. Fortunately this proportion was no more than one in ten in either 1971 or 1978, and satisfaction with health is as a result a less powerful contributor to the total population's feelings of well-being than other domains are.

Being physically attractive is associated with high positive affect, but it is also associated with being young, healthy, intelligent, well-off, and well-educated. This combination of characteristics makes up a syndrome which is difficult to dissect, but when attractiveness is isolated from these other attributes, it still appears to make a small contribution to a person's feelings of well-being. The survey evidence may be said to support the commonplace belief that good looks in themselves are not very central to the major problems of life, but they are hardly ever a disadvantage.

Having a strong sense of controlling one's life is a more dependable predictor of positive feelings of well-being than any of the objective conditions of life we have considered. We have treated the attribute measured by this scale as a quality of personality which intervenes between the outside world and the person's feelings of well-being. We assume that the way people perceive their world and the way they evaluate it is influenced by whether they see themselves as controlling that world or being controlled by it.

One could argue that the feeling of controlling one's life does not precede sense of well-being in a causal sense but is rather in itself a measure of well-being in the same degree that perceived affect and satisfaction are. It is true that feelings of controlling one's life relate nearly as closely to the measures of affect and life satisfaction as these two measures relate to each other, which would suggest that all three are tapping some common factor of psychological well-being in about equal degree. This is not a necessary conclusion, however, and it better fits our picture of how the perception of the outside world is interpreted into feelings of well-being or ill-being to think of feelings of control as intervening between these two points in sequence.

Being satisfied with oneself as a person is unique among the various measures of satisfaction we have considered since it is virtually independent of the social and economic circumstances in which a person lives. People appear to judge themselves in relation to a subjective standard they have in mind and, on the average, this evaluation is no higher or lower in the different educational, economic, racial, age, or other groups in the population. It is by no means a purely random judgment, however, being strongly related to people's general satisfaction with life and somewhat less strongly to the other measure of self-evaluation, sense of personal control.

A positive self-evaluation may be considered to be an aspect of the sense of self-actualization which Allardt takes to be a central component of the "need for being." Those people who achieve a positive feeling about themselves see their lives in a very favorable light, far more favorable than those people who are distinguished only by their economic or educational achievements. And that small number of people who are both dissatisfied with themselves as persons and convinced that their lives are controlled by external forces have one of the most unrelieved patterns of unhappiness and discontent to be found in the entire population.

part 3

The Quality of Life

Kurt Lewin, in his theories of personality and action, emphasized the basic principle that behavior must be understood as the interaction of the person and the environment. People are always influenced by the situation around them, and they always impose their own characteristics on their perception of the situation. They do not behave independently of their environment, and the environment does not entirely control their behavior.

The same principle applies to understanding the sense of well-being. Feelings of well-being or ill-being are not determined exclusively either by the circumstances people find themselves in or by their own expectations, attitudes, or other personal traits. Economic position, marital status, good or bad health, employment or unemployment, and other conditions of life have clearly visible association with the way people evaluate their lives, but in no case do they account for a major part of this evaluation. People bring their own personalities to the situation, and while the mind may not be entirely "its own place," there is no doubt that it contributes substantially to the way people see their lives.

Most of the advanced nations of the world are concerned with attempting to assess the quality of life of their populations, and for this purpose they have depended heavily on a careful monitoring of the economic conditions of their people. More recently they have added measurements of health and environmental and social conditions as additional indicators of the quality of national life. They have now begun to ask whether these measures of the objective conditions of life are adequate to describe the subjective experience of life, as it has become obvious that economic prosperity has not produced the social harmony and felicity that we might have wished.

The interest in measures of the subjective quality of life has led to a burst of research activity by psychologists and sociologists throughout the world. There is still much disagreement about concepts, definitions, techniques of measurement, and even descriptive findings. The field has not yet reached the stage of sophistication at which these questions will have been answered. Exploratory studies have been carried out in many nations, however, and in some there are the beginnings of the kind of continuing programs which will eventually lead to a firmer understanding of the nature of subjective well-being.

The most extensive program of research of this kind carried out in this country is reported in the pages of this book and is summarized in Chapter 14.

14
Well-Being and Ill-Being

Sense of well-being is not a simple experience. It contains affective feelings of happiness, misery, and strain and cognitive impressions of satisfaction and dissatisfaction. It relates to life as a whole and to the specific domains of life. It may have a short-term reference to life these days, or a long-term reference to life up to now. It may be influenced by hopes and expectations concerning events in the future. Whichever of these aspects of well-being we consider, we find that some people are positive and some are negative, and if they are positive in one aspect, they are likely to be positive in the others.

Conventional thinking generally assumes that there is a close and predictable relationship between the quality of the objective circumstances in which people live and the quality of their subjective experience. It attempts to assess the state of national well-being by measuring the objective conditions of life, the average family income, the number of houses and automobiles owned, the average length of the workweek, the number of students in schools and colleges, and the number of doctors and hospitals available. These and other economic and social indicators have become established measures of the quality of national life.

We have argued in this book that the objective conditions of life can be taken as indicators of subjective well-being only in the degree to which they provide positive and satisfying experience. We have assumed that sense of well-being depends on the satisfaction of three basic kinds of need. Following Erik Allardt's language, we have called these the need for having, the need for relating, and the need for being. We have found that no set of objective circumstances fulfills all these needs with very high predictability. Some conditions of life tend to meet the need for having, others the need for relating. There are some patterns of circumstances that are more likely to produce well-being and some that are associated with ill-being, but there is none in which we do not find both happy and miserable people.

The Need for Having

Having the material necessities of life is surely the first requirement of a life of well-being, and it is generally believed that as average family income rises, housing improves in size and amenities, and more consumer goods are owned, people are on the average happier and more satisfied with life. Governments everywhere accept this relationship as self-evident, and much of their activity is intended to increase these material benefits, to satisfy the need for having.

If we had survey evidence of people's feelings of well-being over the last hundred years, we would be able to trace changes in these feelings as material wealth has increased, poverty has been reduced, leisure time has expanded, and the average person's life has become less nasty, brutish, and short. Of course we do not know how people in the 1880s would have answered questions about their happiness and satisfaction with life, and while we may think it likely that they would have answered them less favorably than they do now, we have no assurance that this is in fact true.

We can get some indication of how these feelings of well-being might have differed through time if we compare countries which are still in an early stage of economic development to those like ourselves that are more advanced. The evidence is not substantial, but it does appear that reported well-being is higher in the more prosperous countries than it is in countries where most people are living in or on the edge of poverty. Aspirations and expectations undoubtedly rise as economic levels improve, but on the average people are more satisfied with their lives if they live in an affluent society than if they live in a poor one.

This would seem to suggest that within any of these societies those individuals who are materially well-off will have stronger feelings of well-being than those who are at the bottom of the ladder. This is in fact what surveys have repeatedly found, both in this country and elsewhere. People with high incomes more often describe themselves as happy and satisfied with life than people with low incomes. This is such a central tenet of the conventional wisdom one would hardly think to question it, but the relationship is much weaker than one is likely to think.

Fulfilling the need for having material things and related impersonal resources does not guarantee a high sense of well-being. Images of miserable, impoverished people and the indolent pleasures of the very rich come easily to mind, but these people make up a small fraction of the total population. When we expand our view to include the full range, we find there are people of every degree of happiness and satisfaction at every point in the income scale. High income has its strongest influence on satisfaction in the domains of life most closely associated with the need for having—income, savings, and standard-of-living—but it is totally inadequate as a predictor of satisfaction in domains of life concerned with relating—marriage, family life, and friendships. And it also fails to relate to the most important contributor to satisfaction with life in general, one's satisfaction with self. People who find their marriages or other close relationships unsatisfactory, or find themselves lacking as persons, are not likely to have a very positive view of their lives whatever their income may be.

Over the last 20 years income has tended to lose its force in this country as an indicator of subjective well-being, especially among people with a college education. Why is this true? It is not likely that people have lost interest in having the material things and other benefits that income makes possible, but it does seem probable that as these needs are increasingly fulfilled during a period of rising prosperity, the needs for interpersonal relationships and a favorable self-evaluation become relatively more important. Just as health seems to be a secondary consideration in the life satisfaction of people who are in vigorous good health, income appears to lose priority in the lives of people who have reason to feel financially secure. Those people at the bottom of the income scale are in a different situation; they are still struggling with the needs for having the material necessities of life, and in comparison to the rest of the population, they have much to be dissatisfied with in those domains.

At what point does a person's need for the things that money will buy begin to lose its preeminence in competition with what Maslow called the higher needs and what Allardt has called the needs for relating and being? This must vary from one person to another and from one society to another, but it seems self-evident that as a society becomes more affluent, a larger number of people will pass this point and the significance of income for these people will decline. This appears to have happened in this country during the long period of increasing economic prosperity following the Second World War. We would expect that this has also happened in other countries with a similar economic experience, and evidence from surveys in Western Europe and Canada fulfills this expectation. From their studies of the populations of seven West European countries, Barnes and Inglehart report "a shift from a primary concern with material well-being and physical security toward greater emphasis on the quality of life and self-realization." Atkinson observes from a series of surveys in Canada that "income seems to be losing its effect as a determinant of life satisfaction." The political and social experiences of these countries have been quite different from those of the United States, but they have all enjoyed a substantial rise in economic affluence with consequences which appear to be similar to those in this country.

The Need for Relating

The greatest differences in the degree of well-being or ill-being people perceive in their lives are not found between high income and low income people or between people differing in other aspects of status—education or occupation. The contrasts between people whose patterns of social relationships differ are much sharper.

The basic source of social support among adult Americans is marriage. The need for human relationships can undoubtedly be met in various ways, and countless individuals live what they regard as very satisfactory lives outside of marriage, but on the average, no part of the unmarried population—never married, separated, divorced, widowed—describes itself as a happy and contented with life as that part which is presently married. This may seem curious in light of the probability that a sizable fraction of those married will eventually terminate their marriages in divorce, but the evidence is consistent and substantial: married people see their lives more positively than unmarried people. Despite the fact that attitudes toward marriage are changing in this country, especially among young people, the marriage pattern continues to contribute something uniquely important to the feelings of well-being of the average man and woman.

One of the most important of these changing attitudes is that regarding children. In the space of a single generation prevailing concepts of ideal family size have dropped dramatically and the birthrate has declined to below replacement level. It seems apparent that married couples are increasingly motivated by their own calculations of the benefits and costs of having children rather than by simple acceptance of what their own fertility may produce or by some feeling of duty or social obligation. The fact that such a large majority of married people have at least one child is sufficient evidence that children are desired despite the psychological and economic burden they put on parents. But the fact that the average number of children born to American families is now less than two demonstrates that the perceived benefits of additional children beyond the first diminish rapidly.

The surveys make it quite clear that children are not necessary either for a successful marriage or a happy and satisfying life. Married men and women over 30 who do not have children resemble married people who are parents of grown children in their feelings of well-being, being more positive than the parents of young children and people who are not married. It is not the presence or absence of children that distinguishes the level of well-being of married people from that of unmarried people; it is the presence of the spouse. Being married and having children is still the cultural norm in this country and will probably remain so for the foreseeable future, but it seems probable that an increasing number of men and women will choose to marry but not to have children. There is no reason to believe that this trend will diminish the general level of subjective well-being, and it may well enhance the lives of some of the people who make this choice.

The marital partner is the preeminent source of social support but obviously not the only one, and that sizable portion of the population which is not married is by no means bereft. The "lonely crowd" seems to be made up of people who have a surprising number of relatives and close friends with whom they are in frequent contact. There is, to be sure, a small number of people who live by themselves and have no intimate friend to whom they feel they can confide their problems, and their lack of social support is reflected in their depressed feelings of well-being. Social isolation may suit some few people whose need for relating is not strong, but it does not become the lives of most people for whom supportive human relationships are an essential ingredient of life.

People are surrounded not only by these close interpersonal relationships but also by a broader social context which is less immediate and less important for a sense of well-being than relatives and friends but significant nevertheless. Americans differ in their satisfaction with life according to where they live. It is not the region of the country in which they live that makes a difference, or the vagaries of the weather. These physical aspects of the environment undoubtedly mean a great deal to particular individuals, but they appear to have little general impact. It is the surrounding social environment which is associated with people's sense of well-being—whether they live in a metropolitan center, an outlying suburb, a city, a small town, or in the open country. In general, the larger the surrounding population, the less likely the individual is to express satisfaction, not only with his or her neighborhood and community but also with other domains of life. It is particularly the people in the metropolitan centers, both white and black, who find these aspects of their lives less than satisfying. They see their cities as polluted and dangerous and relatively few speak of them as a very good place to live.

It is apparent, of course, that the large cities have physical attributes that contribute to the dissatisfaction their residents feel. They are noisy and dirty, they lack greenery and open space, their buildings are massive, and they are extensive in area, requiring dependence on impersonal mechanical contrivances, elevators, buses, subways, or commuter trains. But they are also notably lacking in the sociability of the smaller places where people are more likely to know their neighbors, to be free of fear of crime, to feel that they live in a friendly atmosphere. One may assume that both the physical and the psychological characteristics of urban and rural life influence the way people perceive the quality of life in these places, and it cannot be doubted that the feeling of community and its relevance to people's need for relating is an important part of what makes the smaller places more satisfying to people who live there.

The Need for Being

The need for what Allardt calls "being," including what Maslow called "self-fulfillment," is difficult to define and to measure within the context of a population survey. In Allardt's terms, this "category of needs refers to what the individual is and what he does in relation to society—to self-actualization and the obverse of alienation." Central to this definition is the image people have of themselves, including their self-evaluation and their sense of influencing their own fate. Self-fulfillment can only exist in the person's own perceptions of self.

We know as a simple descriptive fact that most people feel they have done at least fairly well in accomplishing what they had hoped for in their lives and in handling the problems they have encountered. They say they come at least fairly close to being the kind of person they would like to be. And while a relatively small number feel completely satisfied with themselves as a person, an even smaller number are on balance dissatisfied with themselves. The intriguing characteristic of these simple self-evaluations is that they are almost completely unrelated to the individual's income, education, age, or marital status—personal qualities which relate strongly to level of satisfaction with other domains of life. These objective conditions of people's lives appear to have little influence on their statements of satisfaction with self.

Satisfaction with self does relate, however, to the individual's sense of controlling his or her own life rather than being controlled by outside forces. Some people see themselves in command of their lives; others feel helpless in the face of external forces. Those who have a strong sense of personal control also express high satisfaction with life. They are not inclined to express negative feelings of well-being, even when the material circumstances of their lives are not favorable. Their positive self-evaluation is clearly more important to their feelings of well-being than their objective situation is.

There are undoubtedly other aspects of "what the individual is" that contribute to the way a person sees the world and evaluates the quality of life. There must be traits of personality that intervene between a person's perception of the world and his or her sense of well-being. National surveys very uncommonly attempt to measure such traits, partly because of the tedious length of most of the standardized measures of personality. But one can hardly doubt that if we had reliable measures of such common characteristics as sociability, ambition, and optimism, we would have a better understanding of why some people are happy and satisfied and others are not.

The Highs and Lows of Well-Being

Studies of subjective well-being throughout the world have repeatedly found that, when total populations are considered, the relationships between the objective conditions of life and the experiences of well-being and ill-being that people report is generally quite weak. A comprehensive study in Scandinavia, for example, concludes, "It is hard to avoid the conclusion that the expressions of satisfaction and dissatisfaction only to a very small degree are directly related to the external social conditions."

A similar conclusion might be drawn from the American studies, although the association appears to be somewhat stronger than that implied in the Scandinavian statement. We have seen in the preceding chapters that the objective conditions of economic and educational status, age, race, marital status, family and friendships, work, place of residence, and health all relate in varying degree not only to satisfaction in the related domains of life but also to the individual's general assessment of affect and satisfaction with life. The only surprising aspect of these relationships is that they are not stronger than they are. If all these objective indicators are taken together as predictors of feelings of well-being, they succeed in accounting for less than a fifth of the variation we see between the individual members of the population in their assessment of their happiness and satisfaction with life.

While it is easy to overestimate the influence that these external conditions of life have on the general sense of well-being of the population, it is nevertheless true that some situations have distinctive characteristics. Scattered through the general population are small pockets of people whose circumstances seem to predispose them to unusual heights or depths of perceived well-being. The objective conditions of life explain only partially the sense of well-being of the total population, but they appear to have a particular impact on the lives of these specific people.

The population tends to be generally positive in its evaluations of life, and there are fewer groups that stand out as distinctively more positive than average than there are that are clearly more negative. Outstanding among the groups who are most positive in their feelings of well-being are young married women who still do not have children. Despite the fact that people under 30 are not generally more positive than older people in any of the measures of well-being, these young women are exceptionally high in both affect and satisfaction with life. While the circumstances of their lives would appear to be very much the same as those of the men they marry, it is a striking fact that men at this stage of life show virtually none of this "honeymoon glow." Young men appear to take the transition from the unmarried state to that of marriage considerably more calmly than young women do.

Among men the most favorable reports of affect and satisfaction come from those living in the empty nest—fathers of grown children and still living with their wife. They do not differ remarkably from other married men of their approximate age who do not have children, but they have a consistently high pattern of perceived well-being. It is a perceptibly more positive pattern, moreover, than that which characterizes women at this stage of the life cycle.

On the opposite side of the well-being scale are the unemployed, the separated and divorced, unmarried mothers, the socially isolated, the physically disabled, and low-income black people. All these population segments find their lives characterized by low positive affect, low satisfaction with life, and high perceived strain. Some parts of the population have a very uneven pattern; widowed people, for example, are not below average in satisfaction with life or absence of strain but neither are they very happy.

If we look at these high and low groups in search of some common quality which distinguishes them from the rest of the population, we are drawn to the fact that they have all had a clear experience in either succeeding or failing to achieve some expectation or relationship to which our society attaches high value. The young married women, for example, have attained the status of wife which society has traditionally regarded as the natural and desirable role for a young woman. It may seem surprising that in the liberated decade of the 1970s, marriage should create such euphoria among these young women, and it makes one wonder whether popular values in this area of life have changed as much as they are sometimes thought to have. The fact that young men do not show this sense of exhilaration reveals something of the different meaning marriage has for men and women in our society.

The situation of the fathers of grown children is not as dramatic as that of recently married young women, but it is also a success story of a different sort. They have come through their period of career development, they have succeeded in maintaining a marriage, in most cases still their first marriage, and they have survived the storm and stress of child-raising. They have reached the peak of their income and occupational accomplishment and have achieved a certain serenity and fulfillment. Women of this stage of life are not so positive; one may guess because for some of them the departure of the children has removed the major preoccupation of their lives.

Those people whose feelings of well-being are distinctively negative are all deprived of some critical element of their lives—social support, good health, employment, or status. In most cases these individuals formerly possessed what they now lack, and their sense of deprivation seems to be acute. There are obviously many things people learn to do without, but for most people marriage, health, and work (if they are in the job market) are major contributors to a positive outlook on life.

It is significant that most of these conditions of life are not specifically economic in nature, although they are all associated with economic deprivation. Divorced and widowed people, most of whom are women, often find themselves in difficult financial circumstances; unemployment and physical disabilities are typically associated with low incomes. Unmarried mothers are also near the bottom of the income scale. Problems of income undoubtedly contribute to the feelings of ill-being these people share, but much of this ill-being remains when the computer removes the influence of income. There is more to these people's situation than low income. They are all lacking an attribute of life which most people have and take for granted; its absence creates a situation which is very difficult to accommodate to and is characterized by unhappiness and dissatisfaction.

The situation of low-income black people is unique; they suffer both from being poor and from being black. Poor white people also have relatively low feelings of well-being, but they are clearly more positive than those of black people in the same low-income category. Black people of all income levels describe their lives less positively than white people do.

A high income raises a black person's sense of well-being, but not to the level of a white person of that income. Black people lack what income alone will not give them, equal social and political status. Their sense of inequity is sharply expressed in the large proportion of black people who feel they have had less than their share of the happiness a person can reasonably expect in life—over twice the proportion found among white people. Being black does not bring the disadvantages it once did in this country, but they are still sufficient to depress the psychological well-being of the black population.

Changes in National Well-being

It is one thing to know the state of public well-being at any particular point in time, but it is another and more interesting thing to know how this state is changing. We are not likely to achieve an understanding of the nature of well-being until we have a series of comparable measurements of its state running through some period of time.

The national measures of perceived well-being recorded by Gurin, Veroff, and Feld in 1957 and by Bradburn in 1965 were both measures of happiness and affect, and they have both been remeasured several times since. The years between 1957 and 1978 were not years of tranquility in this country, and one might have predicted a massive drop in the number of people who called themselves "very happy" during this period. There was indeed a perceptible decline between 1957 and 1972 and thereafter a modest rise. We must assume that a national movement of this kind is the net consequence of positive factors, such as the general economic prosperity during this period, and negative factors such as the Vietnam war, racial confrontations, and rising rates of crime. The lives of many individual Americans must have been influenced dramatically by these events, their feelings of well-being enhanced or diminished, but when these individual changes are aggregated, the total national movement is seen to be rather limited. If we attempt to answer the question of whether the psychological quality of life in this country was improving or deteriorating during these two decades, we would conclude from these statements of happiness that it improved for some parts of the population and declined for others and that the overall balance was moderately negative.

Within the total population there were three significant changes. The relationship between income level and perceived happiness which was quite strong in 1957 was much weaker in 1978. In the same manner the differences in level of happiness reported by people with much or little education declined over this 21-year period. Finally, in 1957 people under 30 years old were much more likely to describe themselves as very happy than people over 60. By 1978 this difference had completely disappeared. It would appear that while self-reported happiness declined somewhat in this country during this period, it was more equally distributed in 1978 than it had been 20 years earlier.

It has been argued that the level of social justice in a society is reflected in the degree to which the satisfaction of individual needs varies within important divisons of society, such as those associated with class, age, and sex. If we accept perceived happiness as an indicator of need-satisfaction, we would conclude that while this country has become less happy since 1957, it has also become more just.

During the period of these surveys, two major social movements created significant changes in the American way of life. The first of these was the civil rights movement which brought a dramatic modification of the patterns of racial segregation and discrimination which have burdened this country for over three hundred years. There is substantial evidence that the economic, educational, occupational, and political status of black people improved between the years of 1957 and 1978 and that the barriers to their participation in the life of the nation have been greatly reduced. These changes, dramatic as they may seem, have not been accompanied by an equally impressive change in the feelings of well-being expressed by black people. The proportion of the black population who describe themselves as "very happy" has remained almost constant throughout this period; the number who say they are "not too happy" has declined gradually and in 1978 was clearly lower than it had been 20 years earlier. But black people as a whole are still substantially less positive in answering this question than white people are. Their objective circumstances have not come up to the equal of those of white people, and neither has their subjective well-being.

The second social movement in recent years has been associated with the liberation of women. The decline in the birthrate, the increase in female employment, and the increase in the number of divorced women and women living in single-adult households are all indicators of the changes which have come about in the situations of American women. In general it may be said that over this period, the choices women make have become less determined by custom, tradition, or the wishes of a husband or other relative and are more dependent on their own preferences and values. Despite the great differences in the way men and women are raised in our society and the differences in their roles and situations, the differences in their general feelings of well-being through the 1957–1978 period seem rather minor. They have not differed in the measures of positive affect and most aspects of satisfaction, although women have persistently shown slightly greater indication of negative affect and strain. Women may find pleasure and satisfaction in different ways than men do, but the total sum seems about the same for both; at least they describe it in similar terms.

Despite the considerable achievements of the women's movement during the 1970s and the ferment of public discussion associated with it, there was very little change in the levels of affect and satisfaction with life expressed by women over this period, and such change as did occur was paralleled by a similar change among men. Certainly the circumstances of many individual women must have changed dramatically, but the net effects on sense of well-being among women in general were not uniquely positive or negative. There were changes of a more specific kind, however, that may presage significant trends in the future. The number of women who expressed satisfaction with housework and the role of homemaker declined during the 1970s. Employed women were more inclined to express a preference for remaining on the job rather than returning to housework, even if economic considerations were no concern. Unemployment became as distressing a circumstance for women as it had been all along for men.

Despite these changes in attitudes and feelings, however, there was little indication that homemaking would soon become a lost art. Most women, whether employed or not, were still favorably disposed to the role of taking care of a home, and most homemakers in both 1971 and 1978 preferred to stay in the home rather than take a job. Many women and some men had no doubt been liberated during this period from traditional expectations and beliefs regarding women's roles, but long established cultural patterns appear to be very resistant to change and one can be as impressed with how much women's attitudes and values have remained the same as by how much they have changed.

Monitoring the National Sense of Well-Being

At a time when a society is in a period of tranquility, it may not feel it important to monitor the minor changes which may be taking place. But when it becomes clear that established patterns of life are changing and simple expectations that earlier patterns will persist become questionable, then it becomes imperative to have systematic information on what these changes are and in what directions society is moving. This country has been experiencing such a period since the Second World War and our realization of that fact has led to a great demand for data describing the economic, political, educational, social, occupational, ecological, and health characteristics of the country and to the creation of mechanisms for monitoring these indicators through time. Our sense that times are changing has also led to the beginnings of a program of monitoring the psychological quality of life, the early steps of which have been the substance of this book.

Historically we have been most diligent about monitoring the economic aspects of American life, and the presence of these data in long-term time depth and in great profusion has led to the development of the system of "national economic accounts" in which the major components of national economic performance are recorded. More recently it has been urged that there be created a parallel system of social accounts, intended to represent the social conditions of the nation.

Whether or not a system of social accounts is feasible at this point, and there are many who think it is not, it is clearly premature at this time to propose a system of psychological accounts. For the immediate future the objective of a program of monitoring the national sense of well-being will be more modest, being primarily intended to improve and refine the methodologies used to measure the relevant variables, to extend our understanding of the nature of subjective well-being through the analysis of change over time, and to raise the consciousness of the national leadership and of the public in general to the presence of this method of evaluating the quality of national life.

It has often been observed that governments seldom do anything about a problem until they have learned to count it. Certainly one of the reasons our government turns so naturally to transfer payments for the impoverished, housing for the poorly housed, job training for the unemployed, or medical care for the old and sick is that it knows how to identify and count these conditions. Its policies follow the principle that whatever the problem may be, the application of an appropriate amount of money will make it better. Governments have a more difficult time with such subjective states as alienation, job dissatisfaction, fear of crime, loneliness, resentment of discrimination, marital discord, or other conditions which diminish the psychological quality of people's lives. They do not have a clear sense of how widespread these problems are or a sure feeling of how to deal with them.

Prior to the late 1930s there was no systematic way of estimating the number of unemployed in this country. The necessity of knowing the extent of unemployment during the Great Depression led to the invention of the research procedures which made possible the unemployment statistics which are now so widely used. The failure of the well-established economic, social, and health indicators to provide an adequate description of the quality of life in this country has led to the development of new methods of assessing directly people's feelings of well-being and ill-being. As these measures become a familiar part of the nation's information about itself, they will heighten the general awareness of the subjective aspects of national life and will contribute to a reassessment of our priorities with a less single-minded preoccupation with the objective circumstances of life and an increasing concern with the subjective experience of life.

The Future

When Edward Tolman predicted in 1940 that this country would move from a time of "economic man" to one of "psychological man," he was assuming that as people's needs for "having" goods and services were met, they would become more concerned with what Allardt later called the needs for "relating" and "being." Whether Tolman specifically anticipated an expanding economy which would make possible an increasingly widespread gratification of the needs for having material things is not possible to say, but most of the prewar predictions regarding the "greening of America" have assumed, at least implicitly, that new patterns of needs and values would be associated with an indefinitely increasing affluence.

For nearly 30 years after the Second World War, Americans did experience a period of increasing material prosperity and their needs for goods and services were satisfied to a degree never before known. But during this same period, economic affluence appeared to lose some of its relationship with happiness and positive affect; the lives of people with high incomes seemed to lose a part of the positive quality they had had, and in their feelings of well-being they became more like those of the rest of the population. Their economic advantage seemed to be less important in determining their sense of well-being in 1978 than it had been in 1957, and it would appear that their psychological need for relating and being began to play a stronger role in this determination over this period of increasing economic affluence.

One cannot be confident, however, that the economic realities of the next few decades will permit this development to continue. If this country is indeed approaching a period of "limits," with shortages and scarcity replacing abundance, as some futurists predict, it is certainly not likely that the need for "having" will diminish in importance in the average American's hierarchy of motives. It has been 50 years since this country experienced a general decline in standard of living, and it is not clear what the social and political implications of a reversal of postwar economic trends would be. The population appears to raise its aspiration levels to keep pace when its achievements are rising; we do not know whether it can as readily adjust its aspirations downward if its achievements begin to recede.

But if the last quarter of the twentieth century turns out to be similar to the third quarter, with expanding economic affluence and increasing numbers of college graduates, we may anticipate the continuing emergence of psychological values, with a declining concentration on enlarging one's command of goods and services and a growing concern with needs associated with relating and being. A part of the population will be liberated from a preoccupation with economic values and Professor Tolman's prediction of the rise of psychological men and women will be increasingly fulfilled.

Appendix

APPENDIX TABLE 1
Percentages of Yes Responses to Bradburn Scale Items of Positive and Negative Affect, 1965, 1972, and 1978

	1965	1972	1978
Positive affect			
During the past few weeks have you ever felt:			
Particularly excited or interested in something	54	64	74
Proud because someone compliments you on something you had done?	71	70	77
Pleased about having accomplished something?	84	80	87
On top of the world?	33	32	42
That things were going your way?	71	68	74
Negative affect			
So restless that you couldn't sit long in a chair?	53	50	48
Very lonely or remote from other people?	26	24	24
Bored?	34	37	30
Depressed or very unhappy?	30	31	30
Upset because someone criticized you?	18	19	22
Number of cases	2787	1072	3692

APPENDIX TABLE 2
Distributions of Domain Satisfactions: 1971 and 1978

	Completely satisfied						Completely dissatisfied	Total	Mean
Domain	1	2	3	4	5	6	7		
Marriage–1971*	58%	25	7	7	2	1	+†	100%	1.73
Marriage–1978	54	27	9	5	2	2	1	100	1.77
Family life–1971	44	30	13	7	3	2	1	100	2.08
Family life–1978	37	32	15	9	4	2	1	100	2.22
Health–1971	45	27	9	9	4	3	3	100	2.22
Health–1978	40	29	12	8	5	3	3	100	2.28
Neighborhood–1971	46	21	13	11	4	2	3	100	2.24
Neighborhood–1978	40	26	13	12	5	2	2	100	2.29
Friendships–1971	37	30	15	12	4	1	1	100	2.26
Friendships–1978	30	35	17	10	5	2	1	100	2.33
Housework–1971‡	44	21	11	15	4	3	2	100	2.29
Housework–1978	35	22	11	19	6	4	3	100	2.65
Work–1971§	36	30	13	13	4	2	2	100	2.33
Work–1978	32	33	15	10	5	3	2	100	2.42
Life in the U.S.–1971	34	25	20	13	5	2	1	100	2.39
Life in the U.S.–1978	31	29	20	13	5	1	1	100	2.38
Community–1971	38	22	15	16	5	2	2	100	2.40
Community–1978	34	26	17	15	5	2	1	100	2.41
Housing–1971	36	26	15	13	5	2	3	100	2.43
Housing–1978	38	27	14	11	5	3	2	100	2.34
Self–1978¶	18	41	23	12	4	1	1	100	2.51
Standard of living–1971	28	25	19	14	7	4	3	100	2.69
Standard of living–1978	23	28	19	16	8	4	2	100	2.78
Family income–1978¶	16	22	20	18	11	7	6	100	3.29
Amount of education–1971	27	15	14	16	9	8	11	100	3.31
Amount of education–1978	20	15	15	18	13	8	11	100	3.57
Savings–1971	19	16	14	15	11	10	15	100	3.73
Savings–1978	14	17	15	16	14	10	14	100	3.78
Life as a whole–1971	22	39	21	11	4	2	1	100	2.45
Life as a whole–1978	22	38	22	11	4	2	1	100	2.46
Number of cases–1971									2146
Number of cases–1978									3692

* Asked only of married people.
† Less than one percent.
‡ Asked only of women, excluding students and retired women.
§ Asked only of people working for pay.
¶ Not asked in 1971.

APPENDIX TABLE 3
Relationship of Individual Domain Satisfaction Scores to Satisfaction with Life in General, 1971-1978

Satisfaction with	Correlation coefficients* 1971	1978
Self		.55
Standard of living	.45	.48
Family life	.50	.45
Marriage	.38	.42
Family income		.40
Friendships	.32	.39
Savings	.36	.38
Work	.36	.37
Housework	.34	.33
Life in the United States	.24	.30
Housing	.30	.30
Neighborhood	.23	.29
Health	.26	.29
Community	.28	.29
Amount of education	.28	.26

*The entries in this table are product moment correlation coefficients between satisfaction with specific domains and satisfaction with life in general.

APPENDIX TABLE 4
Perceived Happiness in Income Groups, 1957-1978, in percent

Family income	1957	1971	1972	1976	1978
	Percent "very happy"				
Highest quartile	47	38	31	44	32
Second quartile	41	29	25	34	32
Third quartile	34	26	22	30	27
Lowest quartile	22	21	20	19	25
	Percent "not too happy"				
Highest quartile	5	5	4	3	5
Second quartile	7	8	6	6	5
Third quartile	10	12	10	12	7
Lowest quartile	20	17	16	21	13
Number of cases	2460	2164	2369	2264	3692

NOTE: These responses were given in answer to the question "Taking all things together, how would you say things are these days—would you say you're very happy, pretty happy, or not too happy these days?"

APPENDIX TABLE 5
Perceived Happiness in Educational Groups, 1957-1978, in percent

Educational level	1957	1971	1972	1976	1978
	Percent "very happy"				
No high school	23	23	19	23	28
Some high school	30	28	25	24	25
High school graduate	46	32	26	32	28
Some college	43	28	24	36	33
College graduate	44	34	29	37	33
	Percent "not too happy"				
No high school	20	14	18	19	13
Some high school	9	11	10	14	9
High school graduate	6	8	7	8	8
Some college	6	9	7	9	5
College graduate	4	7	7	7	6

APPENDIX TABLE 6
Percentage of Marital Compatibility in 1971 and 1978

"How often do you disagree with your (husband-wife) about how much money to spend on various things?"		Never	Rarely	Sometimes	Often	Very often	Total	Number of cases
Women	1971	23	35	30	8	4	100	1,259
	1978	22	36	32	7	3	100	2,151
Men	1971	21	36	33	7	3	100	905
	1978	25	35	28	9	3	100	1,541
"How well do you think your (husband-wife) understands you—your feelings, your likes, and dislikes, and any problems you may have?"			Very well	Fairly well	Not very well	Not well at all		
Women	1971		42	48	7	3	100	
	1978		42	48	7	3	100	
Men	1971		50	44	5	1	100	
	1978		55	40	4	1	100	
"How well do you think you understand your (husband-wife)?"			Very well	Fairly well	Not very well	Not well at all		
Women	1971		50	43	5	2	100	
	1978		46	50	3	1	100	
Men	1971		45	49	5	1	100	
	1978		47	48	4	1	100	
"How much companionship do you and your (husband-wife) have—how often do you do things together?"		All the time	Very often	Often	Sometimes	Hardly ever		
Women	1971	39	30	15	12	4	100	
	1978	37	35	14	10	4	100	
Men	1971	35	32	17	12	4	100	
	1978	34	36	16	12	2	100	

APPENDIX TABLE 7
Percentages of People Living in Communities of Different Size Who Know or Visit Their Neighbors, 1978

"Of the ten families that live closest to you here, how many would you say you know by name?"
"Of these ten families, how many have you ever visited with, either in their home or in yours?"

Number known or visited	Metro centers	Metro suburbs	Large cities	Small cities	Small towns	Rural counties
None						
Known	10	3	10	5	4	2
Visited	17	11	10	11	9	6
One or two						
Known	18	13	16	13	14	7
Visited	33	27	28	28	23	18
Three or four						
Known	15	16	21	17	14	9
Visited	18	27	28	21	20	21
Five or six						
Known	20	22	17	20	16	13
Visited	17	17	18	19	18	16
Seven or eight						
Known	11	13	12	11	11	10
Visited	6	7	7	9	11	11
Nine or ten						
Known	26	33	24	34	41	59
Visited	9	11	9	12	21	28
Total	100	100	100	100	100	100
Number of cases	267	484	535	698	493	1,215

APPENDIX TABLE 8
Trust in Government, 1957-1978, in percent

	Cynical	Mixed	Trusting	Not answered	Total	Number of cases
1958	11	25	58	6	100	1822
1964	19	18	61	2	100	1450
1968	26	24	48	3	100	1348
1970	36	25	38	1	100	1507
1972	36	24	38	2	100	2285
1974	50	24	24	2	100	2523
1976	53	23	22	2	100	2870
1978	52	26	19	3	100	2304

NOTE: The entries in this table are scale values based on answers to the five questions reproduced on page 166.

APPENDIX TABLE 9
Perceived Happiness in Age Groups, 1957-1978, in percent

	Percent "very happy"				
Age	1957	1971	1972	1976	1978
20–29	40	30	26	31	29
30–39	41	31	24	34	31
40–49	33	25	24	32	31
50–59	35	33	22	31	26
60 and over	25	26	25	28	31
	Percent "not too happy"				
20–29	4	8	8	10	8
30–39	8	10	9	9	8
40–49	10	9	8	9	7
50–59	14	12	10	11	9
60 and over	19	11	13	14	8

References

CHAPTER 1

Allardt, E. "Dimensions of Welfare in a Comparative Scandinavian Study." *Acta Sociologica*, Vol. 19, pp. 227–239, 1976.

Maslow, A. *Motivation and Personality*. Harper, New York, 1954.

Mason, R., Faulkenberry, G. and Seidler, A. *The Quality of Life as Oregonians See It*. Oregon State University, Corvallis, 1976.

Tolman, E. C. "Psychological Man." *Journal of Social Psychology*, Vol. 13, 1941, pp. 205–218.

U.S. Department of Health, Education, and Welfare. *Toward a Social Report*. U.S. Government Printing Office, Washington, D.C., 1969.

Part I, Introduction

Wills, G. *Inventing America*. Doubleday, Garden City, N.Y. 1978.

CHAPTER II

Bauer, R. A. (Ed.). *Social Indicators*. MIT Press, Cambridge, 1966.

Bradburn, N. M. *The Structure of Psychological Well-being*. Aldine, Chicago, 1969.

Bradburn, N.M. and Caplovitz, D. *Reports on Happiness*. Aldine, Chicago, 1965.

Campbell, A. and Converse, P. E. (Eds.). *The Human Meaning of Social Change*. Russell Sage Foundation, New York, 1972.

Commission on Critical Choices for Americans. *Qualities of Life: Critical Choices for Americans, Vol. 7*. Lexington Books, Lexington, Mass., 1976.

Duncan, O. D. *Toward Social Reporting: Next Steps.* Russell Sage Foundation, New York, 1969.

Gilmartin, K. J. et al. *Social Indicators: An Annotated Bibliography of Current Literatures.* Garland, New York, 1979.

Gurin, G., Veroff, J. and Feld, S. *Americans View Their Mental Health.* Basic Books, New York, 1960.

Kluckhohn, C. and Murray, H. *Personality in Nature, Society and Culture.* Knopf, New York, 1953.

McKennell, A. C. "Cognition and Affect in Perceptions of Well-being." *Social Indicators Research,* Vol. 5, 1978, pp. 389–426.

Matlin, M. and Stang, D. *The Pollyanna Principle: Selectivity in Language, Memory and Thought.* Schenkman, Cambridge, Mass., 1978.

President's Research Committee on Social Trends. *Recent Social Trends in the United States.* McGraw-Hill, New York, 1933.

The Quality of Life Concept. Environmental Protection Agency, Washington, D.C., 1973.

Sheldon, E. B. and Moore, W. E. *Indicators of Social Change.* Russell Sage Foundation, New York, 1968.

Strupp, H. H. and Hadley, S. W. "A Tripartite Model of Mental Health and Therapeutic Outcomes." *American Psychologist,* Vol. 32, 1977, pp. 187–196.

Taeuber, C. (Ed.). "America in the Seventies: Some Social Indicators." *The Annals.* Vol. 435, 1978, pp. 1–294.

CHAPTER III

Andrews, F. M. and Withey, S. B. *Social Indicators of Well-being.* Plenum Press, New York, 1976.

Brenner, B. "Quality of Affect and Self-evaluated Happiness." *Social Indicators Research,* Vol. 2, 1975, pp. 315–331.

Campbell, A., Converse, P. E. and Rodgers, W. L. *The Quality of American Life.* Russell Sage Foundation, New York, 1976.

Cantril, H. *The Pattern of Human Concerns.* Rutgers University Press, New Brunswick, N.J., 1965.

Duncan, O. D., Schuman, H. and Duncan, B. *Social Change in a Metropolitan Community.* Russell Sage Foundation, New York, 1973.

Easterlin, R. A. "Does Money Buy Happiness?" *Public Interest,* 1973, pp. 3–10.

Gallup, G. H. "Human Needs and Satisfactions: A Global Survey." *Public Opinion Quarterly,* Vol. 40, 1976, pp. 459–467.

Smith, T. W. "Happiness: Time Trends, Seasonal Variations, Intersurvey Differences and Other Mysteries." *Social Psychology Quarterly,* Vol. 42, 1979, pp. 18–30.

Veroff, J., Douvan, E. and Kulka, R. "Americans View Their Mental Health: 1957–1976" (in press). Basic Books, New York.

Watts, W. and Free, L. A. *State of the Nation*. Potomac Associates, Washington, D.C., 1974.

CHAPTER IV

National Research Council. *Toward an Understanding of Metropolitan America*. Canfield Press, San Francisco, 1974.

Quinn, R. and Staines, G. *The 1977 Quality of Employment Survey*. Institute for Social Research, Ann Arbor, Mich., 1979.

Reich, C. A. *The Greening of America*. Random House, New York, 1970.

CHAPTER V

Atkinson, T. H. *Trends in Life Satisfaction among Canadians: 1968–1977* (Occasional Paper No. 7). Institute for Research on Public Policy, Montreal, 1979.

Inglehart, R. *The Silent Revolution*. D. C. Heath, Lexington, Mass., 1974.

Siegel, P. "Prestige in the American Occupational Structure." Dissertation, Department of Sociology, University of Chicago, Chicago, 1971.

CHAPTER VI

Bane, M. J. *Here to Stay*. Basic Books, New York, 1976.

Bernard, J. *The Future of Marriage*. World Publishing, New York, 1972.

Blood, R. O., Jr. and Wolfe, D. M. *Husbands and Wives*. Free Press, Glencoe, Ill., 1960.

Freedman, R., Whelpton, P. K. and Campbell, A. A. *Family Planning, Sterility and Population Growth*, McGraw-Hill, New York, 1959.

Terman, L. M. *Psychological Factors in Marital Happiness*. McGraw-Hill, New York, 1938.

CHAPTER VII

Berkman, L. F. and Syme, S. L. "Social Networks, Host Resistance, and Mortality: A Nine-year Follow-up Study of Alameda County Residents." *American Journal of Epidemiology*, Vol. 109, 1979, pp. 186–204.

Brim, O. G., Jr. and Kagan, J. (Eds.). "Constancy and Change in Human Development" (in press). Harvard University Press, Cambridge, Mass.

Caplan, G. and Killilea, M. *Support Systems and Mutual Help*. Grune and Stratton, New York, 1976.

Cobb, S. "Social Support as a Moderator of Life Stress." *Journal of Psychosomatic Medicine*, Vol. 38, 1976, pp. 300–314.

Fischer, C. S. et al. *Networks and Places: Social Relations in the Urban Setting.* The Free Press, New York, 1977.

Kahn, R. L. and Antonucci, T. C. "Convoys Over the Life Course: Attachment, Roles and Social Support." In *Life-span Development and Behavior, Vol. 3*, P. B. Baltes and O. Brim (Eds.) (in press). Lexington Press, Lexington, Mass.

Lowenthal, M. P. and Haven, C. "Interaction and Adaptation: Intimacy as a Critical Variable." *American Sociological Review*, Vol. 33, 1968, pp. 20–30.

CHAPTER VIII

Quinn, R. P., Staines, G. L. and McCullough, M. R. *Job Satisfaction: Is There a Trend?* (Manpower Research Monograph No. 30). U.S. Department of Labor, U.S. Government Printing Office, Washington.

Robinson, J. P. *How Americans Use Their Time.* Praeger, New York, 1977.

Seashore, S. E. "Job Satisfaction as an Indicator of the Quality of Employment." *Social Indicators Research*, Vol. 1, 1974, pp. 135–168.

Strumpel, B. "Economic Life-styles, Values and Subjective Welfare." In *Economic Means for Human Needs*, B. Strumpel (Ed.). Institute for Social Research, Ann Arbor, Mich., 1976.

CHAPTER IX

Campbell, A. "Women at Home and at Work." In *New Research on Women and Sex Roles*, D. McGuigan (Ed.). Center for Continuing Education of Women, Ann Arbor, Mich., 1976.

Gove, W. R. and Tudor, J. F. "Adult Roles and Mental Illness." In *Changing Women in a Changing Society*, S. Huber (Ed.). Basic Books, New York, 1973.

Hoffman, L. W. and Nye, F. I. *Working Mothers.* Jossey-Bass, San Francisco, 1974.

Van Dusen, R. A. and Sheldon, E. B. "The Changing Status of American Women: A Life Cycle Perspective." *American Psychologist*, Vol. 31, 1976, pp. 106–116.

CHAPTER X

Campbell, A. *White Attitudes Toward Black People.* Institute for Social Research, Ann Arbor, Mich., 1971.

Liu, B. C. *The Quality of Life in the U.S.: 1970.* Midwest Research Institute, Kansas City, Mo., 1973.

Liu, B. C. *Quality of Life Indicators in the U.S. Metropolitan Areas.* Midwest Research Institute, Kansas City, Mo., 1975.

Marans, R. W. and Rodgers, W. L. "Toward an Understanding of Community Satisfaction." In *Metropolitan America: Papers on the State of Knowledge*, A. Hawley and V. Rock (Eds.). National Academy of Sciences, Washington, D.C., 1974.

Marans, R. W. and Sharf, S. "Neighborhood Quality: Concepts, Research and Public Policy Issues" (unpublished), 1980.

Marans, R. W. and Wellman, J. D. *The Quality of Nonmetropolitan Living*. Institute for Social Research, Ann Arbor, Mich., 1978.

Milbrath, L. W. and Sahr, R. C. "Perceptions of Environmental Quality." *Social Indicators Research*, Vol. 1, 1975, pp. 397–438.

White, M. and White, L. *The Intellectual Versus the City: From Thomas Jefferson to Frank Lloyd Wright*. Harvard University Press, Cambridge, Mass., 1962.

Zehner, R. B. *Indicators of the Quality of Life in New Communities*. Ballinger, Cambridge, Mass., 1977.

CHAPTER XI

Campbell, A., et al. *The American Voter*. Wiley, New York, 1960.

Citrin, J. "Political Alienation as a Social Indicator." *Social Indicators Research*, Vol. 4, 1977, pp. 381–419.

Converse, P. E. "Change in the American Electorate." In *The Human Meaning of Social Change*, A. Campbell and P. E. Converse (Eds.). Russell Sage Foundation, New York, 1972.

House, J. S. and Mason, W. M. "Political Alienation in America: 1951–1968." *American Sociological Review*, Vol. 40, 1975, pp. 123–147.

Miller, A. "Current Trends in Political Trust." *Economic Outlook USA*, Vol. 6, 1979, pp. 58–59.

CHAPTER XII

Abrams, M. *Beyond Three-score and Ten*. Age Concern Publications, London, 1978.

Elder, G. H. "Family History and the Life Course." *Journal of Family History*, Vol. 4, 1979, pp. 279–304.

Gould, R. *Transformations: Growth and Change in Adult Life*. Simon and Schuster, New York, 1978.

Levinson, D. *The Seasons of a Man's Life*. Knopf, New York, 1978.

Weiss, R. *Marital Separation*. Basic Books, New York, 1976.

CHAPTER XIII

Gurin, P., Gurin, G. and Morrison, B. M. "Personal and Ideological Aspects of Internal and External Control." *Social Psychology*, Vol. 41, 1978, pp. 275–296.

Rotter, J. B. "Generalized Expectancies for Internal Versus External Control of Reinforcement." *Psychological Monographs*, Vol. 80, 1966, pp. 1–28.

Terman, L. M. et al. (Eds.). "Mental and Physical Traits of a Thousand Gifted Children." In *Genetic Studies of Genius, Vol. I*. Stanford University Press, Stanford, 1947.

Introduction, Part III

Bestuzhev-Lada, I. V. and Blinov, N. M. (Eds.). *The Modern Conceptions of Level of Life, Quality of Life and Way of Life.* Academy of Sciences of the U.S.S.R., Moscow, 1978.

Hall, J. "Subjective Measures of Quality of Life in Britain: 1971 to 1975." In *Social Trends*, No. 7. Burgess and Son, Abington, Oxfordshire, 1976.

Hankiss, E. *Quality of Life Models.* Institute for Culture and Hungarian Academy of Sciences, Budapest, 1976.

Levi, L. and Anderson, L. *Population, Environment and Quality of Life.* Royal Ministry for Foreign Affairs, Stockholm, 1975.

Lewin, K. *A Dynamic Theory of Personality.* McGraw-Hill, New York, 1935.

Research Committee on the Study of Japanese National Character, *Changing Japanese Values.* Institute for Statistical Mathematics, Tokyo, 1977.

Strumpel, B. (Ed.). *Subjective Elements of Well-Being.* Organization for Economic Co-operation and Development, Paris, 1974.

Szanto, M. (Ed.). *Ways of Life.* Corvina Press, Budapest, 1977.

CHAPTER XIV

Barnes, S. and Inglehart, R. "Affluence, Individual Values and Social Change." In *Subjective Elements of Well-Being,* B. Strumpel (Ed.). Organisation for Economic Co-operation and Development, Paris, 1974.

Lane, R. "Markets and the Satisfaction of Human Wants." *Journal of Economic Issues,* Vol. 12, 1978, pp. 799–827.

Scitovsky, T. *The Joyless Economy.* Oxford University Press, New York, 1976.

Walster, E., Walster, G. W. and Berscheid, E. *Equality: Theory and Research.* Allyn and Bacon, Boston, 1978.

Index

About the Author

ANGUS CAMPBELL is the Program Director at the Institute for Social Research, University of Michigan. A member of the National Academy of Sciences, he has also received the Distinguished Scientific Contribution Award of the American Psychological Association. In addition to numerous journal articles, Dr. Campbell is the author of several books, including *The Human Meaning of Social Change*; *White Attitudes Toward Black People*; and *The American Voter*.

THE SENSE OF WELL-BEING IN AMERICA

Recent Patterns and Trends

Angus Campbell

A change of major significance is occurring in this nation. For increasing numbers of people, material well-being is losing its capacity to determine psychological well-being. An income that provides the basic necessities of life is an essential condition for contentment and happiness, but it is not always sufficient. Values other than economics are becoming paramount.

This book explores those other, psychological values. Written in non-technical language, it presents the findings of research conducted for more than twenty years by the Institute for Social Research of the University of Michigan. The results of five national surveys conducted between 1957 and 1978 are described and interpreted skilfully by Dr. Campbell. Central to his findings are those aspects of life that Americans have declared to be crucial to their happiness, satisfaction, or relief from stress.

The book is organized around the theme that the sense of well-being depends on the gratification of three basic needs—having, relating, and being. Dr. Campbell discusses the circumstances of life thought to contribute most significantly to these needs and to the inner quality of our lives: friendships, family life, health, income, community, standard of living, geographic location, housing, marital status, education, and work. Comparisons of the various segments of the population show the relative importance of these conditions, and comparisons of the data show how the ordering has changed over time.

Dr. Campbell breaks new ground in challenging the theme that this country is devoted to the primacy of material values. He demonstrates that the quality of American life can be measured in subjective terms as well. Our attention must be directed increasingly to the concerns revealed in this book: unhappiness, alienation, apathy, loneliness, job dissatisfaction, resentment of injustice, and other psychological states.